D1605748

The Encyclopedia of College & University Name Histories

Morgan G. Brenner

The Scarecrow Press, Inc.
Lanham, Maryland • Toronto • Oxford
2003

SCARECROW PRESS, INC.

Published in the United States of America
by Scarecrow Press, Inc.
A wholly owned subsidary of
The Rowman & Littlefield Publishing Group, Inc.
4501 Forbes Boulevard, Suite 200, Lanham, Maryland 20706
www.scarecrowpress.com

PO Box 317
Oxford
OX2 9RU, UK

Copyright © 2003 by Morgan G. Brenner
Book design and composition by Margaret S. Brenner

British Library Cataloguing in Publication Information Available

Library of Congress Cataloging-in-Publication Data

Brenner, Morgan G.
    The encyclopedia of college and university name histories / Morgan G.
Brenner.
        p. cm.
    ISBN 0-8108-4849-X (alk. paper)
    1. Universities and colleges—United States—Directories. 2. Universities
and colleges—United States—Names. I. Title.

L901.B82 2003
378.73—dc21   2003050693

♾™ The paper used in this publication meets the minimum requirements of
American National Standard for Information Sciences—Permanence of
Paper for Printed Library Materials, ANSI/NISO Z39.48-1992.
Manufactured in the United States of America.

Dedication

To Elsa for forty-four years — and for those to be.

And to Maggie, Dave, and Katie who've "done their old man proud" — oh, so very proud.

Contents

Preface

This book contains the name, merger, and location history of 1,304 United States four-year colleges and universities.

However, it is not all-inclusive. There are over 3,000 post-secondary educational institutions in the United States: four-year, two-year, and various-year trade, or comparable, institutions — accredited and nonaccredited. Only institutions that met the criteria described in "The Data" section are included.

The data for each institution are the following:

- The name at establishment with the year of establishment

- A chronological listing of name changes and/or mergers with other institutions with the year of the name change and/or merger

- A chronological listing of locations of the institution; i.e., different cities, not a different campus in the same city, with the year of each relocation

Conceptually, this book is the result of another one.

While compiling the data during the 1990s for *College Basketball's National Championships: The Complete Record of Every Tournament Ever Played* (Scarecrow Press, 1999), I was working with college basketball records since the early 1900s.

Frequently, I found a college name that I did not recognize and that I could not find in any of the then-current college reference publications.

My concern with these colleges was whether they still were active under the name I had in my records, had closed, had merely changed their name, or had changed their name as a result of a merger. If there had been just a name change, whether the college was still active or had closed, it was important that I credited the data either to the current name or to the last name before closing. If there had been a name change from a merger, it was important that I credited the data either to the new "merged name" or to the old "premerger" name.

In August, 1994, life became considerably easier. I discovered *American Universities and Colleges: A Dictionary of Name Changes*, by Alice H. Songe (Scarecrow Press, 1978). How ironic that I purchased it from the publisher who, four and one-half years later, would publish the basketball book I then was working on and eight years later publish this book.

"The Songe Book," as it became known around my home-office, proved to be extremely valuable. It was, however, twenty-some years old, and a lot of name changes had occurred since its publication. In addition, colleges had closed and/or merged, junior and community colleges had become four-year institutions (some changed their names), and new colleges had opened. Further, through their own research, colleges had refined, updated, and clarified their histories.

As I continued to identify those unrecognized colleges, I built a substantial database of name changes and mergers. At some point during the development of my basketball book, I mentioned "The Songe Book" to my editor. Imagine his surprise when I noted that it had been published by Scarecrow Press, soon to publish my basketball book. Imagine my surprise when shortly thereafter he told me that he had a discussion with the Scarecrow people and that they wanted me to do a new version of "The Songe Book."

So, here it is. What an experience for me. I hope it is valuable.

Morgan G. Brenner
Havertown, PA

The Data

Criteria for Inclusion

1,304 institutions that met each of the following criteria are included in this book:

- Was active in the 2001-02 academic year and was expected to be active in the 2002-03 academic year

- Requires a normal course of study of four or more years

- Was fully accredited by one of the following six regional accrediting associations during the 2000-2001 academic year:
    Middle States Association of Colleges and Schools
    New England Association of Schools and Colleges
    North Central Association of Colleges and Schools
    Northwest Association of Schools and Colleges
    Southern Association of Colleges and Schools
    Western Association of Schools and Colleges

    Institutions that were not fully accredited are in one of the following categories:
    candidate or applicant
    on probation or warning
    accreditation deferred

    Each association maintains a website in which it lists all of its member institutions and their accreditation status. These website lists were used to determine the accreditation status of institutions that met the first two inclusion criteria.

    The accreditation status was as of May 1, 2001; it is possible that changes in accreditation status have occurred between that date and the publication of this book.

- Holds one of the following designations from the Carnegie Foundation (2000 edition):
    Baccalaureate/Associate's Colleges: Baccalaureate de-

grees accounted for at least ten percent of the under-graduate awards (otherwise associate degrees)

Baccalaureate Colleges – General: Awarded less than half of their baccalaureate degrees in liberal arts fields

Baccalaureate Colleges – Liberal Arts: Awarded at least half of their baccalaureate degrees in liberal arts fields

Doctoral/Research Universities – Extensive: Awarded fifty or more doctoral degrees per year across at least fifteen disciplines

Doctoral/Research Universities – Intensive: Awarded at least ten doctoral degrees per year across three or more disci-plines, or at least twenty doctoral degrees per year over-all

Master's Colleges and Universities I: Awarded forty or more master's degrees per year across three or more disciplines

Master's Colleges and Universities II: Awarded twenty or more master's degrees per year

The foundation maintains a website of its 2000 edition in which it lists its designated institutions. This website list was utilized to determine the designations of institutions that met the first three inclusion criteria. The above defini-tions are from the website.

Designations of institutions not included in this book are the following:
art, music, design
business & management
engineering & technical
health
law
medical & medical center
other
teacher
theological seminaries & faith related
tribal

The above designations are from the website.

325 institutions that met all of the above inclusion criteria are not included in this book for one or more of the following reasons:

- Is a "branch campus," or comparable

- Is "nontraditional" in its operation or philosophy

  Nontraditional is defined, for the purposes of this book, as an institution that provides its curricula through television, the internet, etc., with little, if any, on-campus requirements, or whose student body is primarily adult or other specific "nontraditional" groups. It should be noted, however, that a number of "traditional" institutions provide degree-completion through "nontraditional" means or have programs for specific "nontraditional" groups.

- First degree granted is other than a bachelor's
  Associate (primarily); i.e., junior/community/technical colleges
  First professional only
  Master's/doctorate only (graduate only institutions)

- Is located in United States territories such as Puerto Rico, Guam, etc.

Data Acquisition Method

1. Creation of a database with name change and merger histories from "The Songe Book" for the institutions that met the inclusion criteria. Additions and corrections to the database were made from the subsequent steps, below.

2. Access to the "history page" of the internet website of the includible institutions. About five hundred were found. For the most part, the website "history pages" provided confirmations of, or updates to, the Songe data. However, in some cases, there were discrepancies, and there have been name changes since the publication of "The Songe Book." The website information was accepted.

3. A letter to the public relations director of all includible institutions for which no website "history page" was found (about 800). The mailing included a form on which the requested "name his-

tory" information could be entered and returned. About 300 replies were received. Many recipients merely completed the form; others provided brochures or other material.

4. A telephone call to the public relations or comparable office, the "resident historian," or the archivist of all institutions that did not reply to the mailing (about 500). In addition, telephone calls were made to some institutions, even though they have a website "history page" or the form was returned, because information was missing, was unclear, or conflicting information was found in other sources. All information in "The Songe Book" was not necessarily verified in the telephone calls.

There are some institutions for which the information is only from "The Songe Book." If there was no reason to suspect from another source any change in the history, "The Songe Book" information was accepted.

In using the information in this book, it must be understood that not all institutions have complete and accurate information on their history.

Perhaps by the time that this book is published, some included institutions will have undergone a name change, have been involved in a merger, or have closed. It is believed that name changes, mergers, or closures that occurred in 2002 are accounted for. However, in general, if a telephone call was not made to an institution or its website was not accessed after March, 2002, a name change, merger, or closure may not be accounted for.

Otherwise, it is believed that this book provides a complete record of the name history of every currently operating institution of higher education in the United States that met the criteria for inclusion.

Representatives of all included institutions are invited to modify or correct the information herein. Please do so through the publisher.

Guide

Looking for an Institution

If you know the current official name of the institution, alphabetize the name and proceed to the main section of this book.

If you are looking for a former name of an institution, use the Index to Former Names.

Institution Names (Current and Former)

Institutions are presented by their alphabetical name which is the official name, inverted as per standard alphabetizing rules; e.g., The University of Alabama is Alabama, The University of.

Familiar names or initials are not used as the name of the institution. For example, Penn State is Pennsylvania State University, The; Cortland State is New York College at Cortland, State University of; UCLA is California, Los Angeles, University of.

Many of the "A&M" or comparable institutions are known familiarly by the A&M initials. In most cases, the official name uses the words; however, officials at Texas A&M, for example, were emphatic that the official name of the several related institutions is "A&M, no spaces, with ampersand."

It appears that for a number of institutions, "Tech" rather than "Technical" or "Technological," or similar is official. In other cases, the full word is official.

The accuracy of "The" (with a capital "T") in institution names is not guaranteed. There is much use and nonuse of it from publication to publication, and many institutions are uncertain whether its use is official. It seems that in many cases, "The" appeared in an historical reference, perhaps at the beginning of a sentence, and the word just worked itself into use. However, there are institutions for which there is absolutely no question that "The" is a part of the name.

Every attempt was made for total accuracy with institutions that have a campus or city name as part of their over-all name in the use of a comma, a colon, a dash, at, in, or nothing to separate the main name and the location name.

Three editorial liberties were taken with institution names:

- the use of an ampersand (&) for the word "and"

- omission of the period following a person's first and/or middle initial

- spelling the word "Saint," "Mount," "Fort," etc. It is recognized that some institutions officially are "St." and others are "Saint," etc., but spelling the word for all such institutions makes alphabetizing more exact. Interestingly, even among institution officials, there frequently is disagreement as to whether such words are spelled or abbreviated.

Event Years

The year following the event is the year the institution uses for the event.

When the exact year is unknown, "c," circa, is used; i.e., institution officials indicated that the event occurred "about" a given year.

In other cases of an uncertain year "s" is used, i.e., institution officials indicated that the event occurred "during"; e.g., the 1970s.

In a few cases, when no year is known, "UNK" is used; i.e., institution officials indicated that "we just do not know" when the event occurred.

In all cases, the year is the calendar year, not the academic year.

Institutional Data

Heading

Line 1: *Name of the Institution.* This name is the current, official name of the institution, alphabetized.

Line 2: *City where the institution is located.* For simplicity, all communities, regardless of size or legal status, in or near which an institution is located are given the status of "city." However, some institutions are not located in a "legal city," and some, while in a "legal city," use a post office address. If so, the municipality in or near which the institution is located is used.

Line 2: *State where the institution is located.* United States Postal Service abbreviations are used.

Name Histories

Establishment: In the first line, preceded by "Est. as:," is the official name of the institution when it was established — followed by the year when the establishment occurred.

Note that there are instances in which the name of the institution at establishment is unknown or there was no apparent name.

The established year may be the year that the institution was organized, founded, chartered, incorporated, or even the year of first instruction. It is the year, by whatever definition, that the institution uses as its beginning.

For some entries, an asterisk (*) follows the year. It indicates a reference to the end of the entry for clarification.

In such cases, the institution recognizes a year other than the indicated year as its official established year. Usually such a situation occurs when there is a predecessor institution which the institution does not officially consider as part of its history or when an institution considers its beginning when a merger occurred.

It is interesting that while some institutions stretch the imagination to be as old as possible, using the established year of a predecessor institution — even if it was a "noncollegiate" institution, others do not consider the early "academy" or comparable years.

There are authorities who maintain that it is technically inaccurate for institutions to use any established year other than the year when they were first empowered to award collegiate degrees.

Name Changes: Only official name changes are listed. In many cases, institutions have been known by unofficial names, sometimes for athletic purposes, media reference, or "just because," such as easier, location, need for identity amplification, etc. There are instances in which an institution simply has wished to be known by a shortened or other version of its official name. Some institutions even have used unofficial names on their letterheads and campus signs, etc.

Mergers: All recognized official mergers are listed. It should be noted that not all mergers have been complete legal mergers. Some were nothing more than one institution taking over the records of a closed institution and allowing its students to transfer and/or to be considered as alumni. In others, the assets of a closed institution were given or transferred to another institution in a quasimerger. In still others, one institution closed and another took over the campus and established a branch of itself. However, most mergers were a formal, legal merger of two (or more) institutions.

Institution names are affected by a merger in one of several ways:

- one institution assumes another with the former retaining its name and the latter simply being amalgamated and losing its identity; i.e., becoming defunct
- a new "combination name" is created such as Smith-Jones University, with or without the hyphen
- a "brand new" name is created

There are instances of a previously established merger being dissolved at a subsequent time. Such events are noted by "DM."

Notes: For some entries, additional explanatory information is provided at the end of the entry. For a number of institutions, the phrase "was known," or such, indicates an "unofficial" name.

Codes: Following is an explanation of the various codes or abbreviations used in the entries. For convenience, brief explanations are provided at the bottom of most pages.

Est. as: *Established as.* Name of the institution at establishment.

BY MO: *By Merger Of.* Only follows "Est. as:" line or a "Name Change" line; always has at least two "BY MO" lines. An institution was established (created) or acquired a new name by a merger of (not with) other institutions.

DM: *Dissolved Merger With.* Followed by the name of the institution. A previously listed merger with another institution was dissolved.

MW: *Merged With.* Followed by the name of the institution with which the listed institution was merged.

NC: *Name Change To.* Followed by the new name.

Some abbreviations that may appear:

AM&N: Agricultural, Mechanical, & Normal

A&M : Agricultural & Mechanical

A&I : Agricultural & Industrial

Location changes

For institutions that have relocated from one city to another, the one or more locations are listed in chronological order along with the year in which the re-location occurred. This information refers only to relocation from one city to another, not to a new campus in the same city.

If no location history is provided, it can be assumed that the institution always has been located in its current city — although it may have moved its campus within that city.

It should be noted that several of what appear to be a relocation were a name change of the city or a comparable situation.

Abilene Christian University
Abilene, TX

Est. as: Childers Classical Institute – 1906
NC: Abilene Christian College – 1919
MW: Fort Worth Christian College – 1971
MW: Christian College of the Southwest – 1971
DM: Abilene Christian College at Dallas – 1976
NC: Abilene Christian University – 1976

In the 1971 merger, Fort Worth Christian College became Abilene Christian College: Fort Worth Campus; Christian College of the Southwest became Abilene Christian College: Dallas Campus. Fort Worth and Dallas campuses merged in 1976 to become Abilene Christian University at Dallas.

Adams State College
Alamosa, CO

Est. as: State Normal School at Alamosa – 1921
NC: Adams State Normal School – 1923
NC: Adams State Teachers College of Southern Colorado – 1929
NC: Adams State College – 1945

Adelphi University
Garden City, NY

Est. as: Adelphi College – 1896
NC: Adelphi University – 1963

Location changes
Brooklyn, NY – 1896
Garden City, NY – 1929

2

Adrian College
Adrian, MI

Est. as: Adrian College – 1859
MW: Michigan Union College – 1859
MW: Methodist Protestant College – 1916

Agnes Scott College
Decatur, GA

Est. as: Decatur Female Seminary – 1889
NC: Agnes Scott Institute – 1890
NC: Agnes Scott College – 1906

Akron, The University of
Akron, OH

Est. as: Buchtel College – 1870
NC: Municipal University of Akron, The – 1913
NC: University of Akron, The – 1967

Alabama Agricultural & Mechanical University
Normal, AL

Est. as: Huntsville Normal School – 1875
NC: State Normal & Industrial School at Huntsville – 1878
NC: State Agricultural & Mechanical College for Negroes – 1891
NC: State Agricultural & Mechanical Institute for Negroes – 1919
NC: Alabama Agricultural & Mechanical College – 1948
NC: Alabama Agricultural & Mechanical University – 1969

Location changes
Huntsville, AL – 1875
Normal, AL – 1891

Alabama at Birmingham, The University of
Birmingham, AL

Est. as: University of Alabama: Birmingham Extension Center, The – 1936*
NC: University of Alabama in Birmingham, The – 1969
NC: University of Alabama at Birmingham, The – 1984
MW: Walker College – 1994

*Recognizes 1969 as official established year.

By MO: By merger (of) *DM:* Dissolved merger (with) *MW:* Merged with *NC:* Name change (to)

Alabama in Huntsville, The University of
Huntsville, AL

Est. as: University of Alabama's Huntsville Center, The – 1950
NC: University of Alabama's Huntsville Campus, The – 1954
NC: University of Alabama in Huntsville, The – 1967

Alabama State University
Montgomery, AL

Est. as: Lincoln Normal School – 1867
NC: State Normal School & University for Colored Students & Teachers – 1873
NC: Alabama Colored Peoples University – 1887
NC: State Normal School for Colored Students – 1889
NC: State Teachers College – 1929
NC: Alabama State College for Negroes – 1948
NC: Alabama State College – 1954
NC: Alabama State University – 1969

Location changes
Marion, AL – 1867
Montgomery, AL – 1887

Alabama, The University of
Tuscaloosa, AL

Est. as: University of Alabama, The – 1831

Alaska Anchorage, University of
Anchorage, AK

Est. as: University of Alaska, Anchorage – 1954
NC: University of Alaska Anchorage – 1987
MW: Anchorage Community College – 1987
MW: Kenai Community College – 1987
MW: Kodiak College – 1987
MW: Matanuska-Susitna Community College – 1987
MW: Prince William Sound Community College – 1987

By MO: By merger (of) *DM:* Dissolved merger (with) *MW:* Merged with *NC:* Name change (to)

4

Alaska Fairbanks, University of
Fairbanks, AK

Est. as: Alaska Agricultural College & School of Mines, The – 1917
NC: University of Alaska – 1935
NC: University of Alaska, Fairbanks – 1975
NC: University of Alaska Fairbanks – 1987
MW: Bristol Bay Community College – 1987
MW: Chukchi Community College – 1987
MW: Interior Aleutians Campus – 1987
MW: Kuskokwim Community College – 1987
MW: Northwest Community College – 1987
MW: Tanana Valley Community College – 1987

Alaska Pacific University
Anchorage, AK

Est. as: Alaska Methodist University – 1959
NC: Alaska Pacific University – 1978

Closed during 1976-1977 academic year for re-organization.

Alaska Southeast, University of
Juneau, AK

Est. as: Southestern Junior College – 1972
MW: Juneau-Douglas Community College – 1979
NC: University of Alaska, Juneau – 1979
NC: University of Alaska Southeast – 1987
MW: Ketchikan Community College – 1987
MW: Sitka Community College – 1987

Albany State University
Albany, GA

Est. as: Alabama Bible & Manual Training Institute – 1903
NC: Georgia Normal & Agricultural College – 1917
NC: Albany State College – 1943
NC: Albany State University – 1966

Albertson College of Idaho
Caldwell, ID

Est. as: College of Idaho, The – 1891
NC: Albertson College of Idaho – 1991

By MO: By merger (of) **DM:** Dissolved merger (with) **MW:** Merged with **NC:** Name change (to)

Albertus Magnus College
New Haven, CT
Est. as: Albertus Magnus College – 1925

Albion College
Albion, MI
Est. as: Wesleyan Seminary at Albion, The – 1835
NC: Wesleyan Seminary & Female College at Albion – 1857
NC: Albion College – 1861
Location changes
Spring Arbor, MI – 1835
Albion, MI – 1857

In 1850, Albion Female Collegiate Institute was added as a branch of Wesleyan Seminary.

Albright College
Reading, PA
Est. as: Union Seminary – 1856
NC: Central Pennsylvania College – 1887
MW: Albright College of the Pennsylvania Conferences of the United Evangelical Church – 1902
MW: Schuykill College of the East Pennsylvania Conference of the Evangelical Church – 1928
NC: Albright College of the Evangelical Church – 1928
NC: Albright College – 1971
Location changes
New Berlin, PA – 1856
Myerstown, PA – 1902
Reading, PA – 1929

Original Albright College, established in Myerstown in 1895 as Albright Collegiate Institute, was on the campus of the defunct Palantinate College; name changed in 1898 to Albright College of the Pennsylvania Conferences of the Evangelical Church. Schuykill Seminary, established in Reading in 1881, moved to Fredericksburg in 1896 and back to Reading in 1902; name changed in 1923 to Schuykill College of the East Pennsylvania Conference of the Evangelical Church.

Alcorn State University
Lorman, MS

Est. as: Alcorn University – 1871
NC: Alcorn Agricultural & Mechanical College – 1878
NC: Alcorn State University – 1974

Alfred University
Alfred, NY

Est. as: Select School – 1836
NC: Alfred Academy – 1843
NC: Alfred University – 1857

Alice Lloyd College
Pippa Passes, KY

Est. as: Caney Creek Community Center – 1916*
NC: Caney Junior College – 1923
NC: Alice Lloyd College – 1962

*Recognizes 1923 as official established year.

Caney Creek Community Center may have been established in 1917.

Allegheny College
Meadville, PA

Est. as: Allegheny College – 1815

Allen University
Columbia, SC

Est. as: Payne Institute – 1870
NC: Allen University – 1880

Location changes
Cokesbury, SC – 1870
Columbia, SC – 1880

Alliant International University
San Diego, CA

Est. as: California Western University – 1952
NC: United States International University – 1966
MW: Mauna Olu Community College – 1972
MW: Alliant University – 2001
NC: Alliant International University – 2001

At establishment, California Western University may have assumed the charter of Balboa University, established in 1924. Alliant University was a name change in 1990 from California School of Professional Psychology, established in 1969, which remained as a college within the merged institution.

Alma College
Alma, MI

Est. as: Alma College – 1886

Alvernia College
Reading, PA

Est. as: Unnamed teachers seminarium for the education of sisters – 1926*
NC: Alvernia College – 1958

*Recognizes 1958 as official established year.

Alverno College
Milwaukee, WI

Est. as: Saint Joseph Normal School – 1887
NC: Alverno Teachers College – 1936
NC: Alverno College – 1946

*Recognizes 1958 as official established year.

American International College
Springfield, MA

Est. as: French-Protestant College – 1885
NC: French-American College – 1894
NC: American International College – 1905

Location changes
Lowell, MA – 1885
Springfield, MA – 1888

8

American University
Washington, DC

Est. as: American University, The – 1893
NC: American University – 1994

Amherst College
Amherst, MA

Est. as: Amherst College – 1821

Anderson College
Anderson, SC

Est. as: Anderson College – 1911

Anderson University
Anderson, IN

Est. as: Anderson Bible Training School – 1917
NC: Anderson Bible Training School & Seminary – 1925
NC: Anderson College & Technological Seminary – 1929
NC: Anderson College – 1964
NC: Anderson University – 1987

Andrews University
Berrien Springs, MI

Est. as: Battle Creek College – 1874
NC: Emmanuel Missionary College – 1901
MW: Potomac College – 1960
NC: Andrews University – 1960

Location changes
Battle Creek, MI – 1874
Berrien Springs, MI – 1901

Angelo State University
San Angelo, TX

Est. as: San Angelo College – 1928
NC: Angelo State College – 1965
NC: Angelo State University – 1969

By MO: By merger (of) *DM:* Dissolved merger (with) *MW:* Merged with *NC:* Name change (to)

Anna Maria College
Paxton, MA

Est. as: Anna Maria College for Women – 1946
NC: Anna Maria College – 1973

Location changes
Marlboro, MA – 1946
Paxton, MA – 1952

Antioch University
Yellow Springs, OH

Est. as: Antioch College – 1852
NC: Antioch University – 1978

Appalachian State University
Boone, NC

Est. as: Wautaga Academy – 1899
NC: Appalachian Training School for Teachers – 1903
NC: Appalachian State Normal School – 1921
NC: Appalachian State Teachers College – 1929
NC: Appalachian State University – 1967

Aquinas College
Grand Rapids, MI

Est. as: Noviate Normal School – 1886
NC: Sacred Heart College – 1922
NC: Catholic Junior College – 1931
NC: Aquinas College – 1941

Known as Marywood College from 1922-1931; was located at Marywood, Dominican mother house.

Arcadia University
Glenside, PA

Est. as: Beaver Female Seminary – 1853
NC: Beaver College & Musical Institute – 1872
MW: Pittsburgh Female College – 1896
NC: Beaver College – 1907
NC: Arcadia University – 2001
Location changes
Beaver, PA – 1853
Jenkintown, PA – 1925
Glenside, PA – 1928

Arizona State University
Tempe, AZ

Est. as: Arizona Territorial Normal School at Tempe – 1885
NC: Arizona Normal School – 1896
NC: Normal School of Arizona – 1899
NC: Tempe State Teachers College – 1925
NC: Arizona State Teachers College at Tempe – 1928
NC: Arizona State College at Tempe – 1945
NC: Arizona State University – 1958

Arizona, University of
Tucson, AZ

Est. as: University of Arizona – 1885

Arkansas at Little Rock, University of
Little Rock, AR

Est. as: Little Rock Junior College – 1927
NC: Little Rock University – 1957
MW: University of Arkansas – 1969
NC: University of Arkansas at Little Rock – 1969

Arkansas at Monticello, University of
Monticello, AR

Est. as: Fourth District Agricultural School – 1909
NC: Arkansas Agricultural & Mechanical College – 1925
MW: University of Arkansas – 1971
NC: University of Arkansas at Monticello – 1971

By MO: By merger (of) ***DM:*** Dissolved merger (with) ***MW:*** Merged with ***NC:*** Name change (to)

Arkansas at Pine Bluff, University of
Pine Bluff, AR

Est. as: Branch Normal College – 1873
NC: Arkansas Agricultural, Mechanical & Normal College – 1929
MW: University of Arkansas – 1972
NC: University of Arkansas at Pine Bluff – 1972

Arkansas Baptist College
Little Rock, AR

Est. as: Minister's Institute – 1884
NC: Baptist Institute – 1884
NC: Arkansas Baptist College – 1885

Arkansas State University
Jonesboro, AR

Est. as: First District Agricultural School – 1909
NC: First District Agricultural & Mechanical College – 1925
NC: Arkansas State College – 1933
NC: Arkansas State University – 1967

Arkansas Tech University
Russellville, AR

Est. as: Second District Agricultural School – 1909
NC: Arkansas Polytechnic College – 1925
NC: Arkansas Tech University – 1976

Arkansas, University of
Fayetteville, AR

Est. as: Arkansas Industrial University – 1871
NC: University of Arkansas – 1899

Armstrong Atlantic State University
Savannah, GA

Est. as: Armstrong Junior College of Savannah – 1935
NC: Armstrong College – 1940's
NC: Armstrong State College – 1959
NC: Armstrong Atlantic State University – 1996

In early years, was known as Armstrong Memorial College.

By MO: By merger (of) *DM:* Dissolved merger (with) *MW:* Merged with *NC:* Name change (to)

Asbury College
Wilmore, KY

Est. as: Kentucky Holiness College – 1890
NC: Asbury College – 1890

Name change was during the academic year 1890-1891; exact year is unknown.

Ashland University
Ashland, OH

Est. as: Ashland College – 1878
NC: Ashland University – 1989

Assumption College
Worcester, MA

Est. as: Assumption College – 1904

Tornado levelled campus in June, 1953, killing several adults; closed for two years while being rebuilt.

Atlantic Union College
South Lancaster, MA

Est. as: South Lancaster Academy – 1882
NC: Lancaster Junior College – 1918
NC: Atlantic Union College – 1922

Known after founding as "That New England School" from a magazine article which later became the title of a book about the institution.

Atlantic, College of the
Bar Harbor, ME

Est. as: College of the Atlantic – 1969

Auburn University
Auburn, AL

Est. as: East Alabama Male College – 1856
NC: Agricultural & Mechanical College of Alabama – 1872
NC: Alabama Polytechnic Institute – 1899
NC: Auburn University – 1960

By MO: By merger (of) *DM:* Dissolved merger (with) *MW:* Merged with *NC:* Name change (to)

Auburn University at Montgomery
Montgomery, AL

Est. as: Auburn University at Montgomery – 1967

Augsburg College
Minneapolis, MN

Est. as: Augsburg Seminarium – 1869
NC: Augsburg College & Theological Seminary – 1942
NC: Augsburg College – 1963

Location changes
Marshall, WI – 1869
Minneapolis, MN – 1872

Known at establishment as Marshall College, Marshall Seminary & Academy, and Theological Seminary at Marshall.

Augusta State University
Augusta, GA

Est. as: Academy of Richland County – 1783*
NC: Junior College of Augusta – 1925
NC: Augusta College – 1958
NC: Augusta State University – 1996

*Recognizes 1925 as official established year.

Augustana College
Rock Island, IL

Est. as: Augustana Seminary – 1860
NC: Augustana College & Theological Seminary – 1862
NC: Augustana College – 1948

Location changes
Chicago, IL – 1860
Paxton, IL – 1863
Rock Island, IL – 1875

Theological Seminary separated from the college in 1948.

14

Augustana College
Sioux Falls, SD

Est. as: Augustana College & Seminary – 1860
NC: Augustana Seminary & Marshall Academy – 1869
NC: Augustana Seminary & Academy – 1881
NC: Augustana College – 1884
MW: Lutheran Normal School – 1918
NC: Augustana College & Normal School – 1918
NC: Augustana College – 1926

Location changes
Chicago, IL – 1860
Paxton, IL – 1863
Marshall, WI – 1869
Beloit, IA – 1881
Canton, SD – 1884
Sioux Falls, SD – 1918

Aurora University
Aurora, IL

Est. as: Mendota Seminary – 1893
NC: Mendota College – 1912
NC: Aurora College – 1912
NC: Aurora University – 1985
MW: George Williams College – 1992

Location changes
Mendota, IL – 1893
Aurora, IL – 1912

George Williams College became a college of Aurora after the merger.

Austin College
Sherman, TX

Est. as: Austin College – 1849
MW: Texas Presbyterian College – 1930

Location changes
Huntsville, TX – 1849
Sherman, TX – 1876

By MO: By merger (of) *DM:* Dissolved merger (with) *MW:* Merged with *NC:* Name change (to)

Austin Peay State University
Clarksville, TN

Est. as: Austin Peay Normal School – 1927
NC: Austin Peay State College – 1943
NC: Austin Peay State University – 1967

Averett University
Danville, VA

Est. as: Danville Female Institute – 1854*
NC: Baptist Female Seminary – 1859
NC: Union Female College – 1859
NC: Roanoke Female College – 1864
NC: Roanoke College – 1904
NC: Roanoke Institute – 1910
NC: Danville College for Young Women – 1917
NC: Averett College – 1917
NC: Averett University – 2001

*Recognizes 1859 as official established year.

From 1864 to 1893, may have been known as Trustees of Roanoke Female College. Danville College for Young Ladies was name for one month: April, 1917.

Avila College
Kansas City, MO

Est. as: Saint Teresa's Academy – 1867*
NC: Saint Teresa College – 1916
NC: College of Saint Teresa – 1941
NC: Avila College – 1963

*Recognizes 1916 as official established year.

By MO: By merger (of) *DM:* Dissolved merger (with) *MW:* Merged with *NC:* Name change (to)

16

Azusa Pacific University

Azusa, CA

Est. as: Training School for Christian Workers – 1899
NC: Pacific Bible College – 1939
NC: Azusa College – 1957
MW: Los Angeles Pacific College – 1965
NC: Azusa Pacific College – 1965
MW: Arlington College – 1968
NC: Azusa Pacific University – 1981

Location changes

Whittier, CA – 1899
Huntington Park, CA – 1907
Azusa, CA – 1946

B

Baker College
Flint, MI

Est. as: Baker College – 1986*
By MO: Muskegon College – 1986
By MO: Baker Business University – 1986
By MO: Baker College of Owosso – 1986
MW: Jackson Business Institute – 1994

*Recognizes 1986 as official established year; does not recognize histories of merged institutions.

A system of eight campuses in Michigan. Began as Ferris Business Institute in 1888; Baker Business University began in Flint in 1911. Both schools were bought in 1965 by Robert Jewell, and the system developed thereafter. In 1990, the system acquired campuses in Pontiac (now named Auburn Hills campus), Mount Clemens (now named Clinton Township campus), and Port Huron of Pontiac Business Institute which had closed.

Baker University
Baldwin City, KS

Est. as: Baker University – 1858
MW: Missouri Wesleyan College – 1930

Baldwin-Wallace College
Berea, OH

Est. as: Baldwin Institute – 1845
NC: Baldwin University – 1855
MW: German-Wallace College – 1913
NC: Baldwin-Wallace College – 1913

Berea Seminary was founded in 1837 as part of the Lyceum Community with John Wallace as a trustee. When it closed in 1842, Wallace offered the campus to the Methodist Church which then established Baldwin Institute. German Wallace College was created by Baldwin University as its German Department in 1863.

17

18

Ball State University
Muncie, IN

Est. as: Eastern Indiana Normal University – 1899*
NC: Palmer University – 1902
NC: Indiana Normal School & College of Applied Science – 1905
NC: Muncie Normal Institute – 1912
NC: Muncie National Institute – c1914
NC: Indiana State Normal School, Eastern Division – 1918
NC: Ball Teachers College, Indiana State Normal School, Eastern Division – 1922
NC: Muncie Ball State Teachers College – 1929
NC: Ball State University – 1965

*Recognizes 1918 as official established year.

Muncie National Institute declared bankruptcy; purchasers donated its land and buildings to the state for the new institution.

Barber-Scotia College
Concord, NC

Est. as: Scotia Seminary – 1867
NC: Scotia Women's College – 1916
MW: Barber Memorial College – 1930
NC: Barber-Scotia College – 1932

Bard College
Annandale-on-Hudson, NY

Est. as: Saint Stephens College – 1860
MW: Columbia University in the City of New York – 1928
NC: Bard College – 1934
DM: Columbia University in the City of New York – 1944
MW: Simon's Rock Early College – 1979

Merger with Columbia was as an undergraduate college thereof.

Barry University
Miami Shores, FL

Est. as: Barry College – 1940
NC: Barry University – 1981

By MO: By merger (of) *DM:* Dissolved merger (with) *MW:* Merged with *NC:* Name change (to)

Barton College
Wilson, NC

Est. as: Atlantic Christian College – 1902
NC: Barton College – 1990

Bates College
Lewiston, ME

Est. as: Maine State Seminary – 1855
NC: Bates College – 1864

Bay Path College
Longmeadow, MA

Est. as: Bay Path Institute – 1897
NC: Bay Path Secretarial School – 1925
NC: Bay Path Junior College – 1949
NC: Bay Path College – 1989

Location changes
Springfield, MA – 1897
Longmeadow, MA – 1945

Baylor University
Waco, TX

Est. as: Baylor University – 1845
MW: Waco University – 1886

Location changes
Independence, TX – 1845
Waco, TX – 1886

Belhaven College
Jackson, MS

Est. as: Belhaven College for Young Ladies – 1894*
NC: Belhaven College & Industrial Institute – 1911
MW: McComb Female Institute – 1911
NC: Belhaven College – 1915
MW: Mississippi Synodical College – 1939

*Recognizes 1883, when Mississippi Synodical College, Holly Springs, MS, was established as Maury Institute, as official established year.

Destroyed by fire in 1910; title was given to the Presbyterian Church which re-opened the institution in 1911.

Bellarmine University
Louisville, KY

Est. as: Bellarmine College – 1950
MW: Ursuline College – 1968
NC: Bellarmine University – 2000

Bellevue University
Bellevue, NE

Est. as: Bellevue College – 1966
NC: Bellevue University – 1994

There was an earlier, unrelated Bellevue College in Hastings; closed in 1918.

Belmont Abbey College
Belmont, NC

Est. as: Saint Mary's College – 1876
NC: Belmont Abbey College – 1913

Belmont University
Nashville, TN

Est. as: Belmont Junior College – 1890*
MW: Ward Seminary – 1913
NC: Ward-Belmont School – 1913
NC: Belmont College – 1951
NC: Belmont University – 1991

*Recognizes 1951 as official established year.

Beloit College
Beloit, WI

Est. as: Beloit College – 1846

Bemidji State University
Bemidji, MN

Est. as: Bemidji State Normal School – 1919
NC: Bimidji State Teachers College – 1921
NC: Bemidji State College – 1957
NC: Bemidji State University – 1975

By MO: By merger (of) *DM:* Dissolved merger (with) *MW:* Merged with *NC:* Name change (to)

Benedict College
Columbia, SC

Est. as: Benedict Institute – 1870
NC: Benedict College – 1894

Benedictine College
Atchison, KS

Est. as: Saint Benedict's College – 1858
MW: Mount Saint Scholastica College – 1971
NC: Benedictine College – 1971

Benedictine University
Lisle, IL

Est. as: Saint Procopius College – 1887
NC: Illinois Benedictine College – 1971
NC: Benedictine University – 1996

Location changes
Chicago, IL – 1887
Lisle, IL – 1901

Bennington College
Bennington, VT

Est. as: Bennington College – 1932

Bentley College
Waltham, MA

Est. as: Bentley School of Accounting & Finance – 1917
NC: Bentley College of Accounting & Finance – 1961
NC: Bentley College – 1971

Berea College
Berea, KY

Est. as: Berea College – 1855

22

Bernard M Baruch College
of the City University of New York
New York, NY

Est. as: School of Business & Civic Administration of the City College – 1919
NC: Bernard M Baruch School of Business & Public Administration of the City College of New York – 1953
NC: Bernard M Baruch College of the City University of New York – 1968

Berry College
Mount Berry, GA

Est. as: Boy's Industrial School – 1902
NC: Berry School – 1908
NC: Berry Schools, The – 1917
NC: Berry College – 1926

Bethany College
Bethany, WV

Est. as: Bethany College – 1840

Bethany College
Lindsborg, KS

Est. as: Bethany Academy – 1881
NC: Bethany College – 1886

Bethany College of the Assemblies of God
Scotts Valley, CA

Est. as: Glad Tidings Bible Institute – 1919
NC: Bethany Bible College – 1954
NC: Bethany College of the Assemblies of God – 1990

Location changes
San Francisco, CA – 1919
Santa Cruz, CA – 1950
Scotts Valley, CA – 1960s

In 1980s and '90s, was known as Bethany College of California.

By MO: By merger (of) *DM:* Dissolved merger (with) *MW:* Merged with *NC:* Name change (to)

Bethel College
McKenzie, TN

Est. as: Bethel Seminary – 1842
NC: Bethel College – 1850

Location changes
McLemoresville, TN – 1842
McKenzie, TN – 1872

Bethel College
Mishawaka, IN

Est. as: Bethel College – 1947

Bethel College
North Newton, KS

Est. as: Bethel College of the Mennonite Church of North America, The – 1887
NC: Bethel College – 1961

Bethel College
Saint Paul, MN

Est. as: Scandanavian Department of the Baptist Union Theological Seminary of the University of Chicago – 1871
NC: Bethel Academy & Theological Seminary – 1914
NC: Bethel Institute – 1920
NC: Bethel College – 1931
NC: Bethel College & Seminary – 1945
NC: Bethel College – 1974

Bethune-Cookman College
Daytona Beach, FL

Est. as: Daytona Literary & Industrial School for Training Negro Girls – 1904
MW: Cookman Institute for Boys – 1923
NC: Daytona-Cookman Collegiate Institute – 1923
NC: Bethune-Cookman College – 1929

24

Biola University
La Mirada, CA

Est. as: Bible Institute of Los Angeles – 1908
NC: Biola College – 1972
NC: Biola University – 1981

Location changes
Los Angeles, CA – 1908
La Mirada, CA – 1959

Birmingham-Southern College
Birmingham, AL

Est. as: Southern University – 1856
MW: Birmingham College – 1918
NC: Birmingham-Southern College – 1918
MW: Birmingham Conservatory of Music – 1954

Location changes
Greensboro, AL – 1856
Birmingham, AL – 1918

Black Hills State University
Spearfish, SD

Est. as: Spearfish Normal School – 1883
NC: Black Hills Teachers College – 1941
NC: Black Hills State College – 1964
NC: Black Hills State University – 1989

Blackburn University, The
Carlinville, IL

Est. as: Blackburn Theological Seminary – 1837
NC: Blackburn University, The – 1869

In 1930s and '40s, an academy, seminary, and college were incorporated into the university; only the college remains. The name change to Blackburn College, as it is now known, was never official.

By MO: By merger (of) ***DM:*** Dissolved merger (with) ***MW:*** Merged with ***NC:*** Name change (to)

Bloomfield College
Bloomfield, NJ

Est. as: German Theological School – 1868
NC: Bloomfield Theological Seminary – 1913
NC: Bloomfield College & Seminary – 1931
NC: Bloomfield College – 1960

Location changes
Newark, NJ – 1868
Bloomfield, NJ – 1872

Bloomsburg University of Pennsylvania of the State System of Higher Education
Bloomsburg, PA

Est. as: Bloomsburg Academy – 1839
NC: Bloomsburg Literary Institute – 1856
NC: Bloomsburg Literary Institute & State Normal School – 1869
NC: Bloomsburg State Normal School – 1916
NC: Bloomsburg State Teachers College – 1927
NC: Bloomsburg State College – 1960
NC: Bloomsburg University of Pennsylvania of the State System of Higher Education – 1983

Blue Mountain College
Blue Mountain, MS

Est. as: Blue Mountain Female Institute – 1873
NC: Blue Mountain Female College – 1877
NC: Blue Mountain College – 1909

Bluefield State College
Bluefield, WV

Est. as: Bluefield Colored Institute – 1895
NC: Bluefield State Teachers College – 1931
NC: Bluefield State College – 1943

Administrative merger with Concord College, 1973-1976.

Bluffton College
Bluffton, OH

Est. as: Central Mennonite College – 1899
NC: Bluffton College – 1914

By MO: By merger (of) *DM:* Dissolved merger (with) *MW:* Merged with *NC:* Name change (to)

Boise State University
Boise, ID

Est. as: Boise Junior College – 1932
NC: Boise College – 1965
NC: Boise State College – 1969
NC: Boise State University – 1974

Boricua College
New York, NY

Est. as: Boricua College – 1974

Boston College
Chestnut Hill, MA

Est. as: Boston College – 1863
MW: Newton College of the Sacred Heart – 1974

Location changes
Boston, MA – 1863
Chestnut Hill, MA – 1913

Boston University
Boston, MA

Est. as: Newbury Biblical Institute – 1839
NC: Methodist General Biblical Institute – 1846
NC: Boston Theological School – 1867
NC: Boston University – 1869

Location changes
Newbury, VT – 1839
Concord, NH – 1846
Boston, MA – 1867

The 1846 move to Concord and name change may have been in 1847; the 1867 move to Boston and name change may have been in 1866, the name may have been Boston Theological Seminary.

Bowdoin College
Brunswick, ME

Est. as: Bowdoin College – 1794

By MO: By merger (of) **DM:** Dissolved merger (with) **MW:** Merged with **NC:** Name change (to)

Bowie State University
Bowie, MD

Est. as: School 1 – 1865
NC: Baltimore Normal School – 1893
NC: Baltimore Normal School #3 – 1908
NC: Maryland Normal & Industrial School at Bowie – c1914
NC: Maryland Teachers College at Bowie – 1935
NC: Bowie State College – 1963
NC: Bowie State University – 1988

Location changes
Baltimore, MD – 1885
Bowie, MD – c1914

Possible merger with an "Industrial & Architecture School" of Laurel in the mid-1960s; it probably was a "public high school."

Bowling Green State University
Bowling Green, OH

Est. as: Bowling Green State Normal College – 1910
NC: Bowling Green State College – 1929
NC: Bowling Green State University – 1935

Bradley University
Peoria, IL

Est. as: Bradley Polytechnic Institute – 1897
NC: Bradley University – 1946

Brandeis University
Waltham, MA

Est. as: Brandeis University – 1948

Title to Middlesex University was transferred to Brandeis' founding committee in return for its assumption of Middlesex debts; new charter was issued for Brandeis.

Brenau University
Gainesville, GA

Est. as: Georgia Baptist Female Seminary – 1878
NC: Brenau College – 1900
NC: Brenau University – 1992

By MO: By merger (of) **DM:** Dissolved merger (with) **MW:** Merged with **NC:** Name change (to)

28

Brescia University
Owensboro, KY

Est. as: Brescia College – 1950
MW: Mount Saint Joseph Junior College for Women – 1950
NC: Brescia University – 1998

Brevard College
Brevard, NC

Est. as: Oak Hollow Academy – 1853
NC: Rutherford Academy – 1858
NC: Rutherford Seminary – 1861
NC: Rutherford College – 1870
MW: Weaver College – 1934
NC: Brevard College – 1934

Location changes
Rutherford College, NC – 1853
Brevard, NC – 1934

Oak Hollow Academy may have been known as Oak Hollow School.

Brewton-Parker College
Mount Vernon, GA

Est. as: Union Baptist Institute – 1904
NC: Brewton-Parker Institute – 1912
NC: Brewton-Parker Junior College – 1927
NC: Brewton-Parker College – 1978

Briar Cliff University
Sioux City, IA

Est. as: Briar Cliff College – 1930
NC: Briar Cliff University – 2001

Bridgeport, University of
Bridgeport, CT

Est. as: Junior College of Connecticut – 1927
NC: University of Bridgeport – 1947
MW: Weyllister Secretarial Junior College – 1948
MW: Fones School of Dental Hygiene – 1949
MW: Arnold College of Physical Education – 1953

By MO: By merger (of) *DM:* Dissolved merger (with) *MW:* Merged with *NC:* Name change (to)

Bridgewater College
Bridgewater, VA

Est. as: Spring Creek Normal & Collegiate Institute – 1880
NC: Virginia Normal College – 1882
NC: Bridgewater College – 1889
MW: Daleville College – 1923
MW: Blue Ridge College – 1930

Bridgewater State College
Bridgewater, MA

Est. as: Bridgewater Normal School – 1840
NC: Bridgewater State Normal School – 1846
NC: Bridgewater State Teachers College – 1933
NC: State College at Bridgewater – 1960
NC: Bridgewater State College – 1965

Brigham Young University
Provo, UT

Est. as: Brigham Young Academy – 1875
NC: Brigham Young University – 1903

Brigham Young University-Hawaii
Laie, HI

Est. as: Church College of Hawaii, The – 1955
NC: Brigham Young University-Hawaii – 1974

Brooklyn College of the City University of New York
Brooklyn, NY

Est. as: Brooklyn College – 1930*
By MO: City College: Brooklyn Center – 1930
By MO: Hunter College: Brooklyn Center – 1930
NC: Brooklyn College of the City University of New York – 1961

*Recognizes merger year, 1930, as official established year; does not recognize histories of merged institutions.

Brown University
Providence, RI

Est. as: Rhode Island College – 1764
NC: Brown University – 1804

Location changes
Warren, RI – 1764
Providence, RI – 1770

Original name may have been College of Rhode Island. Pembroke, originally was the women's college of Brown; now it is a college within the university. It never was a co-ordinate college like Radcliffe, Newcomb, et al.

Bryan College
Dayton, TN

Est. as: William Jennings Bryan University – 1930
NC: William Jennings Bryan College – 1958
NC: Bryan College – 1993

Bryn Athyn College of the New Church
Bryn Athyn, PA

Est. as: Unnamed theological school – 1876
NC: Academy of the New Church College – 1994
NC: Bryn Athyn College of the New Church – 1997

Bryn Mawr College
Bryn Mawr, PA

Est. as: Bryn Mawr College – 1885

Bucknell University
Lewisburg, PA

Est. as: University at Lewisburg, The – 1846
NC: Bucknell University – 1886

Buena Vista University
Storm Lake, IA

Est. as: Buena Vista College – 1891
NC: Buena Vista University – 1995

Burlington College
Burlington, VT

Est. as: Vermont Institute of Community Involvement – 1972
NC: Burlington College – 1979

Butler University
Indianapolis, IN

Est. as: North Western Christian University – 1855
NC: Butler University – 1879

C

Cabrini College
Radnor, PA
Est. as: Cabrini College – 1957

Caldwell College
Caldwell, NJ
Est. as: Caldwell College for Women – 1939
NC: Caldwell College – 1969

California Baptist University
Riverside, CA
Est. as: California Baptist College – 1950
NC: California Baptist University – 1998
Location changes
El Monte, CA – 1950
Riverside, CA – 1955

California Institute of Technology
Pasadena, CA
Est. as: Throop University – 1891
NC: Throop Polytechnic Institute – 1893
NC: Throop College of Technology – 1913
NC: California Institute of Technology – 1920

California Lutheran University
Thousand Oaks, CA
Est. as: California Lutheran College – 1959
NC: California Lutheran University – 1986

California Polytechnic State University, San Luis Obispo
San Luis Obispo, CA

Est. as: California Polytechnic School – 1901
NC: California State Polytechnic School – 1937
NC: California State Polytechnic College – 1947
NC: California Polytechnic State University, San Luis Obispo – 1972

California State Polytechnic University, Pomona
Pomona, CA

Est. as: Voorhis Unit of the California Polytechnic School – 1938
NC: California State Polytechnic College, Pomona – 1949
NC: California State Polytechnic University, Pomona – 1972

Location changes
San Dimas, CA – 1938
Pomona, CA – 1956

Original campus was site of former Voorhis School for Boys; present site is former ranch of W. K. Kellogg. From 1949 thru 1979 both campuses were operated as Voorhis and Kellogg campus/unit.

California State University, Bakersfield
Bakersfield, CA

Est. as: California State College, Bakersfield – 1970
NC: California State University, Bakersfield – 1987

California State University, Chico
Chico, CA

Est. as: Chico State Normal School – 1887
NC: State Teachers College, Chico – 1921
NC: California State College, Chico – 1935
NC: California State University, Chico – 1972

California State University, Dominquez Hills
Carson, CA

Est. as: California State College, Dominquez Hills – 1960
NC: California State University, Dominguez Hills – 1974

34

California State University, Fresno
Fresno, CA

Est. as: Fresno State Normal School – 1911
NC: State Teachers College, Fresno – 1921
NC: California State College, Fresno – 1935
NC: California State University, Fresno – 1972

From 1921-1948, Fresno Junior College operated on the same campus with the same staff.

California State University, Fullerton
Fullerton, CA

Est. as: Orange County State College – 1957
NC: Orange State College – 1962
NC: California State College at Fullerton – 1964
NC: California State College, Fullerton – 1968
NC: California State University, Fullerton – 1972

California State University, Hayward
Hayward, CA

Est. as: State College for Alameda County – 1957
NC: Alameda County State College – 1961
NC: California State College at Hayward – 1963
NC: California State University, Hayward – 1972

California State University, Long Beach
Long Beach, CA

Est. as: Los Angeles-Orange County State College – 1949
NC: Long Beach State College – 1950
NC: California State College, Long Beach – 1968
NC: California State University, Long Beach – 1972

California State University, Los Angeles
Los Angeles, CA

Est. as: Los Angeles State College – 1947
NC: Los Angeles State College of Applied Arts & Sciences – 1949
NC: California State College at Los Angeles – 1964
NC: California State College, Los Angeles – 1968
NC: California State University, Los Angeles – 1972

By MO: By merger (of) *DM:* Dissolved merger (with) *MW:* Merged with *NC:* Name change (to)

California State University, Northridge
Northridge, CA

Est. as: San Fernando Valley Campus of Los Angeles State College of Applied Arts & Sciences – 1958
NC: San Fernando Valley State College – 1958
NC: California State University, Northridge – 1972

California State University, Sacramento
Sacramento, CA

Est. as: Sacramento State College – 1947
NC: California State University, Sacramento – 1972

California State University, San Bernardino
San Bernardino, CA

Est. as: California State College, San Bernardino – 1965
NC: California State University, San Bernardino – 1984

California State University, San Marcos
San Marcos, CA

Est. as: California State University, San Marcos – 1988

California State University, Stanislaus
Turlock, CA

Est. as: Stanislaus State College – 1957
NC: California State College, Stanislaus – 1972
NC: California State University, Stanislaus – 1985

California University of Pennsylvania of the State System of Higher Education
California, PA

Est. as: California Academy – 1852
NC: South Western Normal School – 1874
NC: California State Normal School – 1914
NC: California State Teachers College – 1927
NC: California State College – 1960
NC: California University of Pennsylvania of the State System of Higher Education – 1983

By MO: By merger (of) ***DM:*** Dissolved merger (with) ***MW:*** Merged with ***NC:*** Name change (to)

California, Berkeley, University of

Berkeley, CA

Est. as: University of California – 1868*
By MO: College of California – 1868
By MO: Agricultural, Mining, & Mechanical Arts College – 1868
NC: University of California, Berkeley – 1952

Location changes

Oakland, CA – 1868
Berkeley, CA – 1873

*Recognizes merger year, 1868, as official established year; does not recognize histories of merged institutions.

California, Davis, University of

Davis, CA

Est. as: University Farm School – 1908
NC: Northern Branch of the College of Agriculture, University of California – 1922
NC: College of Agriculture at Davis – 1938
NC: University of California, Davis – 1959

California, Irvine, University of

Irvine, CA

Est. as: University of California, Irvine – 1965
MW: California College of Medicine – 1967

California, Los Angeles, University of

Los Angeles, CA

Est. as: University of California, Southern Branch – 1919
NC: University of California at Los Angeles – 1927
NC: University of California, Los Angeles – 1958

In 1918, grounds and facilities of Los Angeles State Normal School, established in 1881, were transferred to the University of California and became the Southern Branch of the University of California in 1919.

By MO: By merger (of) **DM:** Dissolved merger (with) **MW:** Merged with **NC:** Name change (to)

California, Riverside, University of
Riverside, CA

Est. as: Citrus Experiment Station – 1907*
NC: University of California, Riverside Campus – 1954
NC: University of California, Riverside – 1958

*Recognizes 1954 as official established year.

California, San Diego, University of
La Jolla, CA

Est. as: Marine Biological Station of San Diego – 1903*
NC: Scripps Institution of Biological Research – 1912
NC: University of California, Scripps Institution of Oceanography – 1925
NC: University of California, San Diego – 1960

*Recognizes 1960 as official established year.

California, Santa Barbara, University of
Santa Barbara, CA

Est. as: Anna S C Blake Manual Training School – 1891*
NC: Santa Barbara State Normal School of Manual Arts & Home Economics – 1909
NC: Santa Barbara State Normal School – 1919
NC: Santa Barbara State Teachers College – 1921
NC: Santa Barbara State College – 1935
NC: Santa Barbara College of the University of California – 1944
NC: University of California, Santa Barbara – 1958

*Recognizes 1909 as official established year.

California, Santa Cruz, University of
Santa Cruz, CA

Est. as: University of California, Santa Cruz – 1965

38

Calumet College of Saint Joseph
Whiting, IN

Est. as: Saint Joseph's College Calumet Center – 1951
NC: Saint Joseph's College Calument Campus – 1960
NC: Saint Joseph's Calumet College – 1971
DM: Saint Joseph's College – 1973
NC: Calumet College – 1973
NC: Calumet College of Saint Joseph – 1987

Location changes
Lake County, IN – 1951
East Chicago, IN – 1960
Whiting, IL – 1976

Calvin College
Grand Rapids, MI

Est. as: Theological School of the Christian Reformed Church, The – 1876
NC: John Calvin Junior College – 1906
NC: Calvin College – 1920

Cameron University
Lawton, OK

Est. as: Cameron State School of Agriculture – 1908
NC: Cameron State Agricultural College – 1927
NC: Cameron College – 1971
NC: Cameron University – 1975

Campbell University
Buies Creek, NC

Est. as: Buie's Creek Academy – 1887
NC: Campbell Junior College – 1926
NC: Campbell College – 1959
NC: Campbell University – 1979

Campbellsville University
Campbellsville, KY

Est. as: Russell Creek Academy – 1906
NC: Campbellsville College – 1924
NC: Campbellsville University – 1996

By MO: By merger (of) *DM:* Dissolved merger (with) *MW:* Merged with *NC:* Name change (to)

Canisius College
Buffalo, NY
Est. as: Canisius College – 1870

Capital University
Columbus, OH
Est. as: Theological Seminary of the Evangelical Lutheran Synod of Ohio – 1830
NC: Capital University – 1850
MW: Franklin University School of Law – 1966
Location changes
Canton, OH – 1830
Columbus, OH – 1831

Cardinal Stritch University
Milwaukee, WI
Est. as: Saint Clare College – 1937
NC: Cardinal Stritch College – 1946
NC: Cardinal Stritch University – 1997

Carleton College
Northfield, MN
Est. as: Northfield College – 1866
NC: Carleton College – 1871

Carlow College
Pittsburgh, PA
Est. as: Mount Mercy College – 1929
NC: Carlow College – 1969

Carnegie Mellon University
Pittsburgh, PA
Est. as: Carnegie Technical Schools – 1900
NC: Carnegie Institute of Technology – 1912
MW: Mellon Institute – 1967
NC: Carnegie Mellon University – 1967

Carroll College
Helena, MT

Est. as: Mount Saint Charles College – 1909
NC: Carroll College – 1932

Carroll College
Waukesha, WI

Est. as: Prairieville Academy – 1840*
NC: Carroll College – 1846

*Recognizes 1846 as official established year.

Carson-Newman College
Jefferson City, TN

Est. as: Mossy Creek Baptist Seminary – 1851
NC: Mossy Creek Baptist College – 1855
NC: Carson College – 1880
MW: Newman College for Women – 1889
NC: Carson-Newman College – 1889

Carthage College
Kenosha, WI

Est. as: Literary & Theological Institute of the Lutheran Church in the Far West – 1847
NC: Hillsboro College – 1847
NC: Illinois State University – 1852
NC: Carthage College – 1870

Location changes
Hillsboro, IL – 1847
Springfield, IL – 1852
Carthage, IL – 1870
Kenosha, WI – 1962

Name change to Hillsboro College was before first classes in 1847. Illinois State University closed in 1869; re-opened in March, 1870, as Carthage College.

By MO: By merger (of) **DM:** Dissolved merger (with) **MW:** Merged with **NC:** Name change (to)

Case Western Reserve University
Cleveland, OH

Est. as: Western Reserve College – 1826
NC: Adelbert College of Western Reserve University – 1882
NC: Western Reserve University – 1884
MW: Cleveland School of Education – 1928
MW: Case Institute of Technology – 1967
NC: Case Western Reserve University – 1967

Location changes
Tallmadge, OH – 1826
Hudson, OH – 1827
Cleveland, OH – 1882

Opened in Tallmadge while facilities were being constructed in Hudson.

Castleton State College
Castleton, VT

Est. as: Rutland County Grammar School – 1787
NC: Vermont Classical High School – 1828
NC: Castleton Seminary – 1830
NC: Castleton Seminary & State Normal School – 1867
NC: State Normal School at Castleton – 1876
NC: Castleton Normal School – 1921
NC: Castleton Teachers College – 1947
NC: Castleton State College – 1962

May have been named Castleton Academy between 1828 and 1830.

Catawba College
Salisbury, NC

Est. as: Catawba College – 1851
NC: Catawba High School – 1865
NC: Catawba College – 1885

Location changes
Newton, NC – 1851
Salisbury, NC – 1925

By MO: By merger (of) ***DM:*** Dissolved merger (with) ***MW:*** Merged with ***NC:*** Name change (to)

42

Catholic University of America, The

Washington, DC

Est. as: Catholic University of America, The – 1887
MW: National Catholic School of Social Services – 1947
MW: Columbus University – 1954

Cazenovia College

Cazenovia, NY

Est. as: Seminary of the Genesee Conference, The – 1824
NC: Seminary of the Genesee & Oneida Conferences, The – 1828
NC: Seminary of the Oneida Conference, The – 1830
NC: Seminary of the New York Conference Seminary, The – 1868
NC: Cazenovia Seminary, The – 1853
NC: Cazenovia Seminary Junior College – 1934
NC: Cazenovia Junior College for Women – 1942
NC: Cazenovia College – 1961

Cedar Crest College

Allentown, PA

Est. as: Allentown Female College – 1867
NC: Allentown College for Women – 1893
NC: Cedar Crest College – 1913

Cedarville University

Cedarville, OH

Est. as: Cedarville College – 1887
MW: Baptist Bible Institute – 1953
NC: Cedarville University – 2000

Centenary College

Hackettstown, NJ

Est. as: Centenary Collegiate Institute – 1867
NC: Centenary Junior College – 1940
NC: Centenary College for Women – 1956
NC: Centenary College – 1976

By MO: By merger (of) ***DM:*** Dissolved merger (with) ***MW:*** Merged with ***NC:*** Name change (to)

Centenary College of Louisiana
Shreveport, LA

Est. as: College of Louisiana – 1825
MW: Centenary College – 1839
NC: Centenary College of Louisiana – 1845

Location changes
Jackson, LA – 1825
Clinton, MS – 1839
Brandon Springs, MS – 1840
Jackson, LA – 1845
Shreveport, LA – 1908

College of Louisiana was established in Jackson in 1925. Centenary College, established in Clinton in 1839, purchased College of Louisiana in 1845 and moved the merged institution to Jackson as Centenary College of Louisiana.

Central Arkansas, University of
Conway, AR

Est. as: Arkansas State Normal School – 1907
NC: Arkansas State Teachers College – 1925
NC: State College of Arkansas – 1967
NC: University of Central Arkansas – 1975

Central College
Pella, IA

Est. as: Central University of Iowa – 1853
NC: Central College – 1994

Central Connecticut State University
New Britain, CT

Est. as: New Britain Normal School – 1849
NC: Teachers College of Connecticut – 1933
NC: Central Connecticut State College – 1959
NC: Central Connecticut State University – 1983

Central Florida, University of
Orlando, FL

Est. as: Florida Technological University – 1963
NC: University of Central Florida – 1978

By MO: By merger (of) *DM:* Dissolved merger (with) *MW:* Merged with *NC:* Name change (to)

Central Methodist College
Fayette, MO

Est. as: Central College – 1854
MW: Northwest Missouri College – 1922
MW: Marvin College – 1924
MW: Central College for Women – 1924
MW: Scarritt-Morrisville College – 1924
MW: Howard Payne College – 1927
NC: Central Methodist College – 1961

Central Michigan University
Mount Pleasant, MI

Est. as: Central Michigan Normal School & Business Institute – 1892
NC: Central Michigan Normal School – 1895
NC: Central State Teachers College – 1927
NC: Central Michigan College of Education – 1940
NC: Central Michigan College – 1957
NC: Central Michigan University – 1959

Central Missouri State University
Warrensburg, MO

Est. as: State Normal School for Second Normal District of Missouri – 1871
NC: Central Missouri State Teachers College – 1919
NC: Central Missouri State College – 1946
NC: Central Missouri State University – 1972

Central Oklahoma, University of
Edmond, OK

Est. as: Territorial Normal School of Oklahoma – 1890
NC: Central State Normal School – 1904
NC: Central State Teachers College – 1919
NC: Central State College – 1939
NC: Central State University – 1971
NC: University of Central Oklahoma – 1991

By MO: By merger (of) *DM:* Dissolved merger (with) *MW:* Merged with *NC:* Name change (to)

Central State University
Wilberforce, OH

Est. as: Combined Normal & Industrial Department at Wilberforce University – 1887
NC: College of Education & Industrial Arts – 1941
DM: Wilberforce University – 1947
NC: Wilberforce State College – 1947
NC: Central State College – 1951
NC: Central State University – 1965

Established as a state supported department of Wilberforce University, a private institution. It became independent of Wilberforce in 1947 but retained Wilberforce in its name until 1951 name change. Central State and Wilberforce are across the street from each other.

Central Washington University
Ellensburg, WA

Est. as: Washington State Normal School – 1890
NC: Central Washington College of Education – 1937
NC: Central Washington State College – 1961
NC: Central Washington University – 1977

Centre College
Danville, KY

Est. as: Centre College – 1819
MW: Central University – 1901
NC: Central University of Kentucky – 1901
DM: Central University of Kentucky – 1918
NC: Centre College – 1918
MW: Kentucky College for Women – 1926

In the merger with Central, both schools retained their own campus. It was a merger of Presbyterian institutions that had different programs and was more administrative than actual.

By MO: By merger (of) *DM:* Dissolved merger (with) *MW:* Merged with *NC:* Name change (to)

Chadron State College
Chadron, NE

Est. as: State Normal School at Chadron, Nebraska – 1911
NC: Nebraska State Normal College at Chadron – 1921
NC: Nebraska State Teachers College at Chadron – 1949
NC: Chadron State College – 1963

Chaminade University of Honolulu
Honolulu, HI

Est. as: Saint Louis Junior College – 1955
NC: Chaminade College of Honolulu – 1957
NC: Chaminade University of Honolulu – 1977

Champlain College
Burlington, VT

Est. as: Burlington Collegiate Institute – 1878
NC: Queen City Business College – 1884
NC: Burlington Business College – 1886
NC: Champlain College of Commerce – 1956
NC: Champlain College – 1958

Known when established as Burlington Commercial School.

Chapman University
Orange, CA

Est. as: Hesperian College – 1861
MW: Berkeley Bible Seminary – 1896
NC: Berkeley Bible Seminary – 1896
NC: California Christian College – 1920
NC: Chapman College – 1934
NC: Chapman University – 1991

Location changes
Woodland, CA – 1861
Los Angeles, CA – 1920
Orange, CA – 1954

By MO: By merger (of) *DM:* Dissolved merger (with) *MW:* Merged with *NC:* Name change (to)

Charleston Southern University
Charleston, SC

Est. as: Baptist College at Charleston – 1964
NC: Charleston Southern University – 1989

Charleston, College of
Charleston, SC

Est. as: College of Charleston – 1770

Charleston, University of
Charleston, WV

Est. as: Barboursville Seminary – 1888
NC: Barboursville College – 1889
NC: Morris Harvey College – 1901
MW: Kanawha Junior College – 1935
MW: Mason College of Fine Arts & Music – 1935
NC: University of Charleston – 1978
Location changes
Barboursville, WV – 1888
Charleston, WV – 1935

Chatham College
Pittsburgh, PA

Est. as: Pennsylvania Female College – 1869
NC: Pennsylvania College for Women – 1890
NC: Chatham College – 1955

Chestnut Hill College
Philadelphia, PA

Est. as: Mount Saint Joseph Academy – 1858*
NC: Mount Saint Joseph Collegiate Institute – 1903
NC: Mount Saint Joseph College – 1904
NC: Chestnut Hill College of the Sisters of Saint Joseph – 1938
NC: Chestnut Hill College – 1972

*Recognizes 1924, when first four-year class was admitted, as official established year.

Cheyney University of Pennsylvania of the State System of Higher Education
Cheyney, PA

Est. as: African Institute, The – 1837
NC: Institute for Coloured Youth – 1837
NC: Cheyney Training School for Teachers – 1914
NC: Cheyney State Normal School – 1920
NC: Cheyney State Teachers College – 1951
NC: Cheyney State College – 1960
NC: Cheyney University of Pennsylvania of the State System of Higher Education – 1983

Location changes
Philadelphia, PA – 1837
Cheyney, PA – 1902

Chicago State University
Chicago, IL

Est. as: Teacher Training School, Blue Island – 1867
NC: Cook County Normal School – 1869
NC: Chicago Normal School Chicago Board of Education – 1897
NC: Chicago Normal College – 1913
NC: Chicago Teachers College – 1938
NC: Chicago Teachers College, South – 1961
NC: Illinois Teachers College: Chicago South – 1965
NC: Chicago State College – 1967
NC: Chicago State University – 1971

Location changes
Blue Island, IL – 1867
Englewood, IL – 1869
Chicago, IL – 1897

Chicago, University of
Chicago, IL

Est. as: University of Chicago – 1891

There was an earlier, unrelated, University of Chicago (1857-1886).

By MO: By merger (of) *DM:* Dissolved merger (with) *MW:* Merged with *NC:* Name change (to)

Chowan College
Murfreesboro, NC

Est. as: Chowan Baptist Female Institute – 1848
NC: Chowan College – 1910

Christendom College
Front Royal, VA

Est. as: Christendom College – 1977
MW: Notre Dame Institute of Alexandria – 1979

Christian Heritage College
El Cajon, CA

Est. as: Christian Heritage College – 1970

Location changes
San Diego, CA – 1970
El Cajon, CA – 1973

Christopher Newport University
Newport News, VA

Est. as: William & Mary College: Newport News Branch – 1960
NC: Christopher Newport College – 1977
NC: Christopher Newport University – 1991

Cincinnati, University of
Cincinnati, OH

Est. as: University of Cincinnati – 1870*
MW: Medical College of Ohio – 1896
MW: Cincinnati College – 1897
MW: Cincinnati College of Pharmacy – 1954
MW: College-Conservatory of Music – 1962
MW: Ohio College of Applied Science – 1969
MW: Ohio Mechanics Institute – 1969

*Recognizes 1819, when Cincinnati College and Drake Medical College of Ohio were established, as official established year.

Citadel, The Military College of South Carolina, The
Charleston, SC

Est. as: South Carolina Military Academy – 1842
NC: Citadel, The Military College of South Carolina, The – 1910

By MO: By merger (of) **DM:** Dissolved merger (with) **MW:** Merged with **NC:** Name change (to)

50

City College of the City University of New York, The
New York, NY

Est. as: New York Free Academy – 1847
NC: College of the City of New York, The – 1866
NC: City College, The – 1929
NC: City College of the City University of New York, The – 1961

Claflin University
Orangeburg, SC

Est. as: Claflin University – 1869
MW: Baker Biblical Institute – c1869
MW: State College of Agriculture & Mechanics – 1872
DM: State College of Agriculture & Mechanics – 1896
NC: Claflin College – 1979
NC: Claflin University – 1996

State College of Agriculture & Mechanics was established by the state legislature as a co-ordinate college of Claflin University. Its name was changed in 1878 to Claflin College; in 1896, it was separated from Claflin to become, eventually, South Carolina State University.

Claremont McKenna College
Claremont, CA

Est. as: Claremont College Undergraduate School for Men – 1946
NC: Claremont Men's College – 1947
NC: Claremont McKenna College – 1976

Clarion University of Pennsylvania of the State System of Higher Education
Clarion, PA

Est. as: Carrier Seminary of Western Pennsylvania – 1867
NC: Clarion State Normal School – 1887
NC: Clarion State Teachers College – 1927
NC: Clarion State College – 1960
NC: Clarion University of Pennsylvania of the State System of Higher Education – 1983

By MO: By merger (of) *DM:* Dissolved merger (with) *MW:* Merged with *NC:* Name change (to)

Clark Atlanta University
Atlanta, GA

Est. as: Clark Atlanta University – 1988*
By MO: Clark College – 1988
By MO: Atlanta University – 1988

*Recognizes merger year, 1988, as official established year; does not recognize histories of merged institutions.

Clark University
Worcester, MA

Est. as: Clark University – 1887
MW: School of the Worcester Art Museum – 1981

Originally a graduate school, it established Clark College, the undergraduate division, in 1902.

Clarke College
Dubuque, IA

Est. as: Saint Mary's Academy – 1843
NC: Saint Joseph Academy – 1846
NC: Mount Saint Joseph Academy and College – 1881
NC: Clarke College – 1928

Clarkson University
Potsdam, NY

Est. as: Thomas S Clarkson Memorial School of Technology – 1896
NC: Thomas S Clarkson Memorial College of Technology – 1913
NC: Clarkson University – 1984

Clayton College & State University
Morrow, GA

Est. as: Clayton State College – 1969
NC: Clayton College & State University – 1996

Clemson University
Clemson, SC

Est. as: Clemson Agricultural College of South Carolina – 1889
NC: Clemson University – 1964

By MO: By merger (of) *DM:* Dissolved merger (with) *MW:* Merged with *NC:* Name change (to)

Cleveland State University
Cleveland, OH

Est. as: Cleveland YMCA School of Technology – 1921*
NC: Fenn College – 1930
NC: Cleveland State University – 1964
MW: Cleveland-Marshall School of Law – 1969

*Recognizes 1923, when first college-level courses were offered, as official established year

Began in 1881 when the local YMCA offered classes which developed into the Cleveland YMCA School of Technology. Fenn College separated from the YMCA in 1951. First college courses were offered in 1923, but the institution technically was established when the state took over Fenn in 1964.

Coastal Carolina University
Conway, SC

Est. as: Coastal Carolina Junior College of the College of Charleston – 1954
NC: Coastal Carolina Junior College – 1958
NC: University of South Carolina at Coastal Carolina – 1960
NC: Coastal Carolina University – 1993

Coe College
Cedar Rapids, IA

Est. as: Cedar Rapids Collegiate Institute – 1851
NC: Coe Collegiate Institute – 1853
NC: Parsons Seminary – 1866
NC: Coe Collegiate Institute – 1875
NC: Coe College – 1881
MW: Leander Clark College – 1919

Cogswell Polytechnical College
Sunnyvale, CA

Est. as: Cogswell Polytechnical College – 1887

Location changes
San Francisco, CA – 1887
Cupertino, CA – 1985
Sunnyvale, CA – 1994

By MO: By merger (of) ***DM:*** Dissolved merger (with) ***MW:*** Merged with ***NC:*** Name change (to)

Coker College
Hartsville, SC

Est. as: Welsh Neck Academy – 1894*
NC: Coker College for Women – 1908
NC: Coker College – 1970

*Recognizes 1908 as official established year.

Colby College
Waterville, ME

Est. as: Maine Literary & Theological Institution – 1813
NC: Waterville College – 1821
NC: Colby University – 1867
NC: Colby College – 1899

Colby-Sawyer College
New London, NH

Est. as: New London Seminary – 1837
NC: New London Literary & Scientific Institution – 1854
NC: Colby Academy, The – 1878
NC: Colby School for Girls – 1928
NC: Colby Junior College for Women – 1933
NC: Colby College-New Hampshire – 1973
NC: Colby-Sawyer College – 1975

Colgate University
Hamilton, NY

Est. as: Hamilton Literary & Theological Institution – 1819
MW: New York Baptist Theological Seminary – 1823
NC: Madison University – 1846
NC: Colgate University – 1890

College Misericordia
Dallas, PA

Est. as: College Misericordia – 1924

Colorado at Boulder, University of
Boulder, CO

Est. as: University at Boulder – 1876
NC: University of Colorado at Boulder – 1972

Colorado at Colorado Springs, University of
Colorado Springs, CO

Est. as: University of Colorado-Colorado Springs Center – 1965
NC: University of Colorado at Colorado Springs – 1972

Colorado at Denver, University of
Denver, CO

Est. as: Department of Correspondence & Extension in Denver – 1912
NC: University of Colorado-Denver Center – 1964
NC: University of Colorado at Denver – 1972

At establishment, was a department of the University of Colorado.

Colorado Christian University
Lakewood, CO

Est. as: Denver Bible Institute – 1914
NC: Denver Bible College – 1945
NC: Rockmont College – 1949
MW: Western Bible College – 1985
NC: Colorado Christian College – 1985
MW: Colorado Baptist University – 1989
NC: Colorado Christian University – 1989

Location changes
Denver, CO – 1914
Longmont, CO – 1949
Lakewood, CO – 1967

Colorado College, The
Colorado Springs, CO

Est. as: Colorado College, The – 1874

Colorado State University
Fort Collins, CO

Est. as: Agricultural College of Colorado – 1870
NC: Colorado State College of Agriculture & Mechanic Arts, The – 1935
NC: Colorado Agricultural & Mechanical College – 1944
NC: Colorado State University – 1957

By MO: By merger (of) *DM:* Dissolved merger (with) *MW:* Merged with *NC:* Name change (to)

Colorado Technical University
Colorado Springs, CO

Est. as: Colorado Electronic Training, Inc. – 1965
NC: Colorado Electronic Technical College – 1970
NC: Colorado Technical College – 1988
NC: Colorado Technical University – 1995

Location changes
Colorado Springs, CO – 1965
Manitou Springs, CO – 1966
Colorado Springs, CO – 1977

Columbia College
Columbia, MO

Est. as: Christian Female College – 1851
NC: Christian College – 1929
NC: Columbia College – 1970

Columbia College
Columbia, SC

Est. as: Columbia Female College, The – 1854
NC: Columbia College – 1905

Administrative merger with Wofford, 1948-1951.

Columbia College Chicago
Chicago, IL

Est. as: Columbia College of Oratory – 1890
NC: Columbia College of Expression – 1907
MW: Pestalozzi-Froebel Teachers College – 1928
NC: Pestalozzi-Froebel Teachers College – 1928
DM: Pestalozzi-Froebel Teachers College – 1944
NC: Columbia College of Chicago – 1944
NC: Columbia College Chicago – UNK

Columbia Union College
Takoma Park, MD

Est. as: Washington Training College – 1904
NC: Washington Foreign Mission Seminary – 1907
NC: Washington Missionary College – 1914
NC: Columbia Union College – 1961

By MO: By merger (of) *DM:* Dissolved merger (with) *MW:* Merged with *NC:* Name change (to)

56

Columbia University in the City of New York
New York, NY

Est. as: King's College of the Province of New York – 1754
NC: Columbia College in the City of New York – 1784
NC: Columbia University in the City of New York – 1912

Known as Columbia University.

Columbus State University
Columbus, GA

Est. as: Columbus College – 1958
NC: Columbus State University – 1996

Concord College
Athens, WV

Est. as: Concord State Normal School – 1872
NC: Concord State Teachers College – 1931
NC: Concord College – 1943

Location changes
Concord, WV – 1872
Athens, WV – 1896

Administrative merger with Bluefield State, 1973-1976. Did not change location in 1896; Concord changed name to Athens.

Concordia College
Bronxville, NY

Est. as: New York Progymnasium – 1881
NC: Concordia Gymnasium – 1905
NC: Concordia College – 1969

Location changes
New York, NY – 1881
Hawthorne, NY – 1894
Bronxville, NY – 1910

Located in New York City for 1908-09 academic year and until January, 1910, while new campus was constructed in Bronxville. College level courses began in 1905. College and junior college may have been known as division/department of Concordia Collegiate Institute from 1918-1969.

By MO: By merger (of) **DM:** Dissolved merger (with) **MW:** Merged with **NC:** Name change (to)

Concordia College
Moorhead, MN
Est. as: Concordia College – 1891
MW: Park Region Luther College – 1917

Concordia College
Selma, AL
Est. as: Alabama Lutheran Academy & College – 1922
NC: Concordia College – 1980

Concordia University
Ann Arbor, MI
Est. as: Concordia Lutheran Junior College – 1962
NC: Concordia Junior College – c1978
NC: Concordia University – 2001

Concordia University
Irvine, CA
Est. as: Christ College Irvine – 1972
NC: Concordia University – 1993

Concordia University
Portland, OR
Est. as: Evangelical Lutheran College at Portland, Oregon, The – 1905
NC: Concordia University – 1995

After becoming a junior college in 1950, was known as Concordia College.

Concordia University
River Forest, IL
Est. as: Concordia Teachers College – 1864
NC: Concordia College – 1979
NC: Concordia University – 1990
Location changes
Addison, IL – 1864
River Forest, IL – 1913

By MO: By merger (of) *DM:* Dissolved merger (with) *MW:* Merged with *NC:* Name change (to)

Concordia University
Seward, NE

Est. as: Lutheran Seminary, The – 1894
NC: Concordia Teachers College – 1924
NC: Concordia College – 1992
NC: Concordia University – 1998

Concordia University at Austin
Austin, TX

Est. as: Lutheran Concordia College – 1926
NC: Concordia Lutheran College – 1965
NC: Concordia University at Austin – 1996

Concordia University Wisconsin
Mequon, WI

Est. as: Concordia College – 1881
NC: Concordia College Wisconsin – 1983
NC: Concordia University Wisconsin – 1989
Location changes
Milwaukee, WI – 1881
Mequon, WI – 1983

Concordia University, Saint Paul
Saint Paul, MN

Est. as: Concordia College – 1893
NC: Concordia University, Saint Paul – 1997

Connecticut College
New London, CT

Est. as: Thames College – 1911
NC: Connecticut College for Women – 1911
NC: Connecticut College – 1969

By MO: By merger (of) **DM:** Dissolved merger (with) **MW:** Merged with **NC:** Name change (to)

Connecticut, University of
Storrs, CT

Est. as: Storrs Agricultural School – 1881
NC: Storrs Agricultural College – 1893
NC: Connecticut Agricultural College – 1899
NC: Connecticut State College – 1933
NC: University of Connecticut – 1939

Converse College
Spartanburg, SC

Est. as: Converse College – 1889

Coppin State College
Baltimore, MD

Est. as: High & Training School – 1900
NC: Fannie Jackson Coppin Normal School – 1926
NC: Coppin Teachers College – 1938
NC: Coppin State Teachers College – 1950
NC: Coppin State College – 1963

Cornell College
Mount Vernon, IA

Est. as: Iowa Conference Seminary – 1853
NC: Cornell College – 1855

Cornell University
Ithaca, NY

Est. as: Cornell University – 1865

60

Cornerstone University
Grand Rapids, MI

Est. as: Baptist Bible Institute of Grand Rapids, Michigan – 1941
NC: Baptist Bible Institute & School of Theology of Grand Rapids Michigan – 1944
NC: Grand Rapids Baptist Theological Seminary & Bible Institute – 1948
NC: Grand Rapids Baptist Bible College & Seminary – 1963
NC: Grand Rapids Baptist College & Seminary – 1972
MW: Grand Rapids Bible & Music College – 1993
NC: Cornerstone College & Grand Rapids Baptist Seminary – 1994
NC: Cornerstone University – 1999

Grand Rapids Bible & Music had closed; Cornerstone assumed control. Legal name of overall operation is Cornerstone Baptist Educational Ministries.

Covenant College
Lookout Mountain, GA

Est. as: Covenant College – 1955

Location changes
Pasadena, CA – 1955
Creve Coeur, MO – 1956
Lookout Mountain, GA – 1964

Creighton University
Omaha, NE

Est. as: Creighton University – 1878
MW: Omaha College of Pharmacy – 1905

Crichton College
Memphis, TN

Est. as: Mid-South Bible Training Center – 1941
NC: Mid-South Bible Institute – 1948
NC: Mid-South Bible College – 1960
NC: Crichton College – 1987

By MO: By merger (of) *DM:* Dissolved merger (with) *MW:* Merged with *NC:* Name change (to)

Crown College
Saint Bonifacius, MN

Est. as: Saint Paul Bible Institute – 1916
NC: Saint Paul Bible College – 1958
NC: Crown College – 1991

Location changes
Saint Paul, MN – 1916
Saint Bonifacius, MN – 1970

Culver-Stockton College
Canton, MO

Est. as: Christian University – 1853
NC: Culver-Stockton College – 1917

Cumberland College
Williamsburg, KY

Est. as: Williamsburg Institute – 1889
MW: Highland College – 1913
NC: Cumberland College – 1913

Cumberland University
Lebanon, TN

Est. as: Cumberland University – 1842
NC: Cumberland College – 1956
NC: Cumberland University – 1984

In 1871-1873, under a contractual relationship, Medical College of Memphis operated a branch on Cumberland campus. In 1951, the College of Liberal Arts was discontinued, but the law school continued. The College of Liberal Arts was re-opened in 1956 as a two-year program and became four-year in 1982. The law school moved to Samford University in 1961.

62

Curry College
Milton, MA

Est. as: School of Expression & Elocution – 1879
NC: School of Expression – 1885
NC: Curry College – 1943
MW: Perry Normal School – 1974
MW: Children's Hospital School of Nursing – 1977

Location changes
Boston, MA – 1879
Milton, MA – 1952

D

Daemen College
Amherst, NY

Est. as: Rosary Hill College – 1947
NC: Daemen College – 1976

Dakota State University
Madison, SD

Est. as: Dakota Normal School – 1881
NC: Madison State Normal School – 1902
NC: Eastern State Normal School – 1921
NC: Eastern State Teachers College – 1927
NC: General Beadle State Teachers College – 1947
NC: General Beadle State College – 1964
NC: Dakota State College – 1969
NC: Dakota State University – 1989

Dakota Wesleyan University
Mitchell, SD

Est. as: Dakota University – 1885
NC: Dakota Wesleyan University – 1904
MW: Black Hills College – 1947

Dallas Baptist University
Dallas, TX

Est. as: Decatur Baptist College – 1898*
NC: Dallas Baptist College – 1965
NC: Dallas Baptist University – 1985

Location changes
Decatur, TX – 1898
Dallas, TX – 1965

*Recognizes 1965 as official established year.

Dallas, The University of
Irving, TX

Est. as: University of Dallas, The – 1956

Original University of Dallas was chartered in 1910 when Vincentian Fathers took that name for Holy Trinity College which they had founded in 1905. Charter became dormant in 1929 (institution may have closed in 1927). Charter was revived in 1955; new University of Dallas opened in 1956 and merged with Our Lady of Victory, a women's junior college in Fort Worth.

Dana College
Blair, NE

Est. as: Trinity Seminary – 1884
MW: Blair College – 1889
NC: Trinity Seminary & Blair College – 1889
NC: Dana College & Trinity Seminary – 1903
NC: Dana College – 1961

Trinity Seminary moved to Dubuque; Dana became autonomous on January 1, 1961.

Daniel Webster College
Nashua, NH

Est. as: New England Aeronautical Institute – 1965
MW: Daniel Webster Junior College – 1977
NC: Daniel Webster College – 1977
1978

New England Aeronautical Institute formed Daniel Webster Junior College in 1967.

Dartmouth College
Hanover, NH

Est. as: Dartmouth College – 1769

Does not recognize Moor's Indian Charity School, founded 1754 in Lebanon, as a predecessor.

David Lipscomb University
Nashville, TN

Est. as: Nashville Bible School – 1891
NC: David Lipscomb College – 1917
NC: David Lipscomb University – 1989

Known as Lipscomb University.

Davidson College
Davidson, NC

Est. as: Davidson College – 1837

Davis & Elkins College
Elkins, WV

Est. as: Davis & Elkins College – 1904

Dayton, University of
Dayton, OH

Est. as: Saint Mary's School for Boys – 1850
NC: Saint Mary's Institute – 1878
NC: Saint Mary's College – 1912
NC: University of Dayton – 1920

Defiance College, The
Defiance, OH

Est. as: Defiance Female Seminary – 1850
NC: Defiance College, The – 1903

Delaware State University
Dover, DE

Est. as: State College for Colored Students – 1891
NC: Delaware State College – 1947
NC: Delaware State University – 1993

Delaware Valley College
Doylestown, PA

Est. as: National Farm School, The – 1896
NC: National Farm School & Junior College, The – 1945
NC: National Agricultural College – 1948
NC: Delaware Valley College of Science & Agriculture – 1960
NC: Delaware Valley College – 1989

Delaware, University of
Newark, DE

Est. as: Alison's Academy – 1743
NC: Academy of Newark, The – 1769
MW: Newark College – 1833
NC: Delaware College – 1843
MW: Women's College of Delaware – 1921
NC: University of Delaware – 1921

Location changes
New London, PA – 1743
Lewisville, DE – 1752
Newark, DE – c1762

Delta State University
Cleveland, MS

Est. as: Delta State Teachers College – 1924
NC: Delta State College – 1955
NC: Delta State University – 1974

Denison University
Granville, OH

Est. as: Granville Literary & Theological Institution – 1831
NC: Granville College – 1845
NC: Denison University – 1854
MW: Shepardson College – 1897

Denver, University of
Denver, CO

Est. as: Colorado Seminary – 1864
NC: University of Denver – 1880
MW: Colorado Women's College – 1982

By MO: By merger (of) **DM:** Dissolved merger (with) **MW:** Merged with **NC:** Name change (to)

DePaul University
Chicago, IL

Est. as: Saint Vincent's College – 1898
NC: DePaul University – 1907
MW: Goodman School of Drama – 1978
MW: Barat College – 2001

Merger with Barat College to be completed for 2003-04 academic year.

DePauw University
Greencastle, IN

Est. as: Indiana Asbury University – 1837
NC: DePauw University – 1884

DeSales University
Center Valley, PA

Est. as: Allentown College of Saint Francis de Sales – 1965
NC: DeSales University – 2001

Detroit Mercy, University of
Detroit, MI

Est. as: University of Detroit Mercy – 1991*
By MO: University of Detroit – 1991
By MO: Mercy University of Detroit – 1991

*Recognizes merger year, 1991, as official established year; does not recognize histories of merged institutions.

DeVry University
Oakbrook Terrace, IL

Est. as: Deforest Training School – 1931
NC: DeVry Technical Institute – 1953
NC: DeVry Institute of Technology – 1968
MW: Keller Graduate School of Management – 1987
MW: Becker CPA Review – 1996
MW: Conviser Duffy CPA Review – UNK
NC: DeVry University – 2002

A system of 22 campuses in the United States and Canada owned by DeVry, Inc. Some campuses were acquisitions of existing similar institutions with their own history; others were opened by DeVry. City of location of Oakbrook Terrace is corporate offices.

By MO: By merger (of) **DM:** Dissolved merger (with) **MW:** Merged with **NC:** Name change (to)

Dickinson College

Carlisle, PA

Est. as: Carlisle Grammar School – 1773
NC: Dickinson College – 1783

Dickinson State University

Dickinson, ND

Est. as: Dickinson Normal School – 1918
NC: Dickinson State Teachers College – 1931
NC: Dickinson State College – 1963
NC: State University of North Dakota-Dickinson – 1987
NC: Dickinson State University – 1987

Dillard University

New Orleans, LA

Est. as: Straight University – 1869
NC: Straight College – UNK
MW: New Orleans University – 1930
NC: Dillard University – 1930

Straight University is considered as the predecessor institution because it was established on June 12, 1869. Union Normal School, which became New Orleans University in 1889 and which merged with Straight in 1930 to form Dillard, was established on July 8, 1869.

District of Columbia, University of the

Washington, DC

Est. as: Normal School for Colored Girls in the City of Washington – 1851*
NC: Institution for the Education of Colored Youth, The – 1863
MW: Howard University – 1871
DM: Howard University – 1877
NC: Miner Normal School – 1879
NC: Miner Teachers College – 1929
MW: Wilson Teachers College – 1955
NC: District of Columbia Teachers College – 1955
MW: Federal City College – 1977
MW: Washington Technical Institute – 1977
NC: University of the District of Columbia – 1977

*Recognizes three established years: 1851 (Miner Teachers College); 1966 (Federal City College & Washington Technical Institute); 1977 (University of the District of Columbia).

Doane College
Crete, NE

Est. as: Doane College – 1872

Fontenelle College, established year unknown, closed in unknown year because of Civil War and drought. Doane is successor institution, but it does not include Fontenelle in its history.

Dominican College
Orangeburg, NY

Est. as: Dominican Junior College of Blauvelt – 1952
NC: Dominican College – 1959

Known as Dominican College of Blauvet for identification purposes only.

Dominican University
River Forest, IL

Est. as: Sinsinawa Academy – 1848*
NC: Saint Clara's College – 1901
NC: Rosary College – 1922
NC: Dominican University – 1997

Location changes
Sinsinawa, WI – 1848
River Forest, IL – 1922

*Recognizes 1901 as official established year.

Dominican University of California
San Rafael, CA

Est. as: Unnamed preparatory school – 1850*
NC: Dominican College of San Rafael – 1890
NC: Dominican University of California – 2000

Location changes
Monterey, CA – 1850
San Rafael, CA – 1890

*Recognizes 1890 as official established year.

By MO: By merger (of) *DM:* Dissolved merger (with) *MW:* Merged with *NC:* Name change (to)

70

Dordt College
Sioux Center, IA

Est. as: Midwest Christian Junior College – 1955
NC: Dordt College – 1956

Dowling College
Oakdale, NY

Est. as: Adelphi Suffolk College – 1955
DM: Adelphi University – 1968
NC: Dowling College – 1968

Location changes
Sayville, NY – 1955
Oakdale, NY – 1963

Began when then Adelphi College, offered extension classes in Port Jefferson, Riverhead, and Sayville.

Drake University
Des Moines, IA

Est. as: Drake University – 1881

Oskaloosa College, established in 1856, is not officially considered as a predecessor institution; it closed in 1880 and was replaced by Drake.

Drew University
Madison, NJ

Est. as: Drew Theological Seminary – 1867
NC: Drew University – 1928

Drexel University
Philadelphia, PA

Est. as: Drexel Institute of Arts, Sciences, & Industry – 1891
NC: Drexel Institute of Technology – 1936
NC: Drexel University – 1970
MW: MCP Hahnemann University – 2002

Assumed management of MCP Hahnemann University in 1998.

By MO: By merger (of) *DM:* Dissolved merger (with) *MW:* Merged with *NC:* Name change (to)

Drury University
Springfield, MO

Est. as: Springfield College – 1873
NC: Drury College – 1873
MW: Iberia Junior College – 1951
NC: Drury University – 2001

Dubuque, University of
Dubuque, IA

Est. as: German Theological School of the Northwest – 1852
NC: German Presbyterian Theological School of the Northwest – 1891
NC: Dubuque German College & Seminary – 1911
NC: University of Dubuque – 1920

Duke University
Durham, NC

Est. as: Brown's Schoolhouse – 1838
NC: Union Institute – 1839
NC: Normal College – 1851
NC: Trinity College – 1859
NC: Duke University – 1924

Location changes
Randolph County, NC – 1838
Durham, NC – 1892

Randolph County is west of Durham in central North Carolina.

Duquesne University of the Holy Ghost
Pittsburgh, PA

Est. as: Pittsburgh Catholic College of the Holy Ghost – 1878
NC: University of the Holy Ghost – 1911
NC: Duquesne University of the Holy Ghost – 1911
NC: Duquesne University – 1935
NC: Duquesne University of the Holy Ghost – 1960

Known as Duquesne University.

By MO: By merger (of) *DM:* Dissolved merger (with) *MW:* Merged with *NC:* Name change (to)

Earlham College
Richmond, IN

Est. as: Friends Boarding School – 1847
NC: Earlham College – 1859

East Carolina University
Greenville, NC

Est. as: East Carolina Teacher Training School – 1907
NC: East Carolina Teachers College – 1921
NC: East Carolina College – 1951
NC: East Carolina University – 1967

East Central University
Ada, OK

Est. as: East Central State Normal School – 1909
NC: East Central State Teachers College – 1919
NC: East Central State College – 1939
NC: East Central Oklahoma State University – 1974
NC: East Central University – 1985

East Stroudsburg University of Pennsylvania of the State System of Higher Education
East Stroudsburg, PA

Est. as: East Stroudsburg Normal School – 1893
NC: East Stroudsburg State Normal School – 1920
NC: East Stroudsburg State Teachers College – 1927
NC: East Stroudsburg State College – 1960
NC: East Stroudsburg University of Pennsylvania of the State System of Higher Education – 1983

East Tennessee State University
Johnson City, TN

Est. as: East Tennessee State Normal School – 1911
NC: East Tennessee State Teachers College – 1924
NC: State Teachers College, Johnson City – 1930
NC: East Tennessee State College – 1943
NC: East Tennessee State University – 1963

East Texas Baptist University
Marshall, TX

Est. as: College of Marshall – 1912
NC: East Texas Baptist College – 1944
NC: East Texas Baptist University – 1984

East-West University
Chicago, IL

Est. as: East-West University – 1978

Eastern Connecticut State University
Willimantic, CT

Est. as: Willimantic State Normal School – 1889
NC: Willimantic State Teachers College – 1937
NC: Willimantic State College – 1959
NC: Eastern Connecticut State College – 1967
NC: Eastern Connecticut State University – 1983

Eastern Illinois University
Charleston, IL

Est. as: Eastern Illinois State Normal School – 1895
NC: Eastern Illinois State Teachers College – 1921
NC: Eastern Illinois State College – 1947
NC: Eastern Illinois University – 1957

Eastern Kentucky University
Richmond, KY

Est. as: Eastern Kentucky State Normal School – 1906
NC: Eastern Kentucky State Normal School & Teachers College – 1922
NC: Eastern Kentucky State Teachers College – 1930
NC: Eastern Kentucky State College – 1948
NC: Eastern Kentucky University – 1966

Eastern Mennonite University
Harrisonburg, VA

Est. as: Eastern Mennonite School – 1917
NC: Eastern Mennonite College and Seminary – 1948
NC: Eastern Mennonite University – 1994

Eastern Michigan University
Ypsilanti, MI

Est. as: Michigan State Normal School – 1849
NC: Michigan State Normal College – 1899
NC: Eastern Michigan College – 1956
NC: Eastern Michigan University – 1959

Eastern Nazarene College
Quincy, MA

Est. as: Unnamed Christian school – 1900
NC: Pentacostal Collegiate Institute – 1902
NC: Eastern Nazarene College – 1918

Location changes
Saratoga Springs, NY – 1900
North Scituate, RI – 1902
Quincy, MA – 1919

Pentacostal Trade School was added in 1910. Massachusetts charter became official in 1930; thereafter students received Eastern Nazarene diploma rather than one from Northwest Nazarene College.

By MO: By merger (of) *DM:* Dissolved merger (with) *MW:* Merged with *NC:* Name change (to)

Eastern New Mexico University
Portales, NM

Est. as: Eastern New Mexico Junior College – 1934
NC: Eastern New Mexico College – 1940
NC: Eastern New Mexico University – 1949

Eastern Oregon University
LaGrande, OR

Est. as: Eastern Oregon Normal School – 1929
NC: Eastern Oregon College of Education – 1939
NC: Eastern Oregon College – 1956
NC: Eastern Oregon State College – 1974
NC: Eastern Oregon University – 1997

Eastern University
Saint Davids, PA

Est. as: Department of Eastern Baptist Theological Seminary – 1932*
NC: Eastern Baptist College – 1952
NC: Eastern College – 1972
NC: Eastern University – 2001

Location changes
Wynnewood, PA – 1932
Saint Davids, PA – 1952

*Recognizes 1952, when separated from Eastern Baptist Theological Seminary, as official established year.

Eastern Washington University
Cheney, WA

Est. as: Benjamin P Cheney Academy – 1882
NC: State Normal School at Cheney – 1890
NC: Eastern Washington College of Education – 1937
NC: Eastern Washington State College – 1961
NC: Eastern Washington University – 1977

Eckerd College
Saint Petersburg, FL

Est. as: Florida Presbyterian College – 1958
NC: Eckerd College – 1972

By MO: By merger (of) *DM:* Dissolved merger (with) *MW:* Merged with *NC:* Name change (to)

76

Edgewood College
Madison, WI

Est. as: Saint Regina Academy – 1881*
NC: Edgewood College of the Sacred Heart – 1927
NC: Edgewood College – 1970

*Recognizes 1927 as official established year.

Edinboro University of Pennsylvania of the State System of Higher Education
Edinboro, PA

Est. as: Edinboro Academy – 1856*
NC: Edinboro Normal School – 1857
NC: Edinboro State Normal School – 1861
NC: Edinboro State Teachers College – 1927
NC: Edinboro State College – 1960
NC: Edinboro University of Pennsylvania of the State System of Higher Education – 1983

*Recognizes 1857 as official established year.

Edward Waters College
Jacksonville, FL

Est. as: Brown Theological Institute – 1866
NC: Brown University – 1874
NC: Edward Waters College – 1891

Elizabeth City State University
Elizabeth City, NC

Est. as: Elizabeth City State Colored Normal School – 1891
NC: Elizabeth City State Teachers College – 1939
NC: Elizabeth City State College – 1963
NC: Elizabeth City State University – 1969

Elizabethtown College
Elizabethtown, PA

Est. as: Elizabethtown College – 1899

Elmhurst College
Elmhurst, IL

Est. as: Elmhurst Pro-Seminary & Academy – 1871
NC: Elmhurst Academy & Junior College – 1919
NC: Elmhurst College – 1924

Elmira College
Elmira, NY

Est. as: Elmira Female College – 1855
NC: Elmira College – 1890

Elms College
Chicopee, MA

Est. as: College of Our Lady of the Elms – 1928
NC: Elms College – 1983

Academy of Our Lady of the Elms (1899-1944) and Our Lady of the Elms Normal School (1899-1934) were related institutions but not predecessors of Elms.

Elon University
Elon, NC

Est. as: Elon College – 1889
NC: Elon University – 2001

Embry-Riddle Aeronautical University
Daytona Beach, FL

Est. as: Embry-Riddle Company, The – 1926
NC: Embry-Riddle International School of Aviation – 1940
NC: Embry-Riddle Aeronautical Institute – 1952
NC: Embry-Riddle Aeronautical University – 1971

Location changes
Cincinnati, OH – 1926
Miami, FL – 1939
Daytona Beach, FL – 1965

78

Emerson College
Boston, MA

Est. as: Boston Conservatory of Oratory – 1880
NC: Monroe College of Oratory – 1881
NC: Emerson College of Oratory – 1890
NC: Emerson College – 1939

Emmanuel College
Boston, MA

Est. as: Emmanuel College – 1919

Emmanuel College
Franklin Springs, GA

Est. as: Franklin Springs Institute – 1919
NC: Emmanuel College & School of Christian Ministry – 1939
NC: Emmanuel College – 1991

Emory University
Atlanta, GA

Est. as: Emory College – 1836
MW: Georgia Conference Manual Labor School – 1840
NC: Emory University – 1915
MW: Wesley Memorial Hospital School of Nursing – 1915
MW: Atlanta Medical College – 1915
MW: Carnegie Library School of Atlanta – 1925
MW: Atlanta-Southern Dental College – 1944

Location changes
Oxford, GA – 1836
Atlanta, GA – 1915

Georgia Conference Manual Labor School was established in 1834; Emory does not recognize that school's history. Emory College became a college of the newly created Emory University in 1915. Move to Atlanta was not completed until 1919.

Emory & Henry College
Emory, VA

Est. as: Emory & Henry College – 1836
MW: Martha Washington College – 1931

Administrative merger of boards of trustees of Emory & Henry and Martha Washington College in 1918; in 1931 Martha Washington closed; students transferred to Emory & Henry. Merger was not technically completed until 1938.

Emporia State University
Emporia, KS

Est. as: Kansas State Normal School – 1863
NC: Kansas State Teachers College – 1923
NC: Emporia Kansas State College – 1974
NC: Emporia State University – 1977

Endicott College
Beverly, MA

Est. as: Endicott Junior College – 1939
NC: Endicott College – 1986

Erskine College
Due West, SC

Est. as: Academy at Due West, The – 1835*
NC: Clark & Erskine Seminary – 1837
NC: Erskine College – 1839
MW: Erskine Theological Seminary – 1926
MW: Due West Female Academy – 1927

*Recognizes 1839 as official established year.

Eureka College
Eureka, IL

Est. as: Walnut Grove Seminary – 1848*
NC: Walnut Grove Academy – 1849
NC: Eureka College – 1855
MW: Abingdon College – 1884

Location changes
Walnut Grove, IL – 1848
Eureka, IL – 1855

*Recognizes 1855 as official established year.

Did not change location in 1855; Walnut Grove changed name to Eureka.

Evangel University of the Assemblies of God
Springfield, MO

Est. as: Evangel College – 1955
NC: Evangel University of the Assemblies of God – 1998

Evansville, University of
Evansville, IN

Est. as: Moores Hill Male & Female Collegiate Institute – 1854
NC: Moores Hill College – 1887
NC: Evansville College – 1919
NC: University of Evansville – 1967

Location changes
Moores Hill, IN – 1854
Evansville, IN – 1919

Evergreen State College, The
Olympia, WA

Est. as: Evergreen State College, The – 1967

By MO: By merger (of) **DM:** Dissolved merger (with) **MW:** Merged with **NC:** Name change (to)

Fairfield University
Fairfield, CT

Est. as: Bellarmine College – 1942
NC: Fairfield University of Saint Robert Bellarmine – 1945
NC: Fairfield University – 1969
MW: Bridgeport Engineering Institute – 1994

Fairleigh Dickinson University
Teaneck, NJ

Est. as: Fairleigh Dickinson Junior College – 1942
NC: Fairleigh Dickinson College – 1948
NC: Fairleigh Dickinson University – 1956

Is one university with several campuses. Original campus in Rutherford closed July, 1994. Teaneck campus opened in 1954 on site of Bergen Junior College. Madison campus opened in 1958. Each campus has its own sports program in different, NCAA divisions. Rutherford and Teaneck campuses had combined sports teams through 1987. Madison campus is now known as College at Florham; Teaneck campus is now known as Metropolitan campus.

Fairmont State College
Fairmont, WV

Est. as: Regency of West Virginia Normal School at Fairmont, The – 1865
NC: Fairmont State Normal School – 1867
NC: Fairmont State Teachers College – 1931
NC: Fairmont State College – 1943

82

Faulkner University
Montgomery, AL

Est. as: Montgomery Bible School – 1942
NC: Alabama Christian College – 1953
NC: Faulkner University – 1985

Fayetteville State University
Fayetteville, NC

Est. as: Howard School – 1867
NC: State Colored Normal School – 1877
NC: State Colored Normal & Industrial School – 1916
NC: State Normal School for the Negro Race – 1921
NC: State Normal School – 1926
NC: Fayetteville State Teachers College – 1939
NC: Fayetteville State College – 1963
NC: Fayetteville State University – 1969

Felician College
Lodi, NJ

Est. as: Immaculate Conception Normal School – 1923*
NC: Immaculate Conception Junior College – 1942
NC: Felician College – 1967
*Recognizes 1942 as official established year.

Ferris State University
Big Rapids, MI

Est. as: Big Rapids Industrial School – 1884
NC: Ferris Industrial School – 1885
NC: Ferris Institute – 1898
NC: Ferris State College – 1963
NC: Ferris State University – 1987
MW: Kendall College of Art & Design – 2001

Ferrum College
Ferrum, VA

Est. as: Ferrum Training School – 1913
NC: Ferrum Training School-Ferrum Junior College – 1940
NC: Ferrum Junior College – 1950
NC: Ferrum College – 1971

Findlay, The University of
Findlay, OH

Est. as: Findlay College – 1882
MW: Findlay Business College – 1893
NC: Nuclear Medicine Institute – 1984
NC: University of Findlay, The – 1989

Fisk University
Nashville, TN

Est. as: Fisk School – 1866
NC: Fisk University – 1867

Fitchburg State College
Fitchburg, MA

Est. as: State Normal School – 1894
NC: State Teachers College – 1932
NC: State College at Fitchburg – 1960
NC: Fitchburg State College – 1965

Five Towns College
Dix Hills, NY

Est. as: Five Towns College – 1972
Location changes
Merrick, NY – 1972
Seaford, NY – c1982
Dix Hills, NY – c1992

Flagler College
Saint Augustine, FL

Est. as: Flagler College – 1968

Florida Agricultural & Mechanical University
Tallahassee, FL

Est. as: State Normal College for Colored Students – 1887
NC: State Normal & Industrial College for Colored Students – 1891
NC: Florida Agricultural & Mechanical College for Negroes – 1909
NC: Florida Agricultural & Mechanical University – 1953

By MO: By merger (of) **DM:** Dissolved merger (with) **MW:** Merged with **NC:** Name change (to)

84

Florida Atlantic University
Boca Raton, FL

Est. as: Florida Atlantic University – 1961

Florida Gulf Coast University
Fort Myers, FL

Est. as: Florida Gulf Coast University – 1997

Florida Institute of Technology
Melbourne, FL

Est. as: Brevard Engineering College – 1958
NC: Florida Institute of Technology – 1966

Florida International University
Miami, FL

Est. as: Florida International University – 1965

Florida Memorial College
Miami, FL

Est. as: Florida Baptist Institute – 1879
NC: Florida Memorial College – 1918
MW: Florida Normal & Industrial Institute – 1941
NC: Florida Normal & Industrial Memorial Institute – 1941
NC: Florida Normal & Industrial College – 1942
NC: Florida Normal & Industrial Memorial College – 1950
NC: Florida Memorial College – 1963

Location changes
Live Oak, FL – 1879
Saint Augustine, FL – 1941
Miami, FL – 1968

Florida State University, The
Tallahassee, FL

Est. as: Seminary West of the Suwannee River, The – 1851
NC: Florida State College, The – 1901
NC: Florida State College for Women, The – 1905
NC: Florida State University, The – 1947

By MO: By merger (of) **DM:** Dissolved merger (with) **MW:** Merged with **NC:** Name change (to)

Florida Southern College
Lakeland, FL

Est. as: South Florida Institute – 1883*
NC: Wesleyan Seminary – UNK
NC: Wesleyan Institute – UNK
NC: High School & College of the Florida Conference – 1886
NC: Florida Conference College – UNK
NC: Florida Seminary – 1902
NC: Southern College – 1906
NC: Florida Southern College – 1935

Location changes
Orlando, FL – 1883
Leesburg, FL – 1886
Southerland (now Palm Harbor), FL – 1902
Clearwater Beach, FL – 1921
Lakeland, FL – 1922

*Recognizes 1885 as official established year.

Florida, University of
Gainesville, FL

Est. as: East Florida Seminary – 1853
NC: University of the State of Florida – 1905
NC: University of Florida – 1909

Location changes
Ocala, FL – 1853
Gainesville, FL – 1866

Act of state legislature in 1905 abolished all schools including East Florida Seminary and Florida Agricultural College which was established in 1884 in Lake City and was the original land-grant institution. It had changed its name in 1903 to University of Florida. Thus, when all new schools were established later in 1905 what is now University of Florida was named University of the State of Florida and took over the land-grant status. East Florida Seminary was closed, officials believe, during the Civil War.

Fontbonne University
Saint Louis, MO

Est. as: Fontbonne College – 1923
NC: Fontbonne University – 2002

Fordham University
Bronx, NY

Est. as: Saint John's College – 1841
NC: Fordham University – 1906
MW: Marymount College – 2002

Fort Hays State University
Hays, KS

Est. as: Kansas Normal School of Emporia, Western Branch – 1902
NC: Fort Hays Kansas State Normal School – 1914
NC: Kansas State Teachers College of Hays – 1923
NC: Fort Hays Kansas State College – 1931
NC: Fort Hays State University – 1977

Fort Lewis College
Durango, CO

Est. as: Unamed Indian boarding school – 1891*
NC: Fort Lewis School – 1911
NC: Fort Lewis Agricultural & Mechanical College – 1933
NC: Fort Lewis College – 1964

Location changes
Fort Lewis, CO – 1891
Durango, CO – 1956

*Recognizes 1911 as official established year.

Originally a branch of Colorado State University.

Fort Valley State University
Fort Valley, GA

Est. as: Fort Valley High & Industrial School – 1895
NC: Fort Valley Normal & Industrial School – 1929
MW: State Teachers & Agricultural College at Forsyth – 1939
NC: Fort Valley State College – 1939
NC: Fort Valley State University – 1996

By MO: By merger (of) *DM:* Dissolved merger (with) *MW:* Merged with *NC:* Name change (to)

Framingham State College
Framingham, MA

Est. as: Unnamed normal school – 1839
NC: State Normal School – 1845
MW: Boston Normal School of Cookery – 1898
NC: Framingham State Teachers College – 1932
NC: State College at Framingham – 1960
NC: Framingham State College – 1968

Location changes
Lexington, MA – 1839
West Newton, MA – 1844
Framingham, MA – 1853

Francis Marion University
Florence, SC

Est. as: Francis Marion College – 1970
NC: Francis Marion University – 1992

Franciscan University of Steubenville
Steubenville, OH

Est. as: College of Steubenville – 1946
NC: University of Steubenville – 1980
NC: Franciscan University of Steubenville – 1987

Franklin College of Indiana
Franklin, IN

Est. as: Indiana Baptist Manual Labor Institute – 1834
NC: Franklin College – 1844
NC: Franklin College of Indiana – 1907

Franklin Pierce College
Rindge, NH

Est. as: Franklin Pierce College – 1962

Franklin & Marshall College
Lancaster, PA

Est. as: Franklin College – 1787
MW: Marshall College – 1853
NC: Franklin & Marshall College – 1853

Freed-Hardeman University
Henderson, TN

Est. as: Henderson Male & Female Institute – 1869
NC: Henderson Masonic Male & Female Institute – 1877
NC: West Tennessee Christian College – 1885
NC: Georgie Robertson Christian College – 1897
NC: National Teachers Normal & Business College – 1907
NC: Freed-Hardeman College – 1919
NC: Freed-Hardeman University – 1990

Georgie Robertson Christian College closed at the end of the spring term, 1907. National Teachers Normal & Business College was incorporated in May, 1907 with A. G. Freed, who had been co-president at Robertson, as president, and N. B. Hardeman, who had been on the Robertson faculty, as vice-president.

Fresno Pacific University
Fresno, CA

Est. as: Pacific Bible Institute – 1944
NC: Pacific College of Fresno – 1960
NC: Fresno Pacific College – 1978
NC: Fresno Pacific University – 1997

Friends University
Wichita, KS

Est. as: Friends University – 1898

Frostburg State University
Frostburg, MD

Est. as: State Normal School 2 at Frostburg – 1898
NC: State Teachers College at Frostburg – 1935
NC: Frostburg State College – 1963
NC: Frostburg State University – 1987

Furman University, The
Greenville, SC

Est. as: Furman Academy & Theological Institution – 1826
NC: Furman Theological Institution – 1833
NC: Furman Institution – 1836
NC: Furman Theological Institution – 1844
NC: Furman University, The – 1851
MW: Greenville Woman's College – 1938

Location changes
Edgefield, SC – 1826
Sumter, SC – 1829
Winnsboro, SC – 1837
Greenville, SC – 1850

Established in 1826; opened in 1827. In 1858, theological department became Southern Baptist Theological Seminary and eventually moved to Louisville.

Gallaudet University
Washington, DC

Est. as: Columbia Institution for the Instruction of the Deaf & Dumb & Blind – 1857*
NC: National College for the Deaf & Dumb – 1864
NC: National Deaf-Mute College – 1865
NC: Gallaudet College – 1893
NC: Galluadet University – 1986

*Recognizes 1864 as official established year.

In 1865 pre-college students transferred to Maryland Institute for the Blind which was re-named Columbia Institution for the Deaf & Dumb; college division was re-named National Deaf-Mute College.

Gannon University
Erie, PA

Est. as: Cathedral College – 1933*
NC: Gannon School of Arts & Sciences – 1941
NC: Gannon College – 1944
NC: Gannon University – 1979
MW: Villa Maria College – 1989

*Recognizes 1925, when Villa Maria College was established, as official established year.

Villa Maria College (women) was established in 1925. Cathedral College (men) was established in 1933 as a department of Saint Vincent's College, Latrobe. In 1941, it came under the Villa Maria charter.

Gardner-Webb University

Boiling Springs, NC

Est. as: Boiling Springs High School – 1905
NC: Gardner-Webb Junior College – 1928
NC: Gardner-Webb College – 1969
NC: Gardner-Webb University – 1993

Geneva College

Beaver Falls, PA

Est. as: Geneva Hall – 1848
NC: Geneva College – 1873

Location changes
New Richland (Northwood), OH – 1848
Beaver Falls, PA – 1880

George Fox University

Newberg, OR

Est. as: Friends Pacific Academy – 1885*
NC: Pacific College – 1891
NC: George Fox College – 1949
MW: Western Evangelical Seminary – 1996
NC: George Fox University – 1996

*Recognizes 1891 as official established year.

George Mason University

Fairfax, VA

Est. as: Northern Virginia Branch of the University of Virginia – 1957*
NC: George Mason College – 1966
DM: University of Virginia – 1972
NC: George Mason University – 1972

*Recognizes 1972 as official established year.

George Washington University, The

Washington, DC

Est. as: Columbian College in the District of Columbia, The – 1821
NC: Columbian University – 1873
NC: George Washington University, The – 1904
MW: Benjamin Franklin University – 1988
MW: Mount Vernon College – 1999

By MO: By merger (of) **DM:** Dissolved merger (with) **MW:** Merged with **NC:** Name change (to)

Georgetown College
Georgetown, KY

Est. as: Royal Springs Academy – 1787*
MW: Rittenhouse Academy – 1829
NC: Rittenhouse Academy – 1829
NC: Georgetown College – 1829

*Recognizes 1829 as official established year.

No official information is available that Royal Springs Academy merged with Rittenhouse Academy; institution officials presume so. Rittenhouse Academy closed, date unknown; facility was taken over by Kentucky Baptist Association, and Georgetown was established.

Georgetown University
Washington, DC

Est. as: Georgetown College – 1789
NC: College of Georgetown in the District of Columbia – 1815
MW: Washington Dental College – 1901
NC: Georgetown College in the District of Columbia – 1944
NC: Georgetown University – 1966

Georgia College & State University
Milledgeville, GA

Est. as: Georgia Normal & Industrial College for Girls – 1889
NC: Georgia State College for Women – 1922
NC: Woman's College of Georgia, The – 1961
NC: Georgia College at Milledgeville – 1967
NC: Georgia College – 1971
NC: Georgia College & State University – 1996

Georgia Institute of Technology
Atlanta, GA

Est. as: Georgia School of Technology – 1885
NC: Georgia Institute of Technology – 1948

By MO: By merger (of) *DM:* Dissolved merger (with) *MW:* Merged with *NC:* Name change (to)

Georgia Southern University
Statesboro, GA

Est. as: First District Agricultural & Mechanical High School – 1906
NC: Georgia Normal School – 1924
NC: South Georgia Teachers College – 1929
NC: Georgia Teachers College – 1939
NC: Georgia Southern College – 1959
NC: Georgia Southern University – 1990

Georgia Southwestern State University
Americus, GA

Est. as: Third District Agricultural & Mechanical School – 1906
NC: Third District Agricultural & Mechanical College – 1926
NC: Georgia Southwestern College – 1932
NC: Georgia Southwestern State University – 1996

Georgia State University
Atlanta, GA

Est. as: Georgia School of Technology Evening School of Commerce – 1913
NC: University System of Georgia Evening School – 1933
NC: University of Georgia Extension Center in Atlanta – 1935
NC: University of Georgia: Atlanta Division – 1947
NC: Georgia State College of Business Administration – 1955
NC: Georgia State College – 1961
NC: Georgia State University – 1969

In 1935, day classes were taught at what was called Atlanta Junior College; night classes were taught at what was called Georgia Evening College.

Georgia, The University of
Athens, GA

Est. as: University of Georgia, The – 1785

Franklin College was an unofficial name in early years; School of Arts & Sciences is now Franklin College of Arts & Sciences.

By MO: By merger (of) *DM:* Dissolved merger (with) *MW:* Merged with *NC:* Name change (to)

94

Georgian Court College
Lakewood, NJ

Est. as: Mount Saint Mary College & Academy – 1908
NC: Georgian Court College – 1924

Location changes
North Plainfield, NJ – 1908
Lakewood, NJ – 1924

Gettysburg College
Gettysburg, PA

Est. as: Pennsylvania College of Gettysburg – 1832
NC: Gettysburg College – 1921

Gettysburg Seminary, established in 1826, was the parent of Pennsylvania College of Gettysburg; Gettysburg Seminary changed its name to Gettysburg Gymnasium in 1828.

Glenville State College
Glenville, WV

Est. as: State Normal School of West Virginia: Glenville Branch – 1872
NC: Glenville State Normal School – 1898
NC: Glenville State Teachers College – 1931
NC: Glenville State College – 1943

Goddard College
Plainfield, VT

Est. as: Green Mountain Central Institute – 1863*
NC: Goddard Seminary – 1870
NC: Goddard School for Girls – 1929
NC: Goddard College – 1938

Location changes
Barre, VT – 1863
Plainfield, VT – 1938

*Recognizes 1938 as official established year.

Gonzaga University
Spokane, WA

Est. as: Gonzaga College – 1887
NC: Gonzaga University – 1912

By MO: By merger (of) *DM:* Dissolved merger (with) *MW:* Merged with *NC:* Name change (to)

Gordon College,
The United College of Gordon & Barrington
Wenham, MA

Est. as: Boston Missionary Training Institute – 1889
NC: Boston Missionary Training School – UNK
NC: Gordon Bible & Missionary Training School – 1895
MW: Newton Theological Institution – 1908
NC: Gordon School of the Newton Theological Institution – 1908
DM: Newton Theological Institution – 1914
NC: Gordon Bible Institute – 1914
NC: Gordon Bible College – 1916
NC: Gordon College of Theology & Missions – 1921
NC: Gordon College & Gordon Divinity School – 1962
NC: Gordon College – 1970
MW: Barrington College – 1985
NC: Gordon College, The United College of Gordon & Barrington –
   1985

Location changes
Boston, MA – 1889
Wenham, MA – 1955

In 1970, the divinity school merged with Conwell Divinity School and relocated to Hamilton; new institution became Gordon Conwell Divinity School.

Goshen College
Goshen, IN

Est. as: Elkhart Institute of Science, Industry, & the Arts – 1894
NC: Goshen College – 1903

Location changes
Elkhart, IN – 1894
Goshen, IN – 1903

By MO: By merger (of) *DM:* Dissolved merger (with) *MW:* Merged with *NC:* Name change (to)

Goucher College
Towson, MD

Est. as: Woman's College of Baltimore City – 1885
NC: Woman's College of Baltimore – 1890
NC: Goucher College – 1910

Location changes
Baltimore, MD – 1885
Towson, MD – 1953

Grace College & Seminary
Winona Lake, IN

Est. as: Grace Theological Seminary, Collegiate Division – 1948
MW: Grace Theological Seminary – 1993
NC: Grace College & Seminary – 1993

Grace University
Omaha, NE

Est. as: Grace Bible Institute – 1943
NC: Grace College of the Bible – 1976
NC: Grace University – 1995

Graceland University
Lamoni, IA

Est. as: Graceland College – 1895
NC: Graceland University – 2000

Grambling State University
Grambling, LA

Est. as: Colored Industrial & Agricultural School – 1901
NC: North Louisiana Agricultural & Industrial School – 1905
NC: Lincoln Parish Training School – 1919
NC: Louisiana Normal & Industrial Institute – 1928
NC: Grambling College – 1946
NC: Grambling State University – 1974

Grand Canyon University
Phoenix, AZ

Est. as: Grand Canyon College – 1949
NC: Grand Canyon University – 1989

Location changes
Prescott, AZ – 1949
Phoenix, AZ – 1951

Grand Valley State University
Allendale, MI

Est. as: Grand Valley State College – 1960
NC: Grand Valley State University – 1987

Grand View College
Des Moines, IA

Est. as: Grand View College – 1896

Gratz College
Melrose Park, PA

Est. as: Gratz College – 1895
MW: Hebrew Education Society – 1928

Location changes
Philadelphia, PA – 1895
Melrose Park, PA – 1989

Great Falls, University of
Great Falls, MT

Est. as: Great Falls Normal College – 1932
NC: Great Falls College of Education – 1940
NC: College of Great Falls – 1950
NC: University of Great Falls – 1995

Green Mountain College
Poultney, VT

Est. as: Troy Conference Academy – 1834
NC: Ripley Female College – 1863
NC: Troy Conference Academy – 1874
NC: Green Mountain Junior College – 1942
NC: Green Mountain College – 1974

By MO: By merger (of) *DM:* Dissolved merger (with) *MW:* Merged with *NC:* Name change (to)

98

Greensboro College
Greensboro, NC

Est. as: Greensboro Female College – 1838
NC: Greensboro College for Women – 1912
NC: Greensboro College – 1920
MW: Davenport College – 1933

Greenville College
Greenville, IL

Est. as: Almira College – 1855*
NC: Greenville College – 1892

*Recognizes 1892 as official established year.

Almira College was purchased by Central Illinois Conference of the Free Methodist Church and given current name.

Grinnell College
Grinnell, IA

Est. as: Iowa College – 1846
MW: Grinnell University – 1859
NC: Grinnell College – 1909

Location changes
Davenport, IA – 1846
Grinnell, IA – 1861

When Iowa College, established in 1846, was merged with Grinnell University, established in 1856, the merged institution was continued at Grinnell under the charter of the older institution. The name of the corporation continued to be The Trustees of Iowa College although the institution had been known as Grinnell College since 1909. As of June 17, 1990, the corporate name was changed to conform with its public identity, Grinnell College. The original Grinnell University apparently never was in operation, but it apparently did have buildings.

Grove City College
Grove City, PA

Est. as: Select School at Pine Grove – 1858*
NC: Pine Grove Normal Academy – 1876
NC: Grove City College – 1884

Location changes
Pine Grove, PA – 1858
Grove City, PA – 1883

*Recognizes 1876 as official established year.

Did not change location in 1883; Pine Grove changed name to Grove City.

Guilford College
Greensboro, NC

Est. as: New Garden Boarding School – 1837
NC: Friends School at New Garden, The – 1883
NC: Guilford College – 1888
MW: Greensboro Evening College – 1953

Gustavus Adolphus College
Saint Peter, MN

Est. as: Academy at Red Wing – 1862
NC: Minnesota Elementary School – 1863
NC: Saint Ansgar's Academy – 1865
NC: Gustavus Adolphus College – 1876

Location changes
Red Wing, MN – 1862
East Union, MN – 1863
Saint Peter, MN – 1876

Gwynedd-Mercy College
Gwynedd Valley, PA

Est. as: Gwynedd-Mercy Junior College – 1948
NC: Gwynedd-Mercy College – 1963

Hamilton College
Clinton, NY

Est. as: Hamilton-Oneida Academy – 1793*
NC: Hamilton College – 1812
MW: Kirkland College – 1978

*Recognizes 1812 as official established year.

Kirkland College had been established by Hamilton as a sister institution for women.

Hamline University
Saint Paul, MN

Est. as: Hamline University – 1854
Red Wing, MN – 1854
Saint Paul, MN – 1880

Hampden-Sydney College
Hampden-Sydney, VA

Est. as: Prince Edward Academy – 1775*
NC: Hampden-Sydney Academy – 1776
NC: Hampden-Sydney College – 1783

*Recognizes 1776 as official established year.

Hampshire College
Amherst, MA

Est. as: Hampshire College – 1965

Hampton University
Hampton, VA

Est. as: Hampton Normal & Agricultural Institute – 1868
NC: Hampton Institute – 1924
NC: Hampton University – 1984

Hannibal-LaGrange College
Hannibal, MO

Est. as: LaGrange Male & Female Seminary – 1858
NC: LaGrange College – c1860
NC: Hannibal-LaGrange College – 1929
MW: Hannibal-LaGrange Extension Center, Saint Louis – 1967
NC: Missouri Baptist College-Hannibal – 1967
DM: Missouri Baptist College-Saint Louis – 1973
NC: Hannibal-LaGrange College – 1973

Location changes
LaGrange, MO – 1858
Hannibal, MO – 1929

Became Hannibal-LaGrange College upon move to Hannibal. The 1967 merger created Missouri Baptist College with two campuses: Hannibal and Saint Louis.

Hanover College
Hanover, IN

Est. as: Hanover Academy – 1827
NC: Hanover College – 1833

Henry C Long College for Women, a co-ordinate college, was established in 1947 and continued until 1978. For the spring semester of 1883-84, then President McMaster opened a new institution, Madison College, in Madison; he felt the location, an Ohio River town, would allow the institution to expand and grow. Most faculty and students moved there, but the original institution remained open; in March, McMaster accepted the presidency of Miami University (OH) and his experiment ended.

Hardin-Simmons University
Abilene, TX

Est. as: Abilene Baptist College – 1891
NC: Simmons College – 1892
NC: Simmons University – 1925
NC: Hardin-Simmons University – 1934

Harding University
Searcy, AR

Est. as: Harding College – 1924*
By MO: Arkansas Christian College – 1924
By MO: Harper College – 1924
NC: Harding University – 1979

Location changes
Morrilton, AR – 1924
Searcy, AR – 1934

*Recognizes merger year, 1924, as official established year; does not recognize histories of merged institutions.

Hartford, University of
West Hartford, CT

Est. as: Hartford Society for Decorative Art – 1877
NC: Hartford Art School – 1940
MW: Hillyer College – 1957
MW: Hartt College of Music – 1957
NC: University of Hartford – 1957
MW: Hartford College for Women – 1991

Hartwick College
Oneonta, NY

Est. as: Hartwick Seminary – 1797
NC: Hartwick College – 1928

Location changes
New York, NY – 1797
Oneonta, NY – 1815

Seminary separated in 1968.

Harvard University
Cambridge, MA

Est. as: Harvard College – 1636
NC: Harvard University – 1782
MW: Radcliffe College – 1999

The state constitution change in 1780 recognized the use of "University" in institution's name; a medical school was established in 1782 to create an official university. Radcliffe had been a co-ordinate college for women.

Harvey Mudd College
Claremont, CA
Est. as: Harvey Mudd College – 1955

Hastings College
Hastings, NE
Est. as: Hastings College – 1882
MW: Bellevue College – 1934

Bellevue College was in Hastings; it had closed in 1918. Hastings College took over Bellevue records in 1934.

Haverford College
Haverford, PA
Est. as: Haverford School – 1833
NC: Haverford College – 1856

Hawaii at Hilo, University of
Hilo, HI
Est. as: University of Hawaii Extension Division – 1947*
NC: University of Hawaii, Hilo College – 1970
NC: University of Hawaii at Hilo – 1970
MW: Hawaii Community College – 1981

*Recognizes 1970 as official established year.

Hawaii at Manoa, University of
Honolulu, HI
Est. as: College of Agriculture & Mechanical Arts – 1907
NC: College of Hawaii – 1911
NC: University of Hawaii – 1920
NC: University of Hawaii at Manoa – 1972

Hawaii Pacific University
Honolulu, HI
Est. as: Hawaii Pacific College – 1965
MW: Honolulu Christian College – 1966
NC: Hawaii Pacific University – 1990
MW: Hawaii Loa College – 1992

Heidelberg College
Tiffin, OH

Est. as: Heidelberg College – 1850
NC: Heidelberg University – 1890
NC: Heidelberg College – 1926

Henderson State University
Arkadelphia, AR

Est. as: Arkadelphia Methodist College – 1890
NC: Henderson College – 1904
NC: Henderson-Brown College – 1911
NC: Henderson State Teachers College – 1929
NC: Henderson State College – 1967
NC: Henderson State University – 1975

After the 1929 merger of Henderson-Brown College with Hendrix College, the campus of Henderson-Brown was turned over to the state. Henderson State Teachers College was opened thereon by the state in 1929.

Hendrix College
Conway, AR

Est. as: Central Institute – 1876
NC: Central Collegiate Institute – 1881
NC: Hendrix College – 1889
MW: Henderson-Brown College – 1929
NC: Hendrix-Henderson College – 1929
NC: Hendrix College – 1931
MW: Galloway Woman's College – 1933

Location changes
Altus, AR – 1876
Conway, AR – 1890

By MO: By merger (of) *DM:* Dissolved merger (with) *MW:* Merged with *NC:* Name change (to)

Herbert H Lehman College
of the City University of New York
Bronx, NY

Est. as: Hunter College in the Bronx – 1931*

NC: Herbert H Lehman College of the City University of New York – 1968

*Recognizes 1968 as official established year.

Originally was women's branch of Hunter College (Manhattan Campus).

Heritage College
Toppenish, WA

Est. as: College of the Holy Names – 1907*
NC: Fort Wright College – 1963
NC: Heritage College – 1982

Location changes
Spokane, WA – 1907
Toppenish, WA – 1982

*Recognizes 1982 as official established year.

High Point University
High Point, NC

Est. as: High Point College – 1924
NC: High Point University – 1991

Hilbert College
Hamburg, NY

Est. as: Immaculata College – 1957
NC: Hilbert College – 1969

Hillsdale College
Hillsdale, MI

Est. as: Michigan Central College – 1844
NC: Hillsdale College – 1853

Location changes
Spring Arbor, MI – 1844
Hillsdale, MI – 1853

By MO: By merger (of) **DM:** Dissolved merger (with) **MW:** Merged with **NC:** Name change (to)

Hiram College
Hiram, OH

Est. as: Western Reserve Eclectic Institute – 1850
NC: Hiram College – 1867

Hobart College
Geneva, NY

Est. as: Geneva Academy – 1796*
NC: Geneva College – 1822
NC: Hobart Free College – 1851
NC: Hobart College – 1860

*Recognizes 1822 as official established year; charter for Geneva College was granted in 1825.

Co-ordinate college with William Smith College (women). The official name, The Colleges of the Senecas, was adopted in 1943.

Hofstra University
Hempstead, NY

Est. as: Nassau College-Hofstra Memorial New York University – 1935
NC: Hofstra College of New York University – 1937
NC: Hofstra College – 1939
NC: Hofstra University – 1963

Hollins University
Roanoke, VA

Est. as: Valley Union Seminary – 1842
NC: Hollins Institute – 1855
NC: Hollins College – 1911
NC: Hollins University – 1998

Holy Cross, College of the
Worcester, MA

Est. as: College of the Holy Cross – 1843

Holy Family College
Philadelphia, PA

Est. as: Holy Family College – 1954

By MO: By merger (of) *DM:* Dissolved merger (with) *MW:* Merged with *NC:* Name change (to)

Holy Names College
Oakland, CA

Est. as: Convent of Our Lady of the Sacred Heart – 1868
NC: Convent & College of the Holy Names – 1880
NC: Holy Names Junior College – 1917
NC: College of the Holy Names – 1956
NC: Holy Names College – 1971

Hood College
Frederick, MD

Est. as: Woman's College of Frederick – 1893
NC: Hood College – 1913

Predecessor institution was Frederick Female Seminary, 1840.

Hope College
Holland, MI

Est. as: Pioneer School – 1851*
NC: Holland Academy, The – 1857
NC: Hope College – 1866

*Recognizes 1866 as official established year.

Hope International University
Fullerton, CA

Est. as: Pacific Bible Seminary – 1928
NC: Pacific Christian College – 1962
NC: Hope International University – 1997

Location changes
Long Beach, CA – 1928
Fullerton, CA – 1972

Pacific Christian College is one of three schools within the university; athletic programs are conducted as Pacific Christian College of Hope International University.

Houghton College
Houghton, NY

Est. as: Houghton Wesleyan Methodist Seminary – 1883
NC: Houghton College – 1923

Houston Baptist University
Houston, TX

Est. as: Houston Baptist College – 1960
NC: Houston Baptist University – 1973

Houston, University of
Houston, TX

Est. as: Houston Junior College – 1927
NC: University of Houston – 1934
NC: University of Houston Central Campus – c1974
NC: University of Houston-University Park – 1983
NC: University of Houston – 1987

University of Houston Central Campus may not have been an official name.

Howard Payne University
Brownwood, TX

Est. as: Howard Payne College – 1889
MW: Daniel Baker College – 1953
NC: Howard Payne University – 1974

Howard University
Washington, DC

Est. as: Howard University – 1867
MW: Institution for the Education of Colored Youth, The – 1871
DM: Institution for the Education of Colored Youth, The – 1877

Humboldt State University
Arcata, CA

Est. as: Humboldt State Normal School – 1913
NC: Humboldt State Teachers College – 1921
NC: Humboldt State College – 1935
NC: California State University at Humboldt – 1972
NC: Humboldt State University – 1974

By MO: By merger (of) *DM:* Dissolved merger (with) *MW:* Merged with *NC:* Name change (to)

Humphreys College
Stockton, CA

Est. as: Stockton Business College, Normal School, & Telegraphic
Institute – 1875*
NC: Humphreys College – 1947

*Recognizes 1896, when John R. Humphreys, Sr., assumed academic administration of the institution, as official established year.

Web site history page indicates that there were several (unlisted) name changes before the current name; the public relations office states that there was only the one indicated name change.

Hunter College of the City University of New York
New York, NY

Est. as: Female Normal & High School – 1870
NC: Hunter College – 1914
NC: Hunter College of the City University of New York – 1961

Huntingdon College
Montgomery, AL

Est. as: Tuskegee Female College – 1854
NC: Alabama Conference Female College – 1872
NC: Women's College of Alabama – 1910
NC: Huntingdon College – 1935

Location changes
Tuskegee, AL – 1854
Montgomery, AL – 1910

Huntington College
Huntington, IN

Est. as: Hartsville Academy – 1850*
NC: Hartsville University – 1851
NC: Hartsville College – 1883
NC: Central College – 1897
NC: Huntington College – 1917

*Recognizes 1897 as official established year.

110

Huron University
Huron, SD

Est. as: Presbyterian University of South Dakota – 1883
NC: Pierre University – 1883
NC: Huron College – 1898
NC: Huron University – 1989

Location changes
Pierre, SD – 1883
Huron, SD – 1898

Husson College
Bangor, ME

Est. as: Shaw School of Business – 1898
NC: Maine School of Commerce – 1925
NC: Husson College – 1947
MW: Eastern Maine General Hospital School of Nursing – 1982
MW: New England School of Communications – 1997

Idaho State University
Pocatello, ID

Est. as: Academy of Idaho, The – 1901
NC: Idaho Technical Institute, The – 1915
NC: University of Idaho-Southern Branch – 1927
NC: Idaho State College – 1947
NC: Idaho State University – 1963

Idaho, University of
Moscow, ID

Est. as: University of Idaho – 1889

Illinois at Chicago, University of
Chicago, IL

Est. as: Chicago Undergraduate Division of the University of Illinois – 1946
NC: University of Illinois, Chicago Circle – 1965
MW: University of Illinois, Medical Center – 1982
NC: University of Illinois at Chicago – 1982

Illinois at Urbana-Champaign, University of
Urbana, IL

Est. as: Illinois Industrial University – 1867
NC: University of Illinois – 1885
NC: University of Illinois at Urbana-Champaign – c1972

Illinois College
Jacksonville, IL

Est. as: Illinois College – 1829

111

112

Illinois Institute of Technology
Chicago, IL

Est. as: Armour Institute – 1890
NC: Armour Institute of Technology – 1895
MW: Lewis Institute – 1940
NC: Illinois Institute of Technology – 1940
MW: Institute of Design – 1949
MW: Chicago-Kent School of Law – 1969
MW: Midwest College of Engineering – 1986

Illinois State University
Normal, IL

Est. as: Illinois State Normal University – 1857
NC: Illinois State University – 1964
MW: Mennonite College of Nursing – 1999

City of location originally was an area known as North Bloomington; it was incorporated and named Normal, for the college, in 1865. There was an earlier, unrelated, Illinois State University (1852-1869).

Illinois Wesleyan University
Bloomington, IL

Est. as: Illinois University – 1850
NC: Illinois Wesleyan University – 1851
MW: Hedding College – 1928

Hedding College had closed; students were admitted to Illinois Wesleyan.

Immaculata University
Malvern, PA

Est. as: Villa Maria Academy for Girls – 1914*
NC: Villa Maria College – 1920
NC: Immaculata College – 1929
NC: Immaculata University – 2002
*Recognizes 1920 as official established year.

By MO: By merger (of) ***DM:*** Dissolved merger (with) ***MW:*** Merged with ***NC:*** Name change (to)

Incarnate Word, University of the

San Antonio, TX

Est. as: Saint Joseph's Orphanage – 1881
NC: Incarnate Word School – 1892
NC: College & Academy of the Incarnate Word – 1909
NC: University of the Incarnate Word – 1996

Academy moved to separate location and was re-named Incarnate Word High School.

Indiana State University

Terre Haute, IN

Est. as: Indiana State Normal School – 1865
NC: Indiana State Teachers College – 1929
NC: Indiana State College – 1961
NC: Indiana State University – 1965

In 1918, what is now Ball State University became the **Eastern Division** of Indiana State Normal School; in 1929, the two divisions were separated into autonomous institutions.

Indiana University

Bloomington, IN

Est. as: Indiana State Seminary – 1820
NC: Indiana College – 1828
NC: Indiana University – 1838

Indiana University of Pennsylvania

Indiana, PA

Est. as: Indiana Normal School – 1875
NC: Indiana State Normal School – 1920
NC: Indiana State Teachers College – 1927
NC: Indiana State College – 1960
NC: Indiana University of Pennsylvania – 1965

Legislation indicates that "of the State System of Higher Education" was not added to institution's name.

114

Indiana University-Purdue University Indianapolis
Indianapolis, IN

Est. as: Indianapolis Downtown Campus – 1916*
NC: Indiana University at Indianapolis – 1968
MW: Indiana University Medical College – 1969
MW: Purdue University: Indianapolis Branch – 1969
NC: Indiana University-Purdue University Indianapolis – 1969
*Recognizes 1969 as official established year.

Indiana Wesleyan University
Marion, IN

Est. as: Marion College – 1920
NC: Indiana Wesleyan University – 1988

Indianapolis, University of
Indianapolis, IN

Est. as: Indiana Central University – 1902
NC: Indiana Central College – 1921
NC: Indiana Central University – 1975
NC: University of Indianapolis – 1986

Iona College
New Rochelle, NY

Est. as: Iona College – 1940
MW: Elizabeth Seton College – 1989

Iowa State University
Ames, IA

Est. as: Iowa Agricultural College & Model Farm – 1858
NC: Iowa State College of Agriculture & Mechanical Arts – 1896
NC: Iowa State University of Science & Technology – 1959
NC: Iowa State University – 1975

By MO: By merger (of) *DM:* Dissolved merger (with) *MW:* Merged with *NC:* Name change (to)

Iowa Wesleyan College
Mount Pleasant, IA

Est. as: Mount Pleasant Literary Institute – 1842
NC: Mount Pleasant Collegiate Institute – 1843
NC: Iowa Wesleyan University – 1855
NC: Iowa Wesleyan College – 1912

Iowa, State University of
Iowa City, IA

Est. as: State University of Iowa – 1847

Known as The University of Iowa and uses such on most documents.

Ithaca College
Ithaca, NY

Est. as: Ithaca Conservatory of Music – 1892
NC: Ithaca Conservatory & Affiliated Schools – 1926
NC: Ithaca College – 1931

J

Jackson State University
Jackson, MS

Est. as: Natchez Seminary – 1877
NC: Jackson College – 1882
NC: Mississippi Negro Training School – 1940
NC: Jackson College for Negro Teachers – 1942
NC: Jackson State College for Negro Teachers – 1954
NC: Jackson State College – 1956
NC: Jackson State University – 1974

Location changes
Natchez, MS – 1877
Jackson, MS – 1882

Jacksonville State University
Jacksonville, AL

Est. as: Jacksonville State Normal School – 1883
NC: Jacksonville State Teachers College – 1930
NC: Jacksonville State College – 1957
NC: Jacksonville State University – 1966

Jacksonville University
Jacksonville, FL

Est. as: William J Porter University – 1934
NC: Jacksonville Junior College – c1935
NC: Jacksonville University – 1956
MW: Jacksonville College of Music – c1957

James Madison University

Harrisonburg, VA

Est. as: Normal & Industrial School for Women at Harrisonburg – 1908
NC: State Normal School for Women at Harrisonburg – 1914
NC: State Teachers College at Harrisonburg – 1924
NC: Madison College – 1938
NC: James Madison University – 1977

Jamestown College

Jamestown, ND

Est. as: Jamestown College – 1883

Jarvis Christian College

Hawkins, TX

Est. as: Jarvis Christian Institute – 1912
NC: Jarvis Christian College – 1928

From 1964 to 1976 was affiliated with Texas Christian University.

John Brown University

Siloam Springs, AR

Est. as: Southwestern Collegiate Institute – 1919
NC: John E Brown College – 1920
MW: Siloam School of the Bible – 1934
MW: John E Brown Vocational College – 1934
NC: John Brown University – 1934

The 1934 merger divisions became a single unit in 1948.

John Carroll University

Cleveland, OH

Est. as: Saint Ignatius College – 1886
NC: Cleveland University – 1923
NC: John Carroll University – 1923
MW: Borromeo College of Ohio – 1991

Johns Hopkins University, The
Baltimore, MD

Est. as: Johns Hopkins University, The – 1876
MW: Paul H Nitze School of Advanced International Studies – 1950
MW: Peabody Conservatory of Music – 1977

Johnson C Smith University
Charlotte, NC

Est. as: Biddle Memorial Institute – 1867
NC: Biddle University – 1876
NC: Johnson C Smith University – 1923

Johnson State College
Johnson, VT

Est. as: Johnson Academy – 1828
NC: Lamoille County Grammar School – 1836
NC: Johnson Normal School – 1866
NC: Johnson Teachers College – 1947
NC: Johnson State College – 1962

Academy was chartered in 1832; grammar school also known as Lamoille Academy.

Johnson & Wales University
Providence, RI

Est. as: Johnson & Wales College of Business – 1914
NC: Johnson & Wales Junior College of Business – 1963
NC: Johnson & Wales College – 1970
NC: Johnson & Wales University – 1988

Some names and some years may not be exact; institution does not have complete records.

Judaism, University of
Bel Air, CA

Est. as: University of Judaism – 1947

Location changes
Los Angeles, CA – 1947
Bel Air, CA – 1979

By MO: By merger (of) *DM:* Dissolved merger (with) *MW:* Merged with *NC:* Name change (to)

Judson College
Elgin, IL

Est. as: Northern Baptist Seminary, College Division – 1920*
NC: Judson College – 1963

Location changes
Chicago, IL – 1920
Elgin, IL – 1963

*Recognizes 1963 as official established year.

Seminary portion of Northern Baptist Seminary, established in 1913, moved from Chicago to Lombard in 1963; the college, which had been established as the college division of the seminary in 1920, was then established in Elgin in 1963.

Judson College
Marion, AL

Est. as: Judson Female Institute – 1838
NC: Judson College – 1903

Juniata College
Huntingdon, PA

Est. as: Huntingdon Normal School – 1876
NC: Juniata College – 1894

K

Kalamazoo College
Kalamazoo, MI

Est. as: Michigan & Huron Institute, The – 1833
NC: Kalamazoo Literary Institute – 1837
NC: University of Michigan: Kalamazoo Branch – 1840
NC: Kalamazoo Literary Institute – 1850
NC: Kalamazoo College – 1855

Kansas State University
Manhattan, KS

Est. as: Kansas State Agricultural College – 1863
NC: Kansas State College of Agriculture & Applied Science – 1931
NC: Kansas State University – 1959
MW: Kansas College of Technology – 1991

Kansas Wesleyan University
Salina, KS

Est. as: Kansas Wesleyan University – 1886
NC: Kansas Wesleyan – 1969
NC: Kansas Wesleyan University – 1990

Kansas, University of
Lawrence, KS

Est. as: University of Kansas – 1866*

*Recognizes 1866 as official established year (when classes began) although 1865, when campus construction began, is on the seal, and 1864 is the year when the school was authorized by the legislature.

Kean University
Union, NJ

Est. as: Newark Normal School – 1855
NC: New Jersey State Normal School at Newark – 1913
NC: Newark State Teachers College – 1935
NC: Newark State College – 1958
NC: Kean College of New Jersey – 1974
NC: Kean University – 1997

Location changes
Newark, NJ – 1855
Union, NJ – 1958

Keene State College
Keene, NH

Est. as: Keene Normal School – 1909
NC: Keene Teachers College – 1939
NC: Keene State College – 1963

Kendall College
Evanston, IL

Est. as: Evanston Collegiate Institute – 1934
NC: Kendall College – 1950

Kennesaw State University
Kennesaw, GA

Est. as: Kennesaw Junior College – 1963
NC: Kennesaw College – 1977
NC: Kennesaw State College – 1988
NC: Kennesaw State University – 1996

Kent State University
Kent, OH

Est. as: Kent State Normal School – 1910
NC: Kent State Normal College – 1915
NC: Kent State College – 1919
NC: Kent State University – 1935

For some years after 1986, was known as Kent University.

Kentucky Christian College
Grayson, KY

Est. as: Christian Normal Institute – 1919
NC: Kentucky Christian College – 1945

Kentucky State University
Frankfort, KY

Est. as: State Normal School for Colored Persons – 1886
NC: Kentucky Normal & Industrial Institute – 1902
NC: Kentucky State Industrial College for Colored Persons – 1926
NC: Kentucky State College for Negroes – 1938
NC: Kentucky State College – 1952
NC: Kentucky State University – 1972

Kentucky Wesleyan College
Owensboro, KY

Est. as: Kentucky Wesleyan College – 1858

Location changes
Millersburg, KY – 1858
Winchester, KY – 1890
Owensboro, KY – 1951

Kentucky, University of
Lexington, KY

Est. as: Kentucky University Agricultural & Mechanical College – 1865
NC: Agricultural & Mechanical College of Kentucky – 1878
NC: State University of Kentucky – 1908
NC: University of Kentucky – 1916

Kentucky University Agricultural & Mechanical College was established by Kentucky University, which later became Transylvania University, along with a College of the Bible and a College of Law. The A&M college was split-off in 1878 and became the University of Kentucky.

Kenyon College
Gambier, OH

Est. as: Theological Seminary of the Protestant Episcopal Church, The – 1824
NC: Kenyon College – 1891

Keuka College
Keuka Park, NY

Est. as: Keuka Institute – 1890
NC: Keuka College – 1896
NC: Keuka College for Women – 1921
NC: Keuka College – 1984

King College
Bristol, TN

Est. as: Bristol High School – 1867
NC: King College – 1869

King's College
Wilkes-Barre, PA

Est. as: King's College – 1946

Knox College
Galesburg, IL

Est. as: Knox Manual Labor College – 1837
NC: Knox College – 1857
MW: Lombard College – 1930

In early years, was known as Prairie College; affectionately known as Old Siwash.

Kutztown University of Pennsylvania of the State System of Higher Education
Kutztown, PA

Est. as: Keystone Normal School – 1866
NC: Kutztown State Teachers College – 1927
NC: Kutztown State College – 1960
NC: Kutztown University of Pennsylvania of the State System of Higher Education – 1983

By MO: By merger (of) *DM:* Dissolved merger (with) *MW:* Merged with *NC:* Name change (to)

La Roche College
Pittsburgh, PA
Est. as: La Roche College – 1963

La Salle University
Philadelphia, PA
Est. as: La Salle College – 1863
NC: La Salle University – 1984

La Sierra University
Riverside, CA
Est. as: La Sierra Academy – 1922
NC: Southern California Junior College – 1928
NC: La Sierra College – 1943
MW: Loma Linda University – 1967
NC: Loma Linda University, Riverside – 1967
DM: Loma Linda University – 1990
NC: La Sierra University – 1991

La Verne, University of
La Verne, CA
Est. as: Lordsburg College – 1891
NC: La Verne College – 1917
NC: University of La Verne – 1977
MW: San Fernando Valley College of Law – 1983

Lafayette College
Easton, PA

Est. as: Lafayette College – 1826

In 1832, The Rev. George Junkin, agreed to move the curriculum and student body of Manual Labor Academy of Pennsylvania from Germantown, a section of Philadelphia, to Easton to assume the Lafayette College charter.

LaGrange College
LaGrange, GA

Est. as: LaGrange Female Academy – 1831
NC: LaGrange Female Institute – 1847
NC: LaGrange Female College – 1851
NC: LaGrange College – 1934

Lake Erie College
Painesville, OH

Est. as: Lake Erie Female Seminary – 1856
NC: Lake Erie Seminary & College – 1898
NC: Lake Erie College – 1908

Lake Forest College
Lake Forest, IL

Est. as: Lind University – 1857
NC: Lake Forest University – 1865
NC: Lake Forest College – 1965

Lake Superior State University
Sault Saint Marie, MI

Est. as: Michigan College of Mining & Technology, Sault Saint Marie Branch – 1946
NC: Lake Superior State College – 1970
NC: Lake Superior State University – 1987

Lakeland College
Sheboygan, WI

Est. as: Mission House – 1862
NC: Lakeland College – 1956

Known at establishment by German founders as Missionhaus.

Lamar University
Beaumont, TX

Est. as: South Park Junior College – 1923
NC: Lamar College – 1932
NC: Lamar State College of Technology – 1951
NC: Lamar University – 1971
NC: Lamar University-Beaumont – 1991
NC: Lamar University – 1995

Lambuth University
Jackson, TN

Est. as: Memphis Conference Female Institute – 1843
NC: Lambuth College – 1924
NC: Lambuth University – 1991

Location changes
Memphis, TN – 1843
Jackson, TN – 1923

Known as Memphis Conference Woman's College in 1919.

Lander University
Greenwood, SC

Est. as: Williamston Female College – 1872
NC: Lander College – 1904
NC: Lander University – 1993

Location changes
Williamston, SC – 1872
Greenwood, SC – 1904

Lane College
Jackson, TN

Est. as: Colored Methodist Episcopal High School – 1882
NC: Lane Institute – 1883
NC: Lane College – 1896

Langston University
Langston, OK

Est. as: Colored Agricultural & Normal University – 1897
NC: Langston University – 1941

By MO: By merger (of) *DM:* Dissolved merger (with) *MW:* Merged with *NC:* Name change (to)

Lasell College
Newton, MA

Est. as: Auburndale Female Seminary – 1851
NC: Lasell Female Seminary – 1852
NC: Lasell Seminary for Young Women – 1874
NC: Lasell Junior College – 1932
NC: Lasell College – 1990

Location changes
Auburndale, MA – 1851
Newton, MA – 1975

Lawrence Technological University
Southfield, MI

Est. as: Lawrence Institute of Technology – 1932
MW: Detroit Institute of Technology – 1981
NC: Lawrence Technological University – 1989

Location changes
Highland Park, MI – 1932
Southfield, MI – 1955

Lawrence University
Appleton, WI

Est. as: Lawrence Institute of Wisconsin – 1847
NC: Lawrence University of Wisconsin – 1849
NC: Lawrence College – 1908
MW: Milwaukee-Downer College – 1964
NC: Lawrence University – 1964

Le Moyne College
Syracuse, NY
Est. as: Le Moyne College – 1946

Lebanon Valley College
Annville, PA
Est. as: Lebanon Valley College – 1866
Known in 1980-90s as Lebanon Valley College of Pennsylvania.

Lee University
Cleveland, TN

Est. as: Unnamed Bible training school – 1918
MW: Murphy Collegiate Institute – 1938
NC: Lee College – 1947
NC: Lee University – 1997
MW: East Coast Bible College – 1999

Location changes
Cleveland, TN – 1918
Sevierville, TN – 1938
Cleveland, TN – 1947

Lee Junior College was established in 1938 as part of the Bible training school; upon move to Cleveland in 1947, it was re-named Lee College.

Lehigh University
Bethlehem, PA

Est. as: Lehigh University – 1865

Lenoir-Rhyne College
Hickory, NC

Est. as: Highland Academy – 1891
NC: Lenoir College – 1892
NC: Lenoir-Rhyne College – 1923

Lesley University
Cambridge, MA

Est. as: Lesley Normal School – 1909
NC: Lesley School, The – 1936
NC: Lesley College – 1943
MW: Art Institute of Boston – 1998
NC: Lesley University – 2000

Under 1998 merger, each institution retained its own name.

LeTourneau University
Longview, TX

Est. as: LeTourneau Technical Institute of Texas – 1946
NC: LeTourneau College – 1961
NC: LeTourneau University – 1989

By MO: By merger (of) **DM:** Dissolved merger (with) **MW:** Merged with **NC:** Name change (to)

Lewis University
Romeoville, IL

Est. as: Holy Name Technical School – 1932
NC: Lewis Holy Name Technical School – 1934
NC: Lewis Holy Name School of Aeronautics – 1935
NC: Lewis School of Aeronautics – 1941
NC: Lewis College of Science & Technology – 1952
NC: Lewis College – 1962
NC: Lewis University – 1973

Location changes
Lockport, IL – 1932
Romeoville, IL – 1977

Did not change location in 1977; campus was annexed into Romeoville for access to municipal water system.

Lewis & Clark College
Portland, OR

Est. as: Albany Collegiate Institute – 1867
NC: Lewis & Clark College – 1942
MW: Northwestern School of Law – 1965

Location changes
Albany, OR – 1867
Portland, OR – 1942

Lewis-Clark State College
Lewiston, ID

Est. as: Lewiston State Normal School – 1893
NC: Northern Idaho College of Education – 1947
NC: Lewis-Clark Normal School – 1955
NC: Lewis-Clark State College – 1971

Liberty University
Lynchburg, VA

Est. as: Lynchburg Baptist College – 1971
NC: Liberty Baptist College – 1975
NC: Liberty University – 1985

By MO: By merger (of) *DM:* Dissolved merger (with) *MW:* Merged with *NC:* Name change (to)

130

Limestone College
Gaffney, SC

Est. as: Limestone Springs School – 1845
NC: Cooper-Limestone Institute – 1881
NC: Limestone College – 1899

Lincoln Memorial University
Harrogate, TN

Est. as: Lincoln Memorial University – 1897

Lincoln University
Jefferson City, MO

Est. as: Lincoln Institute – 1866
NC: Lincoln University – 1921

Lincoln University
Lower Oxford Township, PA

Est. as: Ashmum Institute – 1854
NC: Lincoln University – 1866

Lindenwood University
Saint Charles, MO

Est. as: Lindenwood – 1827
NC: Lindenwood Female College – 1853
NC: Lindenwood College – 1970
NC: Lindenwood University – 1997

Lindsey Wilson College
Columbia, KY

Est. as: Lindsey Wilson Training School – 1903
NC: Lindsey Wilson College – 1923

By MO: By merger (of) *DM:* Dissolved merger (with) *MW:* Merged with *NC:* Name change (to)

Linfield College
McMinnville, OR

Est. as: Oregon City College – 1849
NC: Oregon City University – 1856
NC: Baptist College at McMinnville – 1858
NC: McMinnville College – 1890
NC: Linfield College – 1922

Location changes
Oregon City, OR – 1849
McMinnville, OR – 1858

Livingstone College
Salisbury, NC

Est. as: Zion Wesley Institute – 1879
NC: Zion Wesley College – 1885
NC: Livingstone College – 1887

Location changes
Concord, NC – 1879
Salisbury, NC – 1882

Lock Haven University of Pennsylvania of the State System of Higher Education
Lock Haven, PA

Est. as: Central State Normal School – 1870
NC: Lock Haven State Teachers College – 1927
NC: Lock Haven State College – 1960
NC: Lock Haven University of Pennsylvania of the State System of Higher Education – 1983

Long Island University: Brooklyn Campus
Brooklyn, NY

Est. as: Long Island University – 1926
NC: Long Island University: The Zeckendorf Campus – 1965
NC: Long Island University: Brooklyn Center – 1969
NC: Long Island University: Brooklyn Campus – 1980

132

Longwood College
Farmville, VA

Est. as: Farmville Female Seminary – 1839
NC: State Female Normal School – 1884
NC: State Normal School for Women – 1914
NC: State Teachers College at Farmville – 1924
NC: Longwood College – 1949

Loras College
Dubuque, IA

Est. as: Saint Raphael Seminary – 1839
NC: Mount Saint Bernard – 1850
NC: Saint Joseph's College – 1873
NC: Dubuque College – 1914
NC: Columbia College – 1920
NC: Loras College – 1939

Louisiana at Lafayette, University of
Lafayette, LA

Est. as: Southwestern Louisiana Industrial Institute – 1898
NC: Southwestern Louisiana Institute of Liberal & Technical Learning – 1921
NC: University of Southwestern Louisiana, The – 1960
NC: University of Louisiana – 1984
NC: University of Southwestern Louisiana, The – 1986
NC: University of Louisiana at Lafayette – 1999

In 1984, attempt was made to change name to University of Louisiana; other state educational institutions objected; court action prevented change.

Louisiana at Monroe, University of
Monroe, LA

Est. as: Ouachita Parish Junior College – 1931
NC: Louisiana State University: Northeast Center – 1934
NC: Louisiana State University: Northeast Junior College – 1939
NC: Northeast Louisiana State College – 1950
NC: Northeast Louisiana University – 1970
NC: University of Louisiana at Monroe – 1999

By MO: By merger (of) *DM:* Dissolved merger (with) *MW:* Merged with *NC:* Name change (to)

Louisiana College
Pineville, LA

Est. as: Louisiana College – 1906

Louisiana State University in Shreveport
Shreveport, LA

Est. as: Louisiana State University in Shreveport – 1967

Louisiana State University & Agricultural & Mechanical College
Baton Rouge, LA

Est. as: Seminary of Learning of the State of Louisiana – 1853*
NC: Louisiana State House of Education – 1855
NC: Louisiana State School of Education – 1858
NC: Louisiana State Seminary of Learning & Military Academy – 1860
NC: Louisiana State University, The – 1870
MW: Louisiana Agricultural & Mechanical College – 1877
NC: Louisiana State University & Agricultural & Mechanical College – 1877

Location changes
Near Pineville, LA – 1853
Baton Rouge, LA – 1869

*Recognizes 1860 as official established year.

Closed several times during Civil War; burned on October 15, 1869, re-opened in Baton Rouge on November 1, 1869.

Louisiana Tech University
Ruston, LA

Est. as: Industrial Institute & College of Louisiana – 1894
NC: Louisiana Polytechnic Institute – 1921
NC: Louisiana Tech University – 1970

134

Louisville, University of
Louisville, KY

Est. as: Jefferson Seminary – 1798
MW: Louisville College – 1846
MW: Louisville Medical Institute – 1846
NC: University of Louisville – 1846
MW: Louisville Municipal College – 1951
MW: Kentucky Southern University – 1969
MW: Louisville School of Art – 1983

Jefferson Seminary had closed; Louisville College, formerly Louisville Collegiate Institute, inherited the property in 1844. Merger of Louisville College and Louisville Medical Institute into University of Louisville was administrative; i.e., one board, otherwise autonomous. Louisville Municipal College, a black institution established in 1931, had been a separate institution under the University of Louisville board; the merger provided for the desegregation of the University of Louisville. Louisville School of Art closed and students were admitted to the university.

Lourdes College
Sylvania, OH

Est. as: Extension Campus of the College of Saint Teresa – 1943*
NC: Lourdes Junior College – 1958
NC: Lourdes College – 1973

*Recognizes 1958 as official established year.

Loyola College in Maryland
Baltimore, MD

Est. as: Loyola College – 1852
MW: Mount Saint Agnes College of Women – 1971
NC: Loyola College in Maryland – 1999

Loyola Marymount University
Los Angeles, CA

Est. as: Saint Vincent's College – 1865*
NC: Los Angeles College – 1911
NC: Loyola College of Los Angeles – 1918
NC: Loyola University of Los Angeles – 1930
MW: Marymount College of Los Angeles – 1968
NC: Loyola Marymount University – 1973

*Recognizes 1911 as official established year.

Loyola University New Orleans
New Orleans, LA

Est. as: College of the Immaculate Conception – 1849*
MW: Loyola College – 1911
NC: Loyola University – 1912
MW: New Orleans College of Pharmacy – 1919
MW: New Orleans Conservatory of Music & Dramatic Arts – 1932
NC: Loyola University New Orleans – 1995

*Recognizes 1912 as official established year.

College of the Immaculate Conception also known as the Jesuit School in New Orleans and as the Jesus School.

Loyola University of Chicago
Chicago, IL

Est. as: Saint Ignatius College – 1870
NC: Loyola University Chicago – 1909
MW: Illinois Medical College – 1909
MW: Bennett Medical School – 1910
MW: Chicago College of Medicine & Surgery – 1917
NC: Loyola University of Chicago – 1976
MW: Mallinckrodt College of the North Shore – 1991

Loyola University of Chicago is the official, legal name; in the early 1990s a marketing decision was made to use Loyola University Chicago as the name.

Lubbock Christian University
Lubbock, TX

Est. as: Lubbock Christian College – 1957
NC: Lubbock Christian University – 1987

Luther College
Decorah, IA

Est. as: Luther College – 1861
MW: Decorah College for Women – 1936

Location changes
Halfway Creek (near La Crosse), WI – 1861
Decorah, IA – 1862

Decorah College for Women had closed; graduates received a Luther diploma and were invited to be Luther alumnae.

Lycoming College
Williamsport, PA

Est. as: Williamsport Academy – 1812
NC: Dickinson Seminary – 1848
NC: Dickinson Junior College – 1929
NC: Lycoming College – 1947

Lynchburg College
Lynchburg, VA

Est. as: Virginia Christian College – 1903
NC: Lynchburg College – 1919

Lyndon State College
Lyndonville, VT

Est. as: Lyndon Institute – 1911
NC: Lyndon Teachers College – 1949
NC: Lyndon State College – 1962

By MO: By merger (of) *DM:* Dissolved merger (with) *MW:* Merged with *NC:* Name change (to)

Lynn University

Boca Raton, FL

Est. as: Marymount College – 1962
NC: College of Boca Raton – 1974
NC: Lynn University – 1991
MW: Music Division of Harid Conservatory – 1999

Harid Conservatory had two divisions: music and dance; music was acquired by Lynn (now called Conservatory of Music at Lynn University, a college within the university), but Harid retained the dance division.

Lyon College

Batesville, AR

Est. as: Arkansas College – 1872
NC: Lyon College – 1994

Macalester College
Saint Paul, MN

Est. as: Baldwin School – 1853*
NC: Baldwin University – 1865
NC: Jesus College – 1872
NC: Macalester College – 1874

*Recognizes 1874 as official established year.

MacMurray College
Jacksonville, IL

Est. as: Illinois Female Academy – 1846
NC: Illinois Conference Female Academy – 1851
NC: Illinois Female College – 1863
NC: Illinois Women's College – 1899
NC: MacMurray College for Women – 1930
NC: MacMurray College – 1953
MW: MacMurray College for Men – 1969

Madonna University
Livonia, MI

Est. as: Presentation Blessed Virgin Mary Junior College – 1937*
NC: Madonna College – 1947
NC: Madonna University – 1991

*Recognizes 1947 as official established year.

Maharishi University of Management
Fairfield, IA

Est. as: Maharishi International University – 1971
NC: Maharishi University of Management – 1995

Maine at Augusta, University of

Augusta, ME

Est. as: Regional Center of State Continuing Education Division – 1965

NC: University of Maine at Augusta – 1971

Maine at Farmington, University of

Farmington, ME

Est. as: Western State Normal School – 1863
NC: Northern State Normal School – 1878
NC: Farmington State Normal School – 1903
NC: Farmington State Teachers College – 1945
NC: Farmington State College – 1965
NC: Farmington State College of the University of Maine – 1968
NC: University of Maine at Farmington – 1970

Maine at Fort Kent, University of

Fort Kent, ME

Est. as: Madawaska Training School – 1878
NC: Fort Kent State Normal School – 1955
NC: Fort Kent State Teachers College – 1961
NC: Fort Kent State College – 1965
NC: Fort Kent State College of the University of Maine – 1968
NC: University of Maine at Fort Kent – 1970

Location changes

Fort Kent & Van Buren, ME – 1878
Fort Kent, ME – 1887

Madawaska Training School had two campuses.

Maine at Machias, University of

Machias, ME

Est. as: Washington State Normal School – 1909
NC: Washington State Teachers College – 1952
NC: Washington State College – 1965
NC: Washington State Teachers College of the University of Maine – 1968
NC: University of Maine at Machias – 1970

By MO: By merger (of) **DM:** Dissolved merger (with) **MW:** Merged with **NC:** Name change (to)

Maine at Presque Isle, University of

Presque Isle, ME

Est. as: Aroostook State Normal School – 1903
NC: Aroostook State Teachers College – 1952
NC: Aroostook State College – 1965
NC: Aroostook State College of the University of Maine – 1968
NC: University of Maine at Presque Isle – 1970

Maine, University of

Orono, ME

Est. as: State College of Agriculture & the Mechanical Arts – 1865
NC: University of Maine – 1897
MW: Portland University – 1961
NC: University of Maine at Orono – 1968
NC: University of Maine – 1986

Malone College

Canton, OH

Est. as: Christian Workers Training School for Bible Study & Practical Methods of Work – 1892
NC: Christian Workers Training School – 1895
NC: Friends Bible Institute & Training School, The – 1899
NC: Cleveland Bible Institute & Training School – 1908
NC: Cleveland Bible Institute – 1911
NC: Cleveland Bible College – 1937
NC: Malone College – 1956

Location changes
Cleveland, OH – 1892
Canton, OH – 1957

Manchester College

North Manchester, IN

Est. as: Roanoke Classical Seminary – 1860*
NC: Manchester College – 1889
MW: Mount Morris College – 1932

Location changes
Roanoke, IN – 1860
North Manchester, IN – 1889

*Recognizes 1889 as official established year.

By MO: By merger (of) **DM:** Dissolved merger (with) **MW:** Merged with **NC:** Name change (to)

Manhattan College
Riverdale, NY

Est. as: Academy of the Holy Infancy – 1853
NC: Manhattan Academy – 1861
NC: Manhattan College – 1863

Manhattanville College
Purchase, NY

Est. as: Academy of the Sacred Heart – 1841
NC: College of the Sacred Heart – 1917
NC: Manhattanville College of the Sacred Heart – 1937
NC: Manhattanville College – 1966

Location changes
New York, NY – 1841
Manhattanville, NY – 1847
Purchase, NY – 1952

Mansfield University of Pennsylvania of the State System of Higher Education
Mansfield, PA

Est. as: Mansfield Classical Seminary – 1857
NC: State Normal School, Mansfield – 1862
NC: Mansfield State Normal School – 1920
NC: Mansfield State Teachers College – 1927
NC: Mansfield State College – 1960
NC: Mansfield University of Pennsylvania of the State System of Higher Education– 1983

Marian College
Indianapolis, IN

Est. as: Saint Francis Normal School for Women – 1851
MW: Immaculate Conception Junior College – 1936
NC: Marian College – 1936

Location changes
Oldenburg, IN – 1851
Indianapolis, IN – 1937

Marian College of Fond du Lac

Fond du Lac, WI

Est. as: Marian College – 1936
NC: Marian College of Fond du Lac – 1960
MW: Saint Agnes School of Nursing – 1967

Uses only Marian College as its name except for legal and other official situations.

Marietta College, The

Marietta, OH

Est. as: Institute of Education – 1830*
NC: Marietta Collegiate Institute & Western Teachers Seminary – 1832
NC: Marietta College, The – 1835
MW: Marietta College for Women, The – 1897

*Recognizes 1835 as official established year.

The Marietta College for Women was a co-ordinate college.

Marist College

Poughkeepsie, NY

Est. as: Marist Training School – 1929
NC: Marian College – 1946
NC: Marist College – 1960

Marlboro College

Marlboro, VT

Est. as: Marlboro College – 1946

Marquette University

Milwaukee, WI

Est. as: Marquette College – 1881
NC: Marquette University – 1907

Saint Aloyosius Academy, established in 1857, may have been a predecessor institution.

By MO: By merger (of) **DM:** Dissolved merger (with) **MW:** Merged with **NC:** Name change (to)

Mars Hill College
Mars Hill, NC

Est. as: Frence Broad Baptist Institute – 1856
NC: Mars Hill College – 1859

Marshall University
Huntington, WV

Est. as: Marshall Academy – 1837
NC: Marshall College – 1858
NC: Marshall University – 1961
MW: West Virginia Graduate College – 1997

Location changes
Guyandotte, VA – 1837
Huntington, WV – 1838

Martin Methodist College
Pulaski, TN

Est. as: Martin Female College – 1870
NC: Martin College – c1938
NC: Martin Methodist College – 1987

Martin University
Indianapolis, IN

Est. as: Martin Center College – 1977
NC: Martin University – 1990

Mary Baldwin College
Staunton, VA

Est. as: Augusta Female Academy – 1842
NC: Mary Baldwin Seminary – 1895
NC: Mary Baldwin Junior College – 1916
NC: Mary Baldwin College – 1923

Mary Hardin-Baylor, The University of
Belton, TX

Est. as: Baylor University – 1845*
DM: Baylor University – 1866
NC: Baylor Female College – 1866
NC: Baylor College for Women – 1925
NC: Mary Hardin-Baylor College – 1934
NC: University of Mary-Hardin Baylor, The – 1976

Location changes
Independence, TX – 1845
Belton, TX – 1886

*Recognizes 1845, when Baylor University — from which it evolved — was established, as official established year.

Baylor University had preparatory, female, and male departments. Female Department was chartered separately in 1866 as Baylor Female College.

Mary Washington College
Fredericksburg, VA

Est. as: State Normal & Industrial School for Women, Fredericksburg – 1908
NC: State Teachers College, Fredericksburg – 1924
NC: Mary Washington College – 1938
NC: Mary Washington College of the University of Virginia – 1944
NC: Mary Washington College – 1972

Mary, University of
Bismarck, ND

Est. as: Mary College – 1959
NC: University of Mary – 1986

By MO: By merger (of) *DM:* Dissolved merger (with) *MW:* Merged with *NC:* Name change (to)

Marygrove College
Detroit, MI

Est. as: Saint Mary Academy – 1845*
NC: Saint Mary College – 1905
NC: Marygrove College – 1925

Location changes
Monroe, MI – 1845
Detroit, MI – 1927

*Recognizes 1905 as official established year.

Maryland Eastern Shore, University of
Princess Anne, MD

Est. as: Delaware Conference Academy – 1886
NC: Princess Anne Academy – 1890
NC: Maryland Agricultural College, Eastern Branch of – 1919
NC: Industrial Branch of Morgan State College – 1935
NC: Princess Anne College – 1936
NC: Maryland State College – 1948
NC: University of Maryland: Eastern Shore – 1970
NC: University of Maryland Eastern Shore – 1997

When established, also known as Centenary Biblical Institute.

Maryland, Baltimore County, University of
Baltimore, MD

Est. as: University of Maryland Baltimore County – 1963
NC: University of Maryland, Baltimore County – 1997

Maryland, College Park, University of
College Park, MD

Est. as: Maryland Agricultural College – 1856
NC: Maryland State College of Agriculture – 1916
MW: University of Maryland – 1920
NC: University of Maryland – 1920
NC: University of Maryland, College Park – 1997

The original University of Maryland was in Baltimore and housed the medical and technical departments. After the merger, the various departments became schools within the new institution at College Park.

Marylhurst University
Marylhurst, OR

Est. as: Saint Mary's Academy – 1859*
NC: Saint Mary's Academy & College – 1893
NC: Marylhurst College – 1930
NC: Marylhurst Education Center – 1974
NC: Marylhurst College for Lifelong Learning – 1980
NC: Marylhurst College – 1992
NC: Marylhurst University – 1998

Location changes
Portland, OR – 1859
Marylhurst, OR – 1930

*Recognizes 1893 as official established year.

Marymount Manhattan College
New York, NY

Est. as: Marymount Junior College – 1936*
NC: Marymount Manhattan College – 1961

*Recognizes 1961, when became independent of Marymount College, Tarrytown, NY, as official established year.

Originally established as a junior college branch of Marymount College, Tarrytown, NY. It began to offer extension courses for a 4-year degree in 1946 and may have been known as Marymount College Extension and Marymount College New York.

Marymount University
Arlington, VA

Est. as: Marymount Junior College – 1950
NC: Marymount College of Virginia – 1960
NC: Marymount University – 1986

Maryville College
Maryville, TN

Est. as: Southern & Western Theological Seminary – 1819
NC: Maryville College – 1842

Maryville University of Saint Louis
Saint Louis, MO

Est. as: Convent of the Sacred Heart – 1872
NC: Maryville College & Academy of the Sacred Heart – 1920
NC: Maryville College of the Sacred Heart – 1927
NC: Mercy Junior College – 1970
NC: Maryville College – 1972
NC: Maryville University of Saint Louis – 1991

Marywood University
Scranton, PA

Est. as: Marywood College – 1915
NC: Marywood University – 1997

Massachusetts Amherst, University of
Amherst, MA

Est. as: Massachusetts Agricultural College – 1863
NC: Massachusetts State College – 1931
NC: University of Massachusetts – 1947
NC: University of Massachusetts Amherst – 1991

Massachusetts Boston, University of
Boston, MA

Est. as: University of Massachusetts at Boston – 1964
MW: Boston State College – 1982
NC: University of Massachusetts Boston – 1991

Massachusetts College of Liberal Arts
North Adams, MA

Est. as: North Adams Normal School – 1894
NC: State Teachers College at North Adams – 1932
NC: North Adams State College – 1960
NC: Massachusetts College of Liberal Arts – 1997

148

Massachusetts Dartmouth, University of
North Dartmouth, MA

Est. as: New Bedford Textile School – 1895
NC: New Bedford Technical Institute – 1950
NC: New Bedford Institute of Textiles & Technology – 1955
NC: New Bedford Institute of Technology – 1957
MW: Bradford Durfee College of Technology – 1964
NC: Southwestern Massachusetts Technical Institute – 1964
NC: Southeastern Massachusetts University – 1969
MW: Swain School of Design – 1988
NC: University of Massachusetts Dartmouth – 1991

Location changes
New Bedford, MA – 1895
North Dartmouth, MA – 1964

Proposed merger with Southern New England School of Law for 2002 in discussion stage as of February, 2002.

Massachusetts Institute of Technology
Cambridge, MA

Est. as: Massachusetts Institute of Technology – 1861

Massachusetts Lowell, University of
Lowell, MA

Est. as: Massachusetts State Normal School at Lowell – 1894
NC: State Teachers College at Lowell – 1932
NC: Massachusetts State College at Lowell – 1960
NC: Lowell State College – 1968
MW: Lowell Technological Institute – 1975
NC: University of Lowell – 1975
NC: University of Massachusetts Lowell – 1991

Master's College, The
Santa Clarita, CA

Est. as: Los Angeles Baptist Theological Seminary – 1927
NC: Los Angeles Baptist College – 1959
NC: Master's College, The – 1985

Location changes
Los Angeles, CA – 1927
Santa Clarita, CA – 1961

After the move from Los Angeles in 1927, was located in Newhall which later was incorporated into Santa Clarita.

Mayville State University
Mayville, ND

Est. as: Mayville Normal School – 1889
NC: Mayville State Teachers College – 1925
NC: Mayville State College – 1963
NC: State University of North Dakota-Mayville – 1987
NC: Mayville State University – 1987

McDaniel College
Westminster, MD

Est. as: Western Maryland College – 1867
NC: McDaniel College – 2002

McKendree College
Lebanon, IL

Est. as: Lebanon Seminary – 1828
NC: McKendrian College – 1835
NC: McKedree College – 1839

McMurry University
Abilene, TX

Est. as: McMurry College – 1923
MW: Dallas Institute of Vocal & Dramatic Arts – 1947
NC: McMurry University – 1990

150

McNeese State University
Lake Charles, LA

Est. as: Lake Charles Junior College – 1939
NC: John McNeese Junior College – 1940
NC: McNeese State College – 1950
NC: McNeese State University – 1970

As a junior college, was a division of Louisiana State University; separated in 1950.

McPherson College
McPherson, KS

Est. as: McPherson College & Industrial Institute – 1887
NC: McPherson College – 1898

Medaille College
Buffalo, NY

Est. as: Institute of the Sisters of Saint Joseph – 1875*
NC: Mount Saint Joseph Teachers College – 1937
NC: Mount Saint Joseph College – 1964
NC: Medaille College – 1968

*Recognizes 1937 as official established year.

Medgar Evers College of the City University of New York
Brooklyn, NY

Est. as: Medgar Evers College of the City University of New York – 1968

Memphis, The University of
Memphis, TN

Est. as: West Tennessee Normal School – 1912
NC: West Tennessee State Teachers College – 1925
NC: Memphis State College – 1941
NC: Memphis State University – 1957
NC: University of Memphis, The – 1994

Menlo College
Atherton, CA

Est. as: William Warren School – 1915*
NC: Menlo School & Junior College – 1927
NC: Menlo School & College – 1949
NC: Menlo College – 1986

*Recognizes 1927 as official established year.

Originally a boy's military school which became Menlo School; now separate from the college.

Mercer University
Macon, GA

Est. as: Mercer Institute – 1833
NC: Mercer University – 1837
MW: Southern College of Pharmacy – 1959
MW: Tift College – 1986
MW: Georgia Baptist College of Nursing – 2001

Location changes
Penfield, GA – 1833
Macon, GA – 1871

Mercy College
Dobbs Ferry, NY

Est. as: Mercy Junior College – 1950
NC: Mercy College – 1952

Mercyhurst College
Erie, PA

Est. as: Mercyhurst College – 1926

Meredith College
Raleigh, NC

Est. as: Baptist Female University – 1891
NC: Baptist University for Women – 1905
NC: Meredith College – 1909

Merrimack College
North Andover, MA

Est. as: Augustinian College of the Merrimack Valley – 1947
NC: Merrimack College – 1969

At establishment was known as Augustinian College and as Merrimack College.

Mesa State College
Grand Junction, CO

Est. as: Grand Junction State Junior College – 1925
NC: Mesa College – 1937
NC: Mesa State College – 1989

Messiah College
Grantham, PA

Est. as: Messiah Bible School & Missionary Training Home – 1909
NC: Messiah Bible College – 1924
NC: Messiah College – 1951
MW: Upland College – 1965

Methodist College
Fayetteville, NC

Est. as: Methodist College – 1956

Metropolitan State College of Denver
Denver, CO

Est. as: Metropolitan State College – 1963
NC: Metropolitan State College of Denver – 1990

Metropolitan State University
Saint Paul, MN

Est. as: Minnesota Metropolitan State College – 1971
NC: Metropolitan State University – 1975

By MO: By merger (of) *DM:* Dissolved merger (with) *MW:* Merged with *NC:* Name change (to)

Miami University
Oxford, OH

Est. as: Miami University – 1809
MW: Oxford College for Women – 1928
MW: Western College – 1974

Miami, University of
Coral Gables, FL

Est. as: University of Miami – 1925

Michigan State University
East Lansing, MI

Est. as: Agricultural College of the State of Michigan – 1855
NC: State Agricultural College, The – 1861
NC: Michigan Agricultural College – 1909
NC: Michigan State College of Agriculture & Applied Science – 1925
NC: Michigan State University of Agriculture & Applied Science – 1955
NC: Michigan State University – 1964

Michigan Technological University
Houghton, MI

Est. as: Michigan Mining School – 1885
NC: Michigan College of Mines – 1897
NC: Michigan College of Mining & Technology – 1927
NC: Michigan Technological University – 1964

Michigan, University of
Ann Arbor, MI

Est. as: Catholepistemiad (Universitstis Michigania) – 1817
NC: University of Michigan – 1821

Location changes
Detroit, MI – 1817
Ann Arbor, MI – 1837

Mid-Continent College
Hickory, KY

Est. as: West Kentucky Baptist Bible Institute – 1949
NC: Baptist Bible Institute – 1957
NC: Mid-Continent Baptist Bible College – 1965
NC: Mid-Continent College – 1993

Location changes
Clinton, KY – 1949
Mayfield, KY – 1957
Hickory, KY – 1977

MidAmerica Nazarene University
Olathe, KS

Est. as: MidAmerica Nazarene College – 1966
NC: MidAmerica Nazarene University – 1997

Middle Tennessee State University
Murfreesboro, TN

Est. as: Middle Tennessee State Normal School – 1911
NC: Middle Tennessee State Teachers College – 1926
NC: State Teachers College, Murfreesboro – 1929
NC: Middle Tennessee State College – 1943
NC: Middle Tennessee State University – 1965

Middlebury College
Middlebury, VT

Est. as: Middlebury College – 1800

Midland Lutheran College
Fremont, NE

Est. as: Midland College – 1887*
MW: Fremont College – 1919
MW: Luther Junior College – 1962
NC: Midland Lutheran College – 1962

Location changes
Atchison, NE – 1887
Fremont, NE – 1919

*Recognizes 1883, when Luther Junior College, Wahoo, NE, was established as Luther College & Academy, as official established year.

155

Midway College
Midway, KY

Est. as: Kentucky Female Orphans School – 1847
NC: Pinkerton High School & Midway Junior College – 1942
NC: Midway Junior College – 1972
NC: Midway College – 1978

Midwestern State University
Wichita Falls, TX

Est. as: Wichita Falls Junior College – 1922
NC: Hardin Junior College – 1937
NC: Hardin College – 1946
NC: Midwestern University – 1950
NC: Midwestern State University – 1975

Miles College
Fairfield, AL

Est. as: Miles Memorial College – 1905
NC: Miles College – 1941

Millersville University of Pennsylvania of the State System of Higher Education
Millersville, PA

Est. as: Lancaster County Normal Institute – 1855
NC: Lancaster County Normal School – 1855
NC: First Pennsylvania State Normal School of the Second District – 1859
NC: Millersville State Teachers College – 1927
NC: Millersville State College – 1960
NC: Millersville University of Pennsylvania of the State System of Higher Education – 1983

Trustees of Millersville Academy offered its use to a Wickersham for his Normal Institute; joint decision to continue it as the institute. Does not consider the academy as a predecessor.

Milligan College
Johnson City, TN

Est. as: Buffalo Male & Female Institute – 1866
NC: Milligan College – 1881

Millikin University
Decatur, IL

Est. as: Decatur College & Industrial School of the James Millikin University – 1901
DM: Lincoln University – 1953
NC: Millikin University – 1953

Charter of Lincoln University, established in 1865, was amended to create Decatur College & Industrial School of The James Millikin University. Lincoln University remained as a part of the new institution until the merger was dissolved in 1953.

Mills College
Oakland, CA

Est. as: Young Ladies Seminary of Benecia – 1852
NC: Mills Seminary – 1871
NC: Mills Seminary & College – 1877
NC: Mills College – 1885

Location changes
Benecia, CA – 1852
Oakland, CA – 1871

Millsaps College
Jackson, MS

Est. as: Millsaps College – 1890
MW: Grenada College – 1938
MW: Whitworth College – 1938

Minnesota State University, Mankato
Mankato, MN

Est. as: Mankato State Normal School – 1868
NC: Mankato State Teachers College – 1921
NC: Mankato State College – 1957
NC: Mankato State University – 1975
NC: Minnesota State University, Mankato – 1998

By MO: By merger (of) *DM:* Dissolved merger (with) *MW:* Merged with *NC:* Name change (to)

Minnesota State University, Moorhead

Moorhead, MN

Est. as: Moorhead State Normal School – 1885
NC: Moorhead State Teachers College – 1921
NC: Moorhead State College – 1957
NC: Moorhead State University – 1975
NC: Minnesota State University, Moorhead – 2000

Minnesota, Duluth, University of

Duluth, MN

Est. as: Normal School at Duluth – 1895*
NC: Duluth State Normal School – 1905
NC: Duluth State Teachers College – 1921
NC: University of Minnesota, Duluth – 1947

*Recognizes 1947 as official established year.

Minnesota, Morris, University of

Morris, MN

Est. as: North American Indian Boarding School – 1887*
NC: West Central School of Agriculture – 1910
NC: University of Minnesota, Morris – 1959

*Recognizes 1959 as official established year.

Minnesota, University of

Minneapolis, MN

Est. as: University of Minnesota – 1851

Has two campuses: main one in Minneapolis, another in Saint Paul. Twin Cities Campus is not official name.

Minot State University

Minot, ND

Est. as: Minot Normal School – 1913
NC: Minot State Teachers College – 1924
NC: Minot State College – 1964
NC: Dakota Northwestern University – 1985
NC: Minot State College – 1985
NC: State University of North Dakota-Minot – 1987
NC: Minot State University – 1987

By MO: By merger (of) *DM:* Dissolved merger (with) *MW:* Merged with *NC:* Name change (to)

158

Mississippi College
Clinton, MS

Est. as: Hampstead Academy – 1826
NC: Mississippi Academy – 1827
NC: Mississippi College – 1830
MW: Hillman College – 1942
MW: Clarke College – 1992

Mississippi State University
Starkville, MS

Est. as: Agricultural & Mechanical College of the State of Mississippi – 1878
NC: Mississippi State College – 1932
NC: Mississippi State University – 1958

Mississippi University for Women
Columbus, MS

Est. as: Mississippi Industrial Institute & College – 1884
NC: Mississippi State College for Women – 1920
NC: Mississippi University for Women – 1974

Mississippi Valley State University
Itta Bena, MS

Est. as: Mississippi Vocational College – 1950
NC: Mississippi Valley State College – 1964
NC: Mississippi Valley State University – 1974

Mississippi, The University of
Oxford, MS

Est. as: University of Mississippi, The – 1844

By MO: By merger (of) *DM:* Dissolved merger (with) *MW:* Merged with *NC:* Name change (to)

Missouri Baptist College
Saint Louis, MO

Est. as: Extension Center of Hannibal-LaGrange College – 1957
MW: Hanibal-LaGrange College – 1967
NC: Missouri Baptist College-Saint Louis – 1967
DM: Missouri Baptist College-Hannibal – 1973
NC: Missouri Baptist College – 1973

Known as Saint Louis Baptist College in 1950s and 1960s. Upon merger, Hannibal-LaGrange became Missouri Baptist College-Hannibal. It was one college with two campuses. There was an earlier, unrelated, Missouri Baptist College in Cape Girardeau.

Missouri Southern State College
Joplin, MO

Est. as: Joplin Junior College – 1937
NC: Jasper County Junior College – 1964
NC: Missouri Southern College – 1965
NC: Missouri Southern State College – 1974

Missouri Valley College
Marshall, MO

Est. as: Missouri Valley College – 1889

Missouri Western State College
Saint Joseph, MO

Est. as: Saint Joseph Junior College – 1915
NC: Missouri Western State College – 1969

Missouri-Columbia, University of
Columbia, MO

Est. as: Missouri State University – 1839
NC: University of Missouri – 1900
NC: University of Missouri-Columbia – 1963

Original name may have been University of the State of Missouri.

160

Missouri-Kansas City, University of
Kansas City, MO

Est. as: University of Kansas City – 1929
MW: Kansas City School of Law – 1938
MW: Kansas City-Western Dental College – 1941
MW: Kansas City College of Pharmacy – 1943
MW: Conservatory of Music of Kansas City – 1959
NC: University of Missouri-Kansas City – 1963

Efforts to establish a university in Kansas City involved one group representing Lincoln & Lee (Methodist) and another representing University of Kansas City (non-sectarian). Groups agreed to work together as University of Kansas City.

Missouri-Rolla, University of
Rolla, MO

Est. as: University of Missouri School of Mines & Metalurgy – 1870
NC: University of Missouri-Rolla – 1964

Missouri-Saint Louis, University of
Saint Louis, MO

Est. as: Normandy Residence Center of the University of Missouri – 1963
NC: University of Missouri-Saint Louis – 1965
MW: Barnes College of Nursing – 1994

Mobile, University of
Mobile, AL

Est. as: Mobile College – 1961
NC: University of Mobile – 1993

Molloy College
Rockville Center, NY

Est. as: Molloy Catholic College for Women – 1955
NC: Molloy College – 1971

Monmouth College, The
Monmouth, IL

Est. as: Monmouth Academy, The – 1853
NC: Monmouth College, The – 1857

By MO: By merger (of) *DM:* Dissolved merger (with) *MW:* Merged with *NC:* Name change (to)

Monmouth University
West Long Branch, NJ

Est. as: Mommouth Junior College – 1933
NC: Monmouth College – 1956
NC: Monmouth University – 1995

Montana State University-Billings
Billings, MT

Est. as: Eastern Montana State Normal School – 1927
NC: Eastern Montana College of Education – 1949
NC: Eastern Montana College – 1965
NC: Montana State University-Billings – 1995

Montana State University-Bozeman
Bozeman, MT

Est. as: Agricultural College of the State of Montana – 1893
NC: Montana State College of Agriculture & Mechanic Arts – 1913
NC: Montana State College – 1920
NC: Montana State University – 1965
NC: Montana State University-Bozeman – 1994

Montana State University-Northern
Havre, MT

Est. as: Northern Montana Agricultural & Manual Training School – 1913*
NC: Northern Montana School – 1929
NC: Northern Montana College – 1931
NC: Montana State University-Northern – 1994

*Recognizes 1929 as official established year.

Montana-Missoula, The University of
Missoula, MT

Est. as: University of Montana – 1893
NC: State University of Montana – 1913
NC: Montana State University – 1935
NC: University of Montana – 1965
NC: University of Montana-Missoula, The – 1994

By MO: By merger (of) **DM:** Dissolved merger (with) **MW:** Merged with **NC:** Name change (to)

162

Montana-Western, The University of
Dillon, MT

Est. as: Montana State Normal School – 1893
NC: Montana State Normal College – 1903
NC: Western Montana College of Education – 1949
NC: Western Montana College – 1965
NC: Western Montana College of the University of Montana – 1989
NC: University of Montana-Western, The – 2001

Montclair State University
Upper Montclair, NJ

Est. as: New Jersey Normal School at Montclair – 1908
NC: Montclair State Teachers College – 1927
MW: Panzer College of Physical Education & Hygiene – 1957
NC: Montclair State College – 1958
NC: Montclair State University – 1994

Montevallo, University of
Montevallo, AL

Est. as: Alabama Girls Industrial School – 1896
NC: Alabama Girls Technical Institute – 1911
NC: Alabama College – 1923
NC: University of Montevallo – 1969

May have been known from 1919-1923 as Alabama Technical Institute and College for Women.

Moravian College & Moravian Theological Seminary
Bethlehem, PA

Est. as: Unnamed girls boarding school – 1742
NC: Bethlehem Female Seminary – 1749
NC: Moravian Seminary for Young Ladies – 1863
NC: Moravian Seminary & College for Women – 1913
MW: Moravian College & Theological Seminary – 1954
NC: Moravian College & Moravian Theological Seminary – 1954

Location changes
Germantown (Philadelphia), PA – 1742
Bethlehem, PA – 1742
Nazareth, PA – 1745
Bethlehem, PA – 1749

The girls school is considered as the predecessor institution because it was established on May 4, 1742; the boys school (1954 merger) was established on July 19, 1742.

Morehead State University
Morehead, KY

Est. as: Morehead State Normal School – 1922
NC: Morehead State Normal School & Teachers College – 1926
NC: Morehead State Teachers College – 1930
NC: Morehead State College – 1948
NC: Morehead State University – 1966

Morehead Normal School, a private institution established in 1887, closed in 1922 when the state legislature provided for the state institution.

Morehouse College
Atlanta, GA

Est. as: Augusta Institute – 1867
NC: Atlanta Baptist Seminary – 1879
NC: Atlanta Baptist College – 1897
NC: Morehouse College – 1913

Location changes
Augusta, GA – 1867
Atlanta, GA – 1879

164

Morgan State University
Baltimore, MD

Est. as: Centenary Biblical Institute – 1867
NC: Morgan College – 1890
NC: Morgan State College – 1939
NC: Morgan State University – 1975

Branch in Lynchburg, VA, Virginia Collegiate & Industrial Institute (1891-1917), was abandoned when fire destroyed its buildings. State acquired Morgan in 1939 to avoid desegregating the University of Maryland.

Morningside College
Sioux City, IA

Est. as: University of the Northwest – 1890
NC: Morningside College – 1894
MW: Charles City College – 1914

Morris Brown College
Atlanta, GA

Est. as: Morris Brown College – 1881
NC: Morris Brown University – 1913 ·
NC: Morris Brown College – 1925

Morris College
Sumter, SC

Est. as: Morris College – 1908

Mount Aloysius College
Cresson, PA

Est. as: Saint Aloysius Academy – 1853*
NC: Mount Aloysius Academy – 1897
NC: Mount Aloysius Junior College – 1939
NC: Mount Aloysius College – 1992
Location changes
Loretto, PA – 1853
Cresson, PA – 1897

*Recognizes 1939 as official established year.

By MO: By merger (of) **DM:** Dissolved merger (with) **MW:** Merged with **NC:** Name change (to)

Mount Holyoke College
South Hadley, MA

Est. as: Mount Holyoke Female Seminary – 1837
NC: Mount Holyoke Seminary & College – 1888
NC: Mount Holyoke College – 1893

Mount Ida College
Newton Centre, MA

Est. as: Unnamed junior college – 1899
NC: Mount Ida College – 1982
MW: Chamberlayne Junior College – c1988
MW: New England Institute of Funeral Service Education – c1988
MW: Coyne School of Technical Electricity - c1988

Location changes
Newton Corner, MA – 1899
Newton Center, MA – 1939

Mount Marty College
Yankton, SD

Est. as: Mount Marty Academy – 1922*
NC: Mount Marty Junior College – 1936
NC: Mount Marty College – 1951
MW: Sacred Heart Hospital School of Nursing – 1964

*Recognizes 1936 as official established year.

Mount Mary College
Milwaukee, WI

Est. as: Saint Mary's Institute – 1872*
NC: Saint Mary's College – 1913
NC: Mount Mary College – 1929

Location changes
Prairie du Chien, WI – 1872
Milwaukee, WI – 1929

*Recognizes 1929 as official established year.

Mount Mercy College
Cedar Rapids, IA

Est. as: Saint Joseph's School – 1875*
NC: Sacred Heart Academy – 1906
NC: Mount Mercy Academy – 1924
NC: Mount Mercy Junior College – 1928
NC: Mount Mercy College – 1960

*Recognizes 1928 as official established year.

When Mount Mercy Academy, was known, unofficially, as Mount Mercy of the Pines.

Mount Olive College
Mount Olive, NC

Est. as: Mount Allen Junior College – 1951
NC: Mount Olive Junior College – 1956
NC: Mount Olive College – 1970

Location changes
Cragmont, NC – 1951
Mount Olive, NC – 1953

Mount Saint Clare College
Clinton, IA

Est. as: Mount Saint Clare Academy – 1893*
NC: Mount Saint Clare College – 1918

*Recognizes 1918 as official established year.

Mount Saint Joseph, College of
Cincinnati, OH

Est. as: Mount Saint Joseph Academy – 1906*
NC: College of Mount Saint Joseph-on-the-Ohio – 1920
NC: College of Mount Saint Joseph – 1987

*Recognizes 1920 as official established year.

Originally may have been named Academy of Mount Saint Joseph.

Mount Saint Mary College
Newburgh, NY

Est. as: Mount Saint Mary Normal & Training School – 1930*
NC: Mount Saint Mary College – 1960

*Recognizes 1960 as official established year.

Originally a training school for members of the religious community.

Mount Saint Mary's College
Emmitsburg, MD

Est. as: Mount Saint Mary's College – 1808

Charter is Mount Saint Mary's College; c1990 adopted ...and Seminary. In early days was known as Seminary and as Literary Institute.

Mount Saint Mary's College
Los Angeles, CA

Est. as: Mount Saint Mary's College – 1925

Mount Saint Vincent, College of
Riverdale, NY

Est. as: Academy of Mount Saint Vincent – 1847
NC: College of Mount Saint Vincent – 1910

Location changes
New York, NY – 1847
Riverdale, NY – 1857

Mount Union College
Alliance, OH

Est. as: Select School – 1846
NC: Mount Union Seminary – 1849
NC: Mount Union College – 1858
MW: Scio College – 1911

Mount Vernon Nazarene University
Mount Vernon, OH

Est. as: Mount Vernon Nazarene College – 1964
NC: Mount Vernon Nazarene University – 2002

By MO: By merger (of) *DM:* Dissolved merger (with) *MW:* Merged with *NC:* Name change (to)

Mountain State University

Beckley, WV

Est. as: Beckley College – 1933
NC: College of West Virginia, The – 1991
NC: Mountain State University – 2001

Muhlenberg College

Allentown, PA

Est. as: Allentown Seminary – 1848
NC: Allentown Collegiate & Military Institute – 1864
NC: Allentown Collegiate Institute – 1867
NC: Muhlenberg College – 1867

Military Institute closed; property was sold to Muhlenberg.

Murray State University

Murray, KY

Est. as: Murray State Normal School – 1922
NC: Murray State Normal School & Teachers College – 1926
NC: Murray State Teachers College – 1930
NC: Murray State College – 1948
NC: Murray State University – 1966

Muskingum College, The

New Concord, OH

Est. as: Muskingum College, The – 1837

Does not use "The," but it is official.

By MO: By merger (of) *DM:* Dissolved merger (with) *MW:* Merged with *NC:* Name change (to)

National American University
Rapid City, SD

Est. as: National School of Business – 1941
NC: National College of Business – 1963
NC: National College – 1981
NC: National American University – 1997

National-Louis University
Evanston, IL

Est. as: Miss Harrison's Training School – 1886
NC: Chicago Kindergarten Training School – 1889
NC: Chicago Kindergarten College – 1891
NC: National Kindergarten College – 1912
NC: National Kindergarten & Elementary College – 1916
NC: National College of Education – 1930
NC: National-Louis University – 1990

Location changes
Chicago, IL – 1886
Evanston, IL – 1926

Nazareth College
Rochester, NY

Est. as: Nazareth College – 1924

Nebraska at Kearney, University of
Kearney, NE

Est. as: Nebraska State Normal School at Kearney – 1903
NC: Nebraska State Teachers College at Kearney – 1921
NC: Kearney State College – 1963
MW: University of Nebraska – 1991
NC: University of Nebraska at Kearney – 1991

Nebraska at Omaha, University of
Omaha, NE

Est. as: University of Omaha – 1908
NC: Municipal University of Omaha – 1930
MW: University of Nebraska – 1968
NC: University of Nebraska at Omaha – 1968

Nebraska Wesleyan University, The
Lincoln, NE

Est. as: Cass County University – 1853*
NC: Nebraska Wesleyan University, The – 1887
By MO: Nebraska Central College – 1887
By MO: Mallalieu University – 1887
By MO: York College – 1887

*Recognizes 1887 as official established year.

"The" was unofficially dropped after World War II. York College was also known as Methodist Episcopal College; it is not the existing York College of York, NE.

Nebraska-Lincoln, University of
Lincoln, NE

Est. as: University of Nebraska – 1869
NC: University of Nebraska-Lincoln – 1970's

Neumann College
Aston, PA

Est. as: Our Lady of Angels College – 1965
NC: Neumann College – 1980

Nevada: Las Vegas, University of
Las Vegas, NV

Est. as: University of Nevada, Southern Regional Branch – 1957
NC: Nevada Southern University – 1965
NC: University of Nevada: Las Vegas – 1969

Nevada: Reno, University of
Reno, NV

Est. as: Nevada State University – 1874
NC: University of Nevada – 1887
NC: University of Nevada: Reno – 1969

Location changes
Elko, NV – 1874
Reno, NV – 1886

New College of Florida
Sarasota, FL

Est. as: New College – 1960
MW: University of South Florida – 1975
NC: New College of the University of South Florida – 1975
DM: University of South Florida – 2001
NC: New College of Florida – 2001

Merged with Florida state system and was affiliated with the University of South Florida. State legislature designated institution as autonomous in 2001.

New England College
Henniker, NH

Est. as: New England College – 1946

New England, University of
Biddeford, ME

Est. as: College Seraphique – 1939*
NC: Saint Francis Junior College – c1948
NC: Saint Francis College – 1953
MW: New England College of Osteopathic Medicine – 1978
NC: University of New England – 1983
MW: Westbrook College – 1996

*Recognizes 1953 as official established year although Westbrook College, with which it merged, was established in 1830.

1978 merger was a lease agreement to put the newly created medical school in a building at Saint Francis. 1983 name change was when the 1978 merger was officially completed. Was also known at establishment as Saint Francis High School.

New Hampshire at Manchester, University of
Manchester, NH

Est. as: Marrimack Valley Branch of the University of New Hampshire – 1967*
NC: Merrimack Valley College – 1976
NC: University of New Hampshire at Manchester – 1985

*Recognizes 1985 as official established year.

New Hampshire, University of
Durham, NH

Est. as: New Hampshire College of Agriculture & Mechanical Arts – 1866
NC: University of New Hampshire – 1923

Location changes
Hanover, NH – 1866
Durham, NH – 1893

Originally a part of Dartmouth College; bequest of land and money from Benjamin Thompson provided for new institution in Durham.

New Haven, University of
West Haven, CT

Est. as: New Haven YMCA Junior College – 1920
NC: New Haven College – 1926
NC: University of New Haven – 1970

Location changes
New Haven, CT – 1920
West Haven, CT – 1960

Established by Northeasterm University as a division. Became independent of Northeastern in 1926.

New Jersey City University
Jersey City, NJ

Est. as: New Jersey Normal School of Jersey City – 1927
NC: Jersey City State Teachers College – 1935
NC: Jersey City State College – 1958
NC: New Jersey City University – 1998

New Jersey Institute of Technology
Newark, NJ

Est. as: Newark Technical School – 1881
NC: Newark College of Engineering – 1929
NC: New Jersey Institute of Technology – 1975

New Jersey, The College of
Ewing Township, NJ

Est. as: New Jersey State Normal School – 1855
NC: New Jersey State Normal School at Trenton – 1908
NC: New Jersey State Teachers College & State Normal School at Trenton – 1929
NC: New Jersey State Teachers College at Trenton – 1937
NC: Trenton State College – 1958
NC: College of New Jersey, The – 1996

New Mexico Highlands University
Las Vegas, NM

Est. as: New Mexico Normal School – 1893
NC: New Mexico State Normal University – 1898
NC: New Mexico Highlands University – 1941

New Mexico Institute of Mining & Technology
Socorro, NM

Est. as: New Mexico School of Mines – 1889
NC: New Mexico Institute of Mining & Technology – 1951

New Mexico State University
Las Cruces, NM

Est. as: New Mexico College of Agriculture & Mechanical Arts – 1888
MW: Las Cruces College – 1890
NC: New Mexico State University of Agriculture, Engineering, & Science – 1958
NC: New Mexico State University – 1960

By MO: By merger (of) *DM:* Dissolved merger (with) *MW:* Merged with *NC:* Name change (to)

New Mexico, The University of
Albuquerque, NM

Est. as: University of New Mexico, The – 1889

New Orleans, University of
New Orleans, LA

Est. as: Louisiana State University in New Orleans – 1956
NC: University of New Orleans – 1974

New Rochelle, The College of
New Rochelle, NY

Est. as: College of Saint Angela, The – 1904
NC: College of New Rochelle, The – 1910

New School University
New York, NY

Est. as: New School for Social Research – 1919
MW: Parsons School of Design – 1970
MW: Mannes College of Music – 1989
NC: New School University – 1997

New York College at Brockport, State University of
Brockport, NY

Est. as: Brockport Collegiate Institute – 1836*
NC: Brockport State Normal School – 1867
NC: State Teachers College at Brockport – 1942
NC: State University Teachers College at Brockport – 1948
NC: State University College of Education at Brockport – 1959
NC: State University of New York College at Brockport – 1961

*Recognizes 1867 as official established year.

By MO: By merger (of) *DM:* Dissolved merger (with) *MW:* Merged with *NC:* Name change (to)

New York College at Buffalo, State University of
Buffalo, NY

Est. as: Buffalo Normal School – 1867
NC: State Normal & Training School – 1888
NC: State Teachers College at Buffalo – 1928
NC: New York State College for Teachers at Buffalo – 1946
NC: State University College for Teachers at Buffalo – 1951
NC: State University College of Education at Buffalo – 1959
NC: State University of New York College at Buffalo – 1961

May have been known as Buffalo State Normal School at establishment.

New York College at Cortland, State University of
Cortland, NY

Est. as: Cortland State Normal School – 1868
NC: State Teachers College at Cortland – 1942
NC: State University Teachers College at Cortland – 1948
NC: State University College of Education at Cortland – 1959
NC: State University of New York College at Cortland – 1961

New York College at Fredonia, State University of
Fredonia, NY

Est. as: Fredonia Academy – 1826
NC: State Normal School – 1867
NC: State Teachers College at Fredonia – 1942
NC: State University Teachers College at Fredonia – 1948
NC: State University College of Education at Fredonia – 1959
NC: State University of New York College at Fredonia – 1961

New York College at Geneseo, State University of
Geneseo, NY

Est. as: Wadsworth Normal & Training School – 1871
NC: Geneseo Normal & Training School – 1871
NC: State Teachers College at Geneseo – 1942
NC: State University Teachers College at Geneseo – 1948
NC: State University College of Education at Geneseo – 1959
NC: State University of New York College at Geneseo – 1961

176

New York College at New Paltz, State University of

New Paltz, NY

Est. as: New Paltz Classical School – 1828
NC: New Paltz Academy – 1833
NC: New Paltz Normal School – 1885
NC: State Teachers College at New Paltz – 1942
NC: State University Teachers College at New Paltz – 1948
NC: State University College of Education at New Paltz – 1959
NC: State University of New York College at New Paltz – 1961

New York College at Old Westbury, State University of

Old Westbury, NY

Est. as: State University of New York College at Old Westbury – 1965*

*Recognizes no official established year; no decision on a year has been made by institution officials. Chartered, 1965; first classes, 1968.

New York College at Oneonta, State University of

Oneonta, NY

Est. as: Oneonta State Normal School – 1889
NC: State Teachers College at Oneonta – 1942
NC: State University Teachers College at Oneonta – 1948
NC: State Univ of New York College of Education at Oneonta – 1959
NC: State University of New York College at Oneonta – 1961

New York College at Oswego, State University of

Oswego, NY

Est. as: Oswego Primary Teachers Training School – 1861
NC: Oswego State Normal & Training School – 1865
NC: State Teachers College at Oswego – 1942
NC: State University Teachers College at Oswego – 1948
NC: State University College of Education at Oswego – 1959
NC: State University of New York College at Oswego – 1961

In 1959, may have been named State University College of Arts & Sciences at Oswego.

New York College at Plattsburgh, State University of
Plattsburgh, NY

Est. as: Plattsburgh Academy – 1811*
NC: New York State Normal & Training School at Plattsburgh – 1889
NC: State Teachers College at Plattsburgh – 1942
NC: State University Teachers College at Plattsburgh – 1948
NC: State University College of Education at Plattsburgh – 1959
NC: State University of New York College at Plattsburgh – 1961

*Recognizes 1889 as official established year.

New York College at Potsdam, State University of
Potsdam, NY

Est. as: Saint Lawrence Academy – 1816
NC: Potsdam Normal School – 1868
MW: Crance Normal Institute of Music – 1926
NC: State Teachers College at Potsdam – 1942
NC: State University Teachers College at Potsdam – 1948
NC: State University College of Education at Potsdam – 1959
NC: State University of New York College at Potsdam – 1961

New York College at Purchase, State University of
Purchase, NY

Est. as: State University of New York College at Purchase – 1967

New York College of Environmental Science & Forestry at Syracuse, State University of
Syracuse, NY

Est. as: New York State College of Forestry at Syracuse – 1911
NC: State University College of Forestry at Syracuse University – 1948
NC: State University of New York College of Environmental Science & Forestry at Syracuse – 1972

178

New York City College of Technology
Brooklyn, NY

Est. as: New York State Institute of Applied Arts & Sciences –
1946

NC: New York City Community College of Applied Arts & Sciences –
1953

MW: Vorhees Technical Institute – 1971

NC: New York City Technical College of the City University of New
York – 1980

NC: New York City College of Technology – 2002

Originally was one of five similar institutes created at that time. In
1948, it became part of the State University of New York; in 1964,
it became part of the City University of New York. There may have
been undocumented name changes at those times.

New York College of Technology
at Farmingdale, State University of
Farmingdale, NY

Est. as: State University of New York Agricultural & Technical Institute – 1912

NC: State University of New York College of Technology at Farmingdale – 1988

New York Fashion Institute
of Technology, State University of
New York, NY

Est. as: Central High School of Needle Trade – 1935*

NC: High School for Needle Trade – 1944

NC: State University of New York Fashion Institute of Technology – 1951

*Recognizes 1944 as official established year.

New York Institute of Technology
Old Westbury, NY

Est. as: New York Institute of Technology – 1955

By MO: By merger (of) ***DM:*** Dissolved merger (with) ***MW:*** Merged with ***NC:*** Name change (to)

New York University
New York, NY

Est. as: University of the City of New York – 1831
NC: New York University – 1896

New York University Center at Albany, State University of
Albany, NY

Est. as: New York State Normal School – 1844
NC: New York State Normal College – 1890
NC: New York State College for Teachers – 1914
NC: State University College of Education at Albany – 1959
NC: State University of New York College at Albany – 1961
NC: State University of New York University Center at Albany – 1962

New York University Center at Binghamton, State University of
Binghamton, NY

Est. as: Triple Cities College of Syracuse University – 1946
NC: Harpur College – 1950
NC: State University of New York University Center at Binghamton – 1965

Location changes
Endicott, NY – 1946
Binghamton, NY – 1961

New York University Center at Buffalo, State University of
Buffalo, NY

Est. as: University of Buffalo – 1846
NC: State University of New York University Center at Buffalo – 1962

New York University Center at Stony Brook, State University of
Stony Brook, NY

Est. as: State University of Science & Engineering on Long Island – 1957
NC: State University: Long Island Center – 1960
NC: State University of New York University Center at Stony Brook – 1962

Location changes
Oyster Bay, NY – 1957
Stony Brook, NY – 1962

Newman University
Wichita, KS

Est. as: Sacred Heart Junior College – 1933
NC: Sacred Heart Academy – 1945
NC: Sacred Heart College – 1954
NC: Kansas Newman College – 1973
NC: Newman University – 1998

Predecessor institutions were Saint John's Institute (girls), established in 1902, and Saint John's Academy (boys), established in late 1800s.

Niagara University
Buffalo, NY

Est. as: College & Seminary of our Lady of the Angels – 1856
NC: Niagara University – 1883

Nicholls State University
Thibodaux, LA

Est. as: Francis T Nicholls Junior College of Louisiana State University – 1948
NC: Francis T Nicholls State College – 1956
NC: Nicholls State University – 1970

Norfolk State University
Norfolk, VA

Est. as: Virginia Union University: Norfolk Unit – 1935
NC: Norfolk Polytechnic College – 1942
NC: Virginia State College: Norfolk Division – 1944
NC: Norfolk State College – 1969
NC: Norfolk State University – 1979

North Alabama, University of
Florence, AL

Est. as: LaGrange College – 1830
NC: Wesleyan University – 1855
NC: Florence Normal School – 1872
NC: Florence State Teachers College – 1929
NC: Florence State College – 1957
NC: Florence State University – 1967
NC: University of North Alabama – 1974

Location changes
LaGrange, GA – 1830
Florence, AL – 1855

In 1853, a second LaGrange College was established at Florence; the original remained at LaGrange and was destroyed by Federal troops during the Civil War in 1863.

North Carolina Agricultural & Technical State University
Greensboro, NC

Est. as: A. & M. College for the Colored Race – 1891
NC: Agricultural & Technical College of North Carolina – 1915
NC: North Carolina Agricultural & Technical State University – 1967

Location changes
Raleigh, NC – 1891
Greensboro, NC – 1893

North Carolina at Asheville, The University of
Asheville, NC

Est. as: Buncombe County Junior College – 1927
NC: Biltmore Junior College – 1930
NC: Asheville-Biltmore College – 1936
NC: University of North Carolina at Asheville, The – 1969

North Carolina at Chapel Hill, The University of
Chapel Hill, NC

Est. as: University of North Carolina, The – 1789
NC: University of North Carolina at Chapel Hill, The – 1963

North Carolina at Charlotte, The University of
Charlotte, NC

Est. as: University of North Carolina: Charlotte Center – 1946
NC: Charlotte College – 1949
NC: University of North Carolina at Charlotte, The – 1965

Known as Charlotte University.

North Carolina at Greensboro, The University of
Greensboro, NC

Est. as: State Normal & Industrial School – 1891
NC: State Normal & Industrial College – 1896
NC: North Carolina College for Women – 1919
NC: Women's College of the University of North Carolina, The – 1931
NC: University of North Carolina at Greensboro, The – 1963

North Carolina at Pembroke, The University of
Pembroke, NC

Est. as: Croatan Normal School – 1887
NC: Indian Normal School of Robeson County, The – 1911
NC: Cherokee Indian Normal School of Robeson County, The – 1913
NC: Pembroke State College for Indians – 1941
NC: Pembroke State College – 1949
NC: Pembroke State University – 1969
NC: University of North Carolina at Pembroke, The – 1996

The word "Indian" is part of the institution's name in the enabling legislation, but it is not used not in the institution's records.

By MO: By merger (of) *DM:* Dissolved merger (with) *MW:* Merged with *NC:* Name change (to)

North Carolina at Wilmington, The University of
Wilmington, NC

Est. as: North Carolina College Conference Center – 1946*
NC: Wilmington College – 1947
NC: University of North Carolina at Wilmington, The – 1969

*Recognizes 1947 as official established year.

North Carolina Central University
Durham, NC

Est. as: National Religious Training School & Chatauqua – 1910
NC: National Training School – 1915
NC: Durham State Normal School – 1923
NC: North Carolina College for Negroes – 1925
NC: North Carolina College at Durham – 1947
NC: North Carolina Central University – 1969

North Carolina State University at Raleigh
Raleigh, NC

Est. as: North Carolina College of Agriculture & Mechanic Arts – 1887
NC: North Carolina State College of Agriculture & Engineering – 1917
NC: North Carolina State College of Agriculture & Engineering of the University of North Carolina – 1931
NC: North Carolina State College of the University of North Carolina at Raleigh – 1963
NC: North Carolina State University at Raleigh – 1965

North Central College
Naperville, IL

Est. as: Plainfield College – 1861
NC: North-Western College – 1864
NC: North Central College – 1926

Location changes
Plainfield, IL – 1861
Naperville, IL – 1870

North Dakota State University
Fargo, ND

Est. as: North Dakota Agricultural College – 1890
NC: North Dakota State University – 1961

North Dakota, University of
Grand Forks, ND

Est. as: University of North Dakota – 1883
MW: Wesley College – c1953

North Florida, University of
Jacksonville, FL

Est. as: University of North Florida – 1972

North Georgia College & State University
Dahlonega, GA

Est. as: North Georgia Agricultural College – 1873
NC: North Georgia College – 1926
NC: North Georgia College & State University – 1996

North Greenville College
Tigerville, SC

Est. as: North Greenville High School – 1892
NC: North Greenville Baptist Academy – 1915
NC: North Greenville Junior College – 1950
NC: North Greenville College – 1972

Junior college was established in 1934 as a separate entity from the academy; charter was amended for 1950 name change; academy closed in 1957.

North Park University
Chicago, IL

Est. as: Swedish Evangelical Mission Covenant College & Seminary – 1891
NC: North Park College & Theological Seminary – 1894
NC: North Park University – 1997

Location changes
Minneapolis, MN – 1891
Chicago, IL – 1894

1894 name change occurred after move to Chicago.

North Texas, University of
Denton, TX

Est. as: Texas Normal College & Teacher Training Institute – 1890
NC: North Texas Normal College – 1894
NC: North Texas State Normal College – 1901
NC: North Texas State Teachers College – 1923
NC: North Texas State College – 1949
NC: North Texas State University – 1961
NC: University of North Texas – 1988

Northeastern Illinois University
Chicago, IL

Est. as: Chicago Teachers College, North Side – 1949
NC: Illinois Teachers College: Chicago North – 1965
NC: Northeastern Illinois State College – 1967
NC: Northeastern Illinois University – 1971

Northeastern State University
Tahlequah, OK

Est. as: Cherokee National Female Seminary – 1846*
NC: Northeastern State Normal School – 1909
NC: Northeastern State Teachers College – 1919
NC: Northeastern State College – 1939
NC: Northeastern Oklahoma State University – 1974
NC: Northeastern State University – 1985

*Recognizes 1909 as official established year.

Territory bought building, land, and equipment of Cherokee National Female Seminary for the new institution.

Northeastern University
Boston, MA

Est. as: Evening Institute for Young Men – 1898
NC: Northeastern College – 1916
NC: Northeastern University of the Boston Young Men's Christian Association – 1922
NC: Northeastern University – 1935
MW: Boston Bouve College – 1964

Northern Arizona University
Flagstaff, AZ

Est. as: Northern Arizona Normal School – 1899
NC: Northern Arizona State Teachers College – 1925
NC: Arizona State Teachers College at Flagstaff – 1929
NC: Arizona State College at Flagstaff – 1945
NC: Northern Arizona University – 1966

Northern Colorado, University of
Greeley, CO

Est. as: State Normal School – 1889
NC: Colorado State Teachers College – 1911
NC: Colorado State College of Education – 1935
NC: Colorado State College – 1957
NC: University of Northern Colorado – 1970

Northern Illinois University
DeKalb, IL

Est. as: Northern Illinois State Normal School – 1895
NC: Northern Illinois State Teachers College – 1921
NC: Northern Illinois State College – 1955
NC: Northern Illinois University – 1957

Northern Iowa, University of
Cedar Falls, IA

Est. as: Iowa State Normal School – 1876
NC: Iowa State Teachers College – 1909
NC: State College of Iowa – 1961
NC: University of Northern Iowa – 1967

Northern Kentucky University
Highland Heights, KY

Est. as: Northern Kentucky State College – 1968
MW: Salmon P Chase School of Law – 1972
NC: Northern Kentucky University – 1976

Northern Michigan University
Marquette, MI

Est. as: Northern State Normal School – 1899
NC: Northern State Teachers College – 1927
NC: Northern Michigan College of Education – 1942
NC: Northern Michigan College – 1955
NC: Northern Michigan University – 1963

Northern State University
Aberdeen, SD

Est. as: Industrial Institute of South Dakota – 1889*
NC: Northern Normal & Industrial School – 1901
NC: Northern State Teachers College – 1939
NC: Northern State College – 1964
NC: Northern State University – 1989

*Recognizes 1901 as official established year.

Northland College
Ashland, WI

Est. as: North Wisconsin Academy – 1892
NC: Northland College – 1906

Northwest Christian College
Eugene, OR

Est. as: Eugene Divinity School – 1895
NC: Eugene Bible University – 1908
NC: Eugene Bible College – 1930
MW: Spokane University – 1933
NC: Northwest Christian College – 1933

Northwest College of the Assemblies of God
Kirkland, WA

Est. as: Northwest Bible Institute – 1934
NC: Northwest Bible College – 1949
NC: Northwest College of the Assemblies of God – 1962

Location changes
Seattle, WA – 1934
Kirkland, WA – 1958

Known as Northwest College.

Northwest Missouri State University
Maryville, MO

Est. as: Fifth District Normal School – 1905
NC: Northwest Missouri State Teachers College – 1919
NC: Northwest Missouri State College – 1949
NC: Northwest Missouri State University – 1972

Northwest Nazarene University
Nampa, ID

Est. as: Idaho Holiness School – 1913
NC: Idaho Holiness College – 1913
NC: Northwest Nazarene College – 1917
NC: Northwest Nazarene University – 1999

Northwestern College

Orange City, IA

Est. as: Northwestern Classical Academy – 1882
NC: Northwestern Junior College – 1928
NC: Northwestern College – 1959

Northwestern College

Saint Paul, MN

Est. as: Northwestern Bible & Missionary Training School – 1902
NC: Northwestern Schools – 1951
NC: Northwestern College – 1966

Location changes
Minneapolis, MN – 1902
Saint Paul, MN – 1972

Northwestern Oklahoma State University

Alva, OK

Est. as: Northwestern Territorial Normal School – 1897
NC: Northwestern Normal School – 1904
NC: Northwestern State Normal School – 1907
NC: Northwestern State Teachers College – 1919
NC: Northwestern State College – 1939
NC: Northwestern Oklahoma State University – 1974

Northwestern State University of Louisiana

Natchitoches, LA

Est. as: Louisiana State Normal School – 1884
NC: Louisiana State Normal College – 1918
NC: Northwestern State College of Louisiana – 1944
NC: Northwestern State University of Louisiana – 1970

Northwestern University

Evanston, IL

Est. as: North Western University – 1851
NC: Northwestern University – 1863
MW: Chicago Medical College – 1870
MW: Evanston College for Ladies – 1874

There apparently was no official change to Northwestern (one word) University which was first used in the catalogue in 1863.

By MO: By merger (of) *DM:* Dissolved merger (with) *MW:* Merged with *NC:* Name change (to)

Norwich University
Northfield, VT

Est. as: American Literary, Scientific, & Military Academy – 1819
NC: Norwich University – 1834
NC: Lewis College – 1880
NC: Norwich University – 1884
MW: Vermont College – 1972

Location changes
Norwich, VT – 1819
Middletown, CT – 1825
Norwich, VT – 1829
Northfield, VT – 1866

Notre Dame College
South Euclid, OH

Est. as: Notre Dame College – 1922

Location changes
Cleveland, OH – 1922
South Euclid, OH – 1928

Known as Notre Dame College of Ohio.

Notre Dame de Namur University
Belmont, CA

Est. as: College of Notre Dame – 1851
NC: Notre Dame de Namur University – 2001

Location changes
San Jose, CA – 1851
Belmont, CA – 1923

Notre Dame of Maryland, College of
Baltimore, MD

Est. as: Notre Dame of Maryland Collegiate Institute for Young
  Ladies – 1873
NC: College of Notre Dame of Maryland – 1895

Unnamed predecessor academy may have been established in
1848.

By MO: By merger (of) **DM:** Dissolved merger (with) **MW:** Merged with **NC:** Name change (to)

Notre Dame, University of
South Bend, IN
Est. as: University of Notre Dame – 1842
"The" is used in catalogue, but it is not official.

Nova Southeastern University
Fort Lauderdale, FL
Est. as: Nova Southeastern University – 1964*
By MO: Nova University – 1964
By MO: Southeastern University of Health Sciences – 1964

*Recognizes merger year, 1964, as official established year; does not recognize histories of merged institutions.

Nyack College
Nyack, NY
Est. as: Missionary Training Institute – 1882
NC: Nyack Missionary College – 1956
NC: Nyack College – 1972

Location changes
New York, NY – 1882
Nyack, NY – 1897

Oakland City University
Oakland City, IN

Est. as: Oakland City College – 1885
NC: Oakland City University – 1995

Oakland University
Rochester, MI

Est. as: Michigan State University-Oakland – 1957
NC: Oakland University – 1963

State legislature recognized institution as autonomous in 1970.

Oakwood College
Huntsville, AL

Est. as: Oakwood Industrial School – 1896
NC: Oakwood Manual Training School – 1904
NC: Oakwood Junior College – 1917
NC: Oakwood College – 1943

Oberlin College
Oberlin, OH

Est. as: Oberlin Collegiate Institute – 1833
NC: Oberlin College – 1850

Occidental College
Los Angeles, CA

Est. as: Occidental University of Los Angeles, The – 1887
NC: Occidental College – 1892

Oglethorpe University
Atlanta, GA

Est. as: Oglethorpe University – 1835
NC: Oglethorpe College – 1965
NC: Oglethorpe University – 1972

Location changes
Midway, GA – 1835
Atlanta, GA – 1870

Ohio Dominican College
Columbus, OH

Est. as: Saint Mary's Convent & Academy – 1830*
NC: Ladies Literary Society – 1911
NC: College of Saint Mary of the Springs – 1924
NC: Ohio Dominican College – 1968

Location changes
Somerset, OH – 1830
Columbus, OH – 1866

*Recognizes 1911 as official established year.

Ohio Northern University
Ada, OH

Est. as: Northwestern Ohio Normal School – 1871
NC: Ohio Normal University – 1885
NC: Ohio Northern University – 1903

Ohio State University, The
Columbus, OH

Est. as: Ohio Agricultural & Mechanical College – 1870
NC: Ohio State University, The – 1878

Ohio University
Athens, OH

Est. as: Ohio University – 1804

American Western University had been chartered in 1802 by territorial legislation; it was re-chartered in 1804 by the state legislature as Ohio University.

By MO: By merger (of) *DM:* Dissolved merger (with) *MW:* Merged with *NC:* Name change (to)

Ohio Valley College
Parkersburg, WV

Est. as: Ohio Valley College – 1958
MW: Northeastern Christian Junior College – 1993

Ohio Wesleyan University
Delaware, OH

Est. as: Ohio Wesleyan University – 1842
MW: Ohio Wesleyan Female College – 1877

Oklahoma Baptist University, The
Shawnee, OK

Est. as: Baptist University of Oklahoma, The – 1910
NC: Oklahoma Baptist University, The – 1921

Oklahoma Christian University
Oklahoma City, OK

Est. as: Central Christian College – 1950
NC: Oklahoma Christian College – 1958
NC: Oklahoma Christian University of Science & Arts – 1990
NC: Oklahoma Christian University – 1993

Location changes
Bartlesville, OK – 1950
Oklahoma City, OK – 1958

Oklahoma City University
Oklahoma City, OK

Est. as: Epworth University – 1904
MW: Fort Worth University – 1911
NC: Methodist University of Oklahoma, The – 1911
NC: Oklahoma City College – 1919
NC: Oklahoma City University – 1924

Location changes
Oklahoma City, OK – 1904
Guthrie, OK – 1911
Oklahoma City, OK – 1919

Epworth University and Fort Worth University closed; reformed as The Methodist University of Oklahoma which then closed and was re-formed as Oklahoma City College.

By MO: By merger (of) *DM:* Dissolved merger (with) *MW:* Merged with *NC:* Name change (to)

Oklahoma Panhandle State University
Goodwell, OK

Est. as: Pan-Handle Agricultural Institute – 1909
NC: Panhandle Agricultural & Mechanical College – 1921
NC: Oklahoma Panhandle State College of Agriculture & Applied Sciences – 1967
NC: Oklahoma Panhandle State University – 1974

From 1967-1974 was known as Panhandle State College.

Oklahoma State University
Stillwater, OK

Est. as: Oklahoma Agricultural & Mechanical College – 1890
NC: Oklahoma State University – 1957

Oklahoma Wesleyan University
Bartlesville, OK

Est. as: Rocky Mountain Missionary & Evangelistic School – 1905*
NC: Western Holiness College & Bible Training School – 1910
NC: Colorado Springs Bible Training School – 1925
MW: Spokane Pilgrim Bible School – 1941
NC: Colorado Springs Bible College – 1959
NC: Central Pilgrim College – 1959
MW: Western Pilgrim College – 1960
NC: Bartlesville Wesleyan College – 1968
MW: Miltonvale Wesleyan College – 1972
NC: Oklahoma Wesleyan University – 2001

Location changes
Colorado Springs, CO – 1910
Bartlesville, OK – 1959

*Recognizes 1910 as official established year.

Oklahoma, University of
Norman, OK

Est. as: University of Oklahoma – 1890

Old Dominion University
Norfolk, VA

Est. as: Norfolk Division of the College of William & Mary – 1930
NC: Norfolk College of the College of William & Mary of the Colleges of William & Mary – 1961
NC: Old Dominion College – 1962
NC: Old Dominion University – 1969

Olivet College
Olivet, MI

Est. as: Olivet College – 1844
NC: Olivet Institute – 1847
NC: Olivet College – 1859

Olivet Nazarene University
Bourbonnais, IL

Est. as: Illinois Holiness University – 1907
NC: Olivet University – 1915
NC: Olivet College – 1923
NC: Olivet Nazarene College – 1940
NC: Olivet Nazarene University – 1986

Location changes
Georgetown, IL – 1907
Bourbonnais, IL – 1940

Oral Roberts University
Tulsa, OK

Est. as: Oral Roberts University – 1963

Oregon State University
Corvallis, OR

Est. as: Corvallis Academy – 1856*
NC: Corvallis College – 1858
NC: Corvallis College & Agricultural College of Oregon – 1868
NC: Corvallis State Agricultural College – 1872
NC: State Agricultural College – 1876
NC: Corvallis College & State Agricultural College – 1879
NC: Corvallis Agricultural College – 1881
NC: Corvallis College & Oregon State Agricultural College – 1882
NC: Corvallis College & Oregon Agricultural College – 1885
NC: State Agricultural College of Oregon – 1886
NC: State Agricultural College of the State of Oregon – 1888
NC: Oregon Agricultural College – 1890
NC: Agricultural College of the State of Oregon – 1896
NC: Oregon Agricultural College – 1908
NC: Oregon State Agricultural College – 1927
NC: Oregon State College – 1937
NC: Oregon State University – 1961

*Recognizes 1868 as official established year.

In 1868, Corvallis College was re-incorporated as a degree-granting institution and designated as the agricultural college of Oregon. Corvallis College may have been part of the 1876 name. In 1885, president's letterhead used State Agricultural College of Oregon, and in 1897, president's letterhead used Oregon Agricultural College. Oregon State College was name in common use in 1933 and by legislative action in 1953.

Oregon, University of
Eugene, OR
Est. as: University of Oregon – 1876

198

Ottawa University
Ottawa, KS

Est. as: Ottawa University – 1865

Charter granted in 1861 for Roger Williams University which never opened. New charter granted in 1865 for Ottawa University. Does not recognize Roger Williams University as a predecessor institution.

Otterbein College
Westerville, OH

Est. as: Otterbein University – 1847
MW: Mount Pleasant College – 1858
NC: Otterbein College – 1917

Blendon's Young Men's Seminary, established in 1839, closed; grounds were purchased for Otterbein University.

Ouachita Baptist University
Arkadelphia, AR

Est. as: Ouachita Baptist College – 1886
NC: Ouachita Baptist University – 1965

Our Lady of Holy Cross College
New Orleans, LA

Est. as: Academy of the Holy Angels Normal School – 1916
NC: Holy Cross Normal College – 1931
NC: Academy of the Holy Angels College Department – 1941
NC: Our Lady of Holy Cross College – 1960

Our Lady of the Lake University of San Antonio
San Antonio, TX

Est. as: Our Lady of the Lake Academy – 1895
NC: Our Lady of the Lake College – 1912
NC: Our Lady of the Lake University of San Antonio – 1975

Ozarks, College of the
Point Lookout, MO

Est. as: School of the Ozarks – 1906
NC: College of the Ozarks – 1990

By MO: By merger (of) *DM:* Dissolved merger (with) *MW:* Merged with *NC:* Name change (to)

Ozarks, University of the

Clarksville, AR

Est. as: Cane Hill College – 1834
NC: Arkansas Cumberland College – 1891
NC: College of the Ozarks, The – 1920
NC: University of the Ozarks – 1987

Location changes

Cane Hill, AR – 1834
Clarksville, AR – 1891

Cane Hill College closed (date unknown); Arkansas Cumberland College was the successor institution.

Pace University
New York, NY

Est. as: Pace Institute – 1906
NC: Pace School of Accountancy – UNK
NC: Pace College – 1948
NC: Pace University – 1973
MW: College of White Plains – 1975
MW: Briarcliffe College – 1977
MW: World Trade Institute – 1997

Pace School of Accountancy may not have been an official name.

Pacific Lutheran University
Parkland, WA

Est. as: Pacific Lutheran Academy – 1890
MW: Columbia College – 1920
NC: Pacific Lutheran College – 1920
MW: Spokane College – 1929
NC: Pacific Lutheran University – 1960

Spokane College had closed.

Pacific Union College
Angwin, CA

Est. as: Heraldsburg Academy – 1882
NC: Heraldsburg College – 1899
NC: Pacific Union College – 1906

Location changes
Heraldsburg, CA – 1882
Angwin, CA – 1909

Pacific University
Forest Grove, OR

Est. as: Tualatin Academy – 1849
NC: Tualatin Academy & Pacific University – 1854
NC: Pacific University – 1915

Tualatin Academy closed in 1915.

Pacific, University of the
Stockton, CA

Est. as: California Wesleyan University – 1851
NC: University of the Pacific, The – 1852
MW: Napa College – 1896
NC: College of the Pacific, The – 1911
NC: University of the Pacific – 1961
MW: College of Physicians & Surgeons – 1962
MW: McGeorge School of Law – 1962

Location changes
Santa Clara, CA – 1851
San Jose, CA – 1871
Stockton, CA – 1924

Paine College
Augusta, GA

Est. as: Paine Institute – 1882
NC: Paine College – 1903

Palm Beach Atlantic College
West Palm Beach, FL

Est. as: Palm Beach Atlantic College – 1968

Park University
Parkville, MO

Est. as: Park College – 1875
NC: Park University – 2000

By MO: By merger (of) ***DM:*** Dissolved merger (with) ***MW:*** Merged with ***NC:*** Name change (to)

Patten College
Oakland, CA

Est. as: Oakland Bible Institute – 1944
NC: Patten School of Religion – 1953
NC: Patten Bible College – 1966
NC: Patten College – 1979

Paul Quinn College
Dallas, TX

Est. as: Paul Quinn College – 1872

Location changes
Austin, TX – 1872
Waco, TX – 1881
Dallas, TX – 1990

Peace College
Raleigh, NC

Est. as: Peace College – 1857

Pennsylvania College of Technology
Williamsport, PA

Est. as: Williamsport Technical Institute – 1941
NC: Williamsport Area Community College – 1965
NC: Pennsylvania College of Technology – 1989

Pennsylvania State University, The
State College, PA

Est. as: Farmer's High School – 1855
NC: Agricultural College of Pennsylvania – 1862
NC: Pennsylvania State College, The – 1874
NC: Pennsylvania State University, The – 1953
MW: Dickinson School of Law – 1997

By MO: By merger (of) *DM:* Dissolved merger (with) *MW:* Merged with *NC:* Name change (to)

Pennsylvania, University of
Philadelphia, PA

Est. as: Academy of Philadelphia – 1749*
NC: College & Academy & Charitable School in the Province of Philadelphia – 1755
NC: University of the State of Pennsylvania – 1779
NC: University of Pennsylvania – 1791

*Recognizes 1740 as official established year.

In 1740, a group of citizens created an educational trust and began construction of a building. In 1741, the operation declared insufficient funds. In 1750, the Academy of Philadelphia purchased the site for a charity school which became part of the 1755 name change. In 1779, the charter for the College & Academy of Philadelphia was revoked; a new charter was granted for the University of the State of Pennsylvania (situation was a question of Tories and revolutionaries on the board). In 1788, the Tories recanted and signed a "loyalty" agreement. The original charter for the College & Academy of Philadelphia was restored, but the one for the University of the State of Pennsylvania was not revoked. The two separate physical institutions existed until 1791 when, technically, the College & Academy was merged into the University of Pennsylvania. In late 1800s, an official university resolution declared 1740 as the founding date.

Pepperdine University
Malibu, CA

Est. as: George Pepperdine College – 1937
NC: Pepperdine University – 1971

Location changes
Los Angeles, CA – 1937
Malibu, CA – 1971

Peru State College
Peru, NE

Est. as: Mount Vernon College – 1865*
NC: Nebraska State Normal School – 1867
NC: Peru State Teachers College – 1921
NC: Nebraska State Teachers College at Peru – 1949
NC: Peru State College – 1963

*Recognizes 1867, when state assumed control of institution, as official established year.

204

Pfeiffer University
Misenheimer, NC

Est. as: Oberlin Home & School – 1885
NC: Ebenezer Mitchell Home & School – 1903
NC: Mitchell Junior College – 1934
NC: Pfeiffer Junior College – 1935
NC: Pfeiffer College – 1954
NC: Pfeiffer University – 1996

Location changes
Lick Mountain, NC – 1885
Lenoir, NC – 1908
Misenheimer, NC – 1910

Philadelphia University
Philadelphia, PA

Est. as: Philadelphia Textile School, The – 1884
MW: Philadelphia Museum & School of Industrial Art – 1884
NC: Textile Division of the Philadelphia Museum & School of Industrial Art – 1884
NC: Philadelphia Textile Institute – 1942
DM: Philadelphia Museum of Art – 1949
NC: Philadelphia College of Textiles & Science – 1960
NC: Philadelphia University – 1999

Established name is uncertain. Merger with Philadelphia Museum & School of Industrial Art made institution a division thereof. In 1938, Philadelphia Museum & School of Industrial Art became Philadelphia Museum of Art.

Philander Smith College
Little Rock, AR

Est. as: Walden Seminary – 1877
NC: Philander Smith College – 1882
MW: George R Smith College – 1933

Piedmont College
Demerest, GA

Est. as: J & S Green Collegiate Institute – 1897
NC: J S Green College – 1899
NC: Piedmont College – 1903

By MO: By merger (of) *DM:* Dissolved merger (with) *MW:* Merged with *NC:* Name change (to)

Pikeville College
Pikeville, KY

Est. as: Pikeville Collegiate Institute – 1889
NC: Pikeville College – 1909

Pine Manor College
Chestnut Hill, MA

Est. as: Post-secondary division of Dana Hall School – 1911
NC: Pine Manor Junior College – 1930
NC: Pine Manor College – 1977

Location changes
Wellesley, MA – 1911
Chestnut Hill, MA – 1965

Pittsburg State University
Pittsburg, KS

Est. as: Kansas State Manual Training Normal School Auxiliary – 1903
NC: Kansas State Manual Training Normal School – 1913
NC: Kansas State Teachers College of Pittsburg – 1923
NC: Kansas State College of Pittsburg – 1959
NC: Pittsburg State University – 1977

Originally a branch of Emporia State.

Pittsburgh, University of
Pittsburgh, PA

Est. as: Pittsburgh Academy – 1787
NC: Western University of Pennsylvania – 1819
NC: University of Pittsburgh – 1908

Official name apparently includes "...of the Commonwealth System of Higher Education," effective in 1965 or 1966. Institution officials discourage the use of the name "Pitt."

Pitzer College
Claremont, CA

Est. as: Pitzer College – 1963

Plymouth State College
Plymouth, NH

Est. as: Plymouth Normal School – 1871
NC: Plymouth Teachers College – 1939
NC: Plymouth State College – 1963

Point Loma Nazarene University
San Diego, CA

Est. as: Pacific Bible College – 1902
NC: Nazarene University – 1910
NC: Pasadena College – 1924
NC: Point Loma College – 1973
NC: Point Loma Nazarene College – 1983
NC: Point Loma Nazarene University – 1998

Location changes
Los Angeles, CA – 1902
Pasadena, CA – 1910
San Diego, CA – 1973

Point Park College
Pittsburgh, PA

Est. as: Point Park Junior College – 1960
NC: Point Park College – 1966

Polytechnic University
Brooklyn, NY

Est. as: Brooklyn Collegiate & Polytechnic Institute – 1854
NC: Polytechnic Institute of Brooklyn – 1889
MW: New York University School of Engineering & Science – 1973
NC: Polytechnic Institute of New York – 1973
NC: Polytechnic University – 1985

Known as Brooklyn Poly and Brooklyn Tech.

Pomona College

Claremont, CA

Est. as: Pomona College – 1887

Location changes
Pomona, CA – 1887
Claremont, CA – 1889

City of original location known also as Piedmont and/or North Pomona.

Portland State University

Portland, OR

Est. as: Vanport Extension Center of the Oregon State System of Higher Education – 1946
NC: Portland State College – 1955
NC: Portland State University – 1969

Location changes
Vanport, OR – 1946
Portland, OR – 1952

Portland, University of

Portland, OR

Est. as: Columbia University – 1901
NC: University of Portland – 1935

Prairie View A&M University

Prairie View, TX

Est. as: Alta Vista Agricultural College – 1876
NC: Prairie View State Normal & Industrial College – 1889
NC: Prairie View University – 1945
NC: Prairie View Agricultural & Mechanical College – 1947
NC: Prairie View A&M University – 1973

Pratt Institute

Brooklyn, NY

Est. as: Pratt Institute – 1887

Presbyterian College
Clinton, SC

Est. as: Clinton College – 1880
NC: Presbyterian College of South Carolina – 1890
NC: Presbyterian College – 1928

Prescott College
Prescott, AZ

Est. as: Prescott College – 1966
NC: Prescott Center College – 1975
NC: Prescott College – 1981

Original institution declared bankruptcy in December, 1974; faculty and students began new institution, Prescott College Center, in January, 1975. Prescott Center for Alternative Education was corporate name. Embry-Riddle University had purchased the bankrupt campus; in 1981, its board gave name of Prescott College to the Center to use as a trade name.

Princeton University
Princeton, NJ

Est. as: College of New Jersey – 1746
NC: Princeton University – 1896
Location changes
Elizabethtown (now Elizabeth), NJ – 1746
Newark, NJ – 1747
Princeton, NJ – 1756

Principia College
Elsah, IL

Est. as: Principia College – 1910
Location changes
Saint Louis, MO – 1910
Elsah, IL – 1935

Providence College
Providence, RI

Est. as: Providence College – 1917

Puget Sound, University of
Tacoma, WA

Est. as: Puget Sound University – 1888
NC: University of Puget Sound – 1903
NC: College of Puget Sound – 1914
NC: University of Puget Sound – 1960

Operated as a consolidation with Portland University in 1890s until Portland closed in 1899.

Purdue University
West Lafayette, IN

Est. as: Purdue University – 1869

Queens College
Charlotte, NC

Est. as: Charlotte Female Institute – 1857
NC: Seminary for Girls – 1891
NC: Presbyterian Female College – 1895
NC: Presbyterian College for Women – 1910
NC: Queens College – 1914
MW: Chicora College – 1930
NC: Queens-Chicora College – 1930
NC: Queens College – 1939

Charlotte Female Institute was preceded by Charlotte Female Academy, and other names, 1821-1851; closed in 1851, re-opened as the institute in 1857.

Queens College of the City University of New York
Flushing, NY

Est. as: Queens College of the City of New York – 1937
NC: Queens College of the City University of New York – 1961

Quincy University
Quincy, IL

Est. as: College of Saint Francis Solano – 1860
NC: Quincy College & Seminary – 1918
NC: Quincy College – 1970
NC: Quincy University – 1992

Quinnipiac University
Hamden, CT

Est. as: Connecticut College of Commerce – 1929
NC: Junior College of Commerce – 1935
NC: Quinnipiac College – 1951
MW: Larson College – 1952
MW: University of Bridgeport School of Law – 1995
NC: Quinnipiac University – 2000

Location changes
New Haven, CT – 1929
Hamden, CT – 1966

Radford University
Radford, VA

Est. as: State Normal & Industrial School for Women at Radford – 1910

NC: State Teachers College – 1924

MW: Virginia Agricultural & Mechanical College & Polytechnic Institute – 1944

NC: Virginia Agricultural & Mechanical College & Polytechnic Institute: Women's Division – 1944

DM: Virginia Agricultural & Mechanical College & Polytechnic Institute – 1964

NC: Radford College – 1964

NC: Radford University – 1979

Ramapo College of New Jersey
Mahwah, NJ

Est. as: Ramapo College of New Jersey – 1969

Randolph-Macon College
Ashland, VA

Est. as: Randolph-Macon College – 1830

Location changes
Boydton, VA – 1830
Ashland, VA – 1868

Randolph-Macon Woman's College
Lynchburg, VA

Est. as: Randolph-Macon Woman's College – 1891

Redlands, University of
Redlands, CA
Est. as: University of Redlands – 1907

Reed College
Portland, OR
Est. as: Reed College – 1909
Chartered as Reed Institute but designated as Reed College.

Regis College
Weston, MA
Est. as: Regis College for Women – 1927
NC: Regis College – 1971

Regis University
Denver, CO
Est. as: Las Vegas College – 1877
MW: College of the Sacred Heart – 1884
NC: College of the Sacred Heart – 1884
NC: Sacred Heart College – 1888
NC: Regis College – 1921
NC: Regis University – 1991
Location changes
Las Vegas, NM – 1877
Morrison, CO – 1884
Denver, CO – 1888

Reinhardt College
Waleska, GA
Est. as: Reinhardt College – 1883
May have been called Reinhardt Academy when established.

Rensselaer Polytechnic Institute
Troy, NY
Est. as: Rensselaer School – 1824
NC: Rensselaer Institute – 1837
NC: Rensselaer Polytechnic Institute – 1861

Rhode Island College
Providence, RI

Est. as: Rhode Island State Normal School – 1854
NC: Rhode Island College of Education – 1920
NC: Rhode Island College – 1959

Rhode Island, University of
Kingston, RI

Est. as: State Agricultural School – 1888*
NC: Rhode Island College of Agricultural & Mechanical Arts – 1892
NC: Rhode Island State College – 1909
NC: University of Rhode Island – 1951

*Recognizes 1892 as official established year.

Rhodes College
Memphis, TN

Est. as: Masonic University of Tennessee – 1848
NC: Montgomery Masonic College – 1850
NC: Stewart College – 1855
NC: Southwestern Presbyterian University – 1875
NC: Southwestern College – 1925
NC: Southwestern at Memphis – 1945
NC: Rhodes College – 1984

Location changes
Clarksville, TN – 1848
Memphis, TN – 1925

Rice University, William Marsh
Houston, TX

Est. as: William Marsh Rice Institute for the Advancement of
Letters, Science, & Art – 1891
NC: William Marsh Rice University – 1960

Recognizes Rice University as official name.

Richard Stockton College of New Jersey, The
Pomona, NJ

Est. as: Stockton State College – 1969
NC: Richard Stockton College of New Jersey, The – 1993

By MO: By merger (of) **DM:** Dissolved merger (with) **MW:** Merged with **NC:** Name change (to)

Richmond, University of
Richmond, VA

Est. as: Dunlora Academy – 1830
NC: Virginia Baptist Seminary – 1832
NC: Richmond College – 1840
MW: Westhampton College – 1914
NC: University of Richmond – 1920

Rider University
Lawrenceville, NJ

Est. as: Trenton Business College – 1865
NC: Rider Business College, The – 1897
MW: Stewart Business College – 1901
NC: Rider-Moore & Stewart School of Business – 1917
NC: Rider College – 1921
MW: Westminster Choir College – 1992
NC: Rider University – 1994

Location changes
Trenton, NJ – 1865
Lawrenceville, NJ – 1960

In early days was sometimes known as Capital City Business College.

Rio Grande, University of
Rio Grande, OH

Est. as: Rio Grande College – 1876
NC: University of Rio Grande – 1988

Ripon College
Ripon, WI

Est. as: Lyceum of Ripon – 1850*
NC: Brockway College – 1851
NC: Ripon College – 1864

*Recognizes 1851 as official established year.

Rivier College
Nashua, NH

Est. as: Rivier College – 1933

Location changes
Hudson, NH – 1933
Nashua, NH – 1941

Roanoke College
Salem, VA

Est. as: Virginia Institute, The – 1842
NC: Virginia Collegiate Institute, The – 1844
NC: Roanoke College – 1853

Location changes
Staunton, VA – 1842
Salem, VA – 1847

Robert Morris University
Moon Township, PA

Est. as: Pittsburgh School of Accountancy – 1921
NC: Robert Morris School, The – 1935
NC: Robert Morris Junior College – 1962
NC: Robert Morris College – 1969
NC: Robert Morris University – 2002

Roberts Wesleyan College
Rochester, NY

Est. as: Chili Seminary – 1866
NC: A M Chesbrough Seminary – 1885
NC: Roberts Junior College – 1945
NC: Roberts Wesleyan College – 1949

Rochester College
Rochester Hills, MI

Est. as: North Central Christian College – 1959
NC: Michigan Christian Junior College – 1961
NC: Michigan Christian College – 1978
NC: Rochester College – 1997

By MO: By merger (of) *DM:* Dissolved merger (with) *MW:* Merged with *NC:* Name change (to)

Rochester Institute of Technology

Rochester, NY

Est. as: Athenaeum, The – 1829
MW: Rochester Literary Company – 1830
MW: Young Men's Society – 1834
MW: Young Men's Association – 1838
NC: Rochester Athenaeum & Young Men's Association – 1838
MW: Mechanics Literary Association – 1847
NC: Rochester Athenaeum & Mechanics Association – 1847
MW: Mechanics Institute, The – 1891
NC: Rochester Athenaeum & Mechanics Institute – 1891
NC: Rochester Institute of Technology – 1944
MW: Eisenhower College – 1979

Preceded by Franklin Institute, 1821; not recognized as a predecessor.

Rochester, University of

Rochester, NY

Est. as: University of Rochester – 1850

Rockford College

Rockford, IL

Est. as: Rockford Female Seminary – 1847
NC: Rockford Seminary – 1887
NC: Rockford College – 1892

Rockhurst University

Kansas City, MO

Est. as: Rockhurst University & High School – 1910
NC: Rockhurst University – 1998

Rocky Mountain College

Billings, MT

Est. as: Montana Collegiate Institute – 1878
NC: College of Montana – 1882
MW: Montana Wesleyan University – 1923
NC: Intermountain Union College – 1923
MW: Billings Polytechnic Institute – 1947
NC: Rocky Mountain College – 1947

Location changes
Deer Lake, MT – 1878
Helena, MT – 1923
Great Falls, MT – 1935
Billings, MT – 1936

Roger Williams University

Bristol, RI

Est. as: Northeastern University School of Commerce & Finance: Providence Branch – 1919*
NC: Providence Institute of Engineering & Finance – 1940
NC: YMCA Institute of Engineering & Finance – 1945
NC: YMCA Institute – UNK
NC: Roger Williams Junior College – 1956
NC: Roger Williams College – 1968
NC: Roger Williams University – 1992

Location changes
Providence, RI – 1919
Bristol, RI – 1968

*Recognizes 1956 as official established year.

Established name was not necessarily official. The branch was opened at the YMCA. In 1920, Northeastern opened its School of Law, and in 1938, it opened Providence Technical Institute, also at the YMCA. These branches separated from Northeastern in 1940.

Rollins College

Winter Park, FL

Est. as: Rollins College – 1885

Roosevelt University
Chicago, IL

Est. as: Thomas Jefferson College of Chicago – 1945
NC: Roosevelt College of Chicago – 1945
MW: Chicago Musical College – 1954
NC: Roosevelt University – 1954

Board of Central YMCA College had imposed minority admission quotas and other requirements. President was opposed to them; took faculty and students and opened what became Roosevelt University.

Rosemont College
Rosemont, PA

Est. as: Rosemont College – 1921

Rowan University
Glassboro, NJ

Est. as: New Jersey State Normal School at Glassboro – 1923
NC: New Jersey State Teachers College at Glassboro – 1937
NC: Glassboro State College – 1958
NC: Rowan College of New Jersey – 1992
NC: Rowan University – 1997

Russell Sage College
Troy, NY

Est. as: Russell Sage College – 1916

Rust College
Holly Springs, MS

Est. as: Shaw School – 1866
NC: Shaw University – 1870
NC: Rust University – 1882
NC: Rust College – 1915

220

Rutgers, The State University of New Jersey
New Brunswick, NJ

Est. as: Queen's College – 1766
NC: Rutgers College – 1825
NC: Rutgers University – 1925
NC: Rutgers, The State University of New Jersey – 1945
MW: University of Newark – 1946
MW: College of South Jersey – 1950

Sacred Heart University
Fairfield, CT
Est. as: Sacred Heart University – 1963

Saginaw Valley State University
Saginaw, MI
Est. as: Saginaw Valley College – 1963
NC: Saginaw Bay State College – 1965
NC: Saginaw Valley State College – 1975
NC: Saginaw Valley State University – 1987

Saint Ambrose University
Davenport, IA
Est. as: Saint Ambrose Seminary – 1882
NC: Saint Ambrose College – 1892
NC: Saint Ambrose University – 1987

Saint Andrews Presbyterian College
Laurinburg, NC
Est. as: Consolidated Presbyterian College – 1958*
By MO: Flora MacDonald College – 1958
By MO: Presbyterian Junior College – 1958
NC: Saint Andrews Presbyterian College – 1960

*Recognizes merger year, 1958, as official established year; does not recognize histories of merged institutions.

Merged institutions continued to operate in Red Springs and Maxton until Laurinburg campus opened in fall of 1961.

Saint Anselm College
Manchester, NH

Est. as: Saint Anselm's College – 1889
NC: Saint Anselm College – 1981

Saint Augustine's College
Raleigh, NC

Est. as: Saint Augustine's Normal School & Collegiate Institute – 1867
NC: Saint Augustine's School – 1893
NC: Saint Augustine's Junior College – 1919
NC: Saint Augustine's College – 1928

Saint Benedict, College of
Saint Joseph, MN

Est. as: Saint Benedict's Academy – 1867*
NC: Saint Benedict's College & Academy – 1913
NC: College of Saint Benedict – 1927

*Recognizes 1913 as official established year.

Saint Bonaventure University
Olean, NY

Est. as: Saint Bonaventure College & Seminary – 1858
NC: Saint Bonaventure University – 1950

Saint Catherine, College of
Saint Paul, MN

Est. as: College of Saint Catherine – 1905

Saint Cloud State University
Saint Cloud, MN

Est. as: Third State Normal School – 1869
NC: State Normal School at Saint Cloud – 1894
NC: Saint Cloud State Teachers College – 1921
NC: Saint Cloud State College – 1957
NC: Saint Cloud State University – 1975

Saint Edward's University
Austin, TX

Est. as: Saint Edward's Academy – 1870*
NC: Saint Edward's College – 1885
NC: Saint Edward's University – 1925
MW: Maryhill College – 1970

*Recognizes 1885 as official established year.

Saint Elizabeth, College of
Morristown, NJ

Est. as: College of Saint Elizabeth – 1899

Saint Francis College
Brooklyn, NY

Est. as: Saint Francis Academy – 1858*
NC: Saint Francis Monestary of the City of Brooklyn – 1868
NC: Saint Francis College – 1884

*Recognizes 1884 as official established year.

Saint Francis University
Loretto, PA

Est. as: Saint Francis Academy – 1847
NC: Saint Francis College – 1920
NC: Saint Francis University – 2001

Saint Francis, University of
Fort Wayne, IN

Est. as: Saint Francis Normal School – 1890
NC: Saint Francis College – 1940
NC: University of Saint Francis – 1998
MW: Lutheran College of Health Professions – 1999

Location changes
Lafayette, IN – 1890
Fort Wayne, IN – 1944

By MO: By merger (of) *DM:* Dissolved merger (with) *MW:* Merged with *NC:* Name change (to)

Saint Francis, University of
Joliet, IL

Est. as: New College, The – 1920
NC: Assissi Junior College – 1925
NC: College of Saint Francis – 1930
MW: Saint Joseph College of Nursing – 1997
NC: University of Saint Francis – 1998

Saint Gregory's University
Shawnee, OK

Est. as: Sacred Heart Boys School & College – 1875
NC: Saint Gregory's High School & College – 1915
NC: Saint Gregory's College – 1965
NC: Saint Gregory's University – 1997

Location changes
Konawa, OK – 1875
Shawnee, OK – 1915

Saint John Fisher College
Rochester, NY

Est. as: Saint John Fisher College – 1948

Saint John's College
Annapolis, MD

Est. as: King William's School – 1696*
NC: Saint John's College – 1784

*Recognizes 1784 as official established year.

Saint John's University
Collegeville, MN

Est. as: Saint John's Seminary – 1857
NC: Saint John's University – 1883

Saint John's University
Jamaica, NY

Est. as: Saint John's College – 1870
NC: Saint John's University, Brooklyn – 1933
NC: Saint John's University – 1954
MW: Notre Dame College of Staten Island – 1971
MW: College of Insurance – 2001

Location changes
Brooklyn, NY – 1870
Jamaica, NY – 1958

Saint Joseph College
West Hartford, CT

Est. as: Mount Saint Joseph College – 1932
NC: Saint Joseph College – 1935

Saint Joseph's College
Brooklyn, NY

Est. as: Saint Joseph's College for Women – 1916
NC: Saint Joseph's College – 1970

Saint Joseph's College
Rensselaer, IN

Est. as: Saint Joseph's College – 1891

Saint Joseph's College
Standish, ME

Est. as: Saint Joseph's College – 1912
NC: College of Our Lady of Mercy – 1949
NC: Saint Joseph's College – 1956

Location changes
Portland, ME – 1912
Standish, ME – 1956

Saint Joseph's University
Philadelphia, PA

Est. as: Saint Joseph's College – 1851
NC: Saint Joseph's University – 1978

By MO: By merger (of) *DM:* Dissolved merger (with) *MW:* Merged with *NC:* Name change (to)

226

Saint Joseph, College of
Rutland, VT

Est. as: Saint Joseph Teachers College – 1956
NC: College of Saint Joseph the Provider, The – 1960
NC: College of Saint Joseph – 1983

Saint Lawrence University
Canton, NY

Est. as: Saint Lawrence University – 1856

Saint Leo University
Saint Leo, FL

Est. as: St. Leo's College – 1889
NC: St. Leo Military Academy – 1890
NC: St. Leo College – 1903
NC: St. Leo College & Preparatory School – 1917
NC: Saint Leo College – 1918
NC: St. Leo High School – 1920
NC: St. Leo Academy – 1923
NC: Benedictine High School – 1927
NC: Saint Leo College Preparatory School – 1929
NC: Saint Leo College – 1959
NC: Saint Leo University – 1999

"Saint" was officially spelled and abbreviated at different times.

Saint Louis University
Saint Louis, MO

Est. as: Saint Louis Academy – 1818
NC: Saint Louis College – 1820
NC: Saint Louis University – 1832
MW: Parks College of Engineering & Aviation – 1946

From 1920s through 1960, had a relationship with other schools in the area as affiliated corporate colleges of Saint Louis: Notre Dame College (a junior college), Saint Mary's Junior College, Mercy Junior College, Marilac Junior College, all now closed, and with Fontbonne, Webster, and Maryville, all active.

By MO: By merger (of) *DM:* Dissolved merger (with) *MW:* Merged with *NC:* Name change (to)

Saint Martin's College
Lacey, WA
Est. as: Saint Martin's College – 1895

Saint Mary College
Leavenworth, KS
Est. as: Saint Mary's Academy – 1860*
NC: Saint Mary Junior College – 1923
NC: Saint Mary College – 1930
*Recognizes 1923 as official established year.

Saint Mary's College
South Bend, IN
Est. as: Saint Mary's Academy – 1844
NC: Saint Mary's College – 1903

Location changes
Bertrand, MI – 1844
South Bend, IN – 1855

Saint Mary's College of California
Moraga, CA
Est. as: Saint Mary's – 1863
NC: Saint Mary's College of California – 1870

Location changes
San Francisco CA – 1863
Oakland CA – 1868
Moraga CA1928

Originally a residential high school.

Saint Mary's College of Maryland
Saint Mary's City, MD
Est. as: Saint Mary's Female Seminary – 1840
NC: Saint Mary's Seminary Junior College – 1949
NC: Saint Mary's College of Maryland – 1964

Saint Mary's University of Minnesota
Winona, MN

Est. as: Saint Mary's College – 1912
NC: Saint Mary's College of Minnesota – 1990
NC: Saint Mary's University of Minnesota – 1995

Saint Mary's University of San Antonio
San Antonio, TX

Est. as: Saint Mary's Institute – 1852
NC: Saint Louis College – 1894
NC: Saint Mary's University – 1927
NC: Saint Mary's University of San Antonio – 1976

Saint Mary, College of
Omaha, NE

Est. as: College of Saint Mary – 1923

Saint Mary-of-the-Woods College
Terre Haute, IN

Est. as: Saint Mary's Female Institute – 1840
NC: Saint Mary-of-the-Woods College – 1909

Saint Michael's College
Winooski Park, VT

Est. as: Saint Michael's Institute – 1904
NC: Saint Michael's College – 1913

Saint Norbert College
De Pere, WI

Est. as: Saint Norbert College – 1898

Saint Olaf College
Northfield, MN

Est. as: Saint Olaf's School – 1874
NC: Saint Olaf College – 1889
MW: College Department of United Church Seminary – 1900
MW: College Department of Red Wing Seminary – 1917

Saint Paul's College
Lawrenceville, VA

Est. as: Saint Paul's Normal & Industrial School – 1888
NC: Saint Paul's Polytechnic Institute – 1941
NC: Saint Paul's College – 1951

Saint Peter's College
Jersey City, NJ

Est. as: Saint Peter's College – 1872

Saint Rose, The College of
Albany, NY

Est. as: College of Saint Rose, The – 1920

Saint Scholastica, The College of
Duluth, MN

Est. as: College of Saint Scholastica, The – 1912

Saint Thomas Aquinas College
Sparkill, NY

Est. as: Saint Thomas Aquinas College – 1952

Saint Thomas University
Miami, FL

Est. as: Biscayne College – 1961
NC: Saint Thomas University – 1984

Saint Thomas, University of
Houston, TX

Est. as: University of Saint Thomas – 1947

Saint Thomas, University of
Saint Paul, MN

Est. as: Saint Thomas Aquinas Seminary – 1885
NC: College of Saint Thomas – 1894
MW: Saint Paul Seminary – 1987
NC: University of Saint Thomas – 1990

By MO: By merger (of) *DM:* Dissolved merger (with) *MW:* Merged with *NC:* Name change (to)

Saint Vincent College
Latrobe, PA

Est. as: Saint Vincent College – 1846

May have been established as Saint Vincent Archabbey & College.

Saint Xavier University
Chicago, IL

Est. as: Saint Francis Academy for Females – 1847
NC: Saint Xavier College for Women – 1912
NC: Saint Xavier College – 1956
NC: Saint Xavier University – 1992

Salem Academy & College
Winston-Salem, NC

Est. as: Salem School for Girls – 1772
NC: Salem Female Academy – 1886
NC: Salem Academy & College – 1907

Salem International University
Salem, WV

Est. as: Salem College – 1888
MW: Teikyo Yamanashi Education & Welfare Foundation – 1989
NC: Salem-Teikyo University – 1989
NC: Salem International University – 2000

Salem State College
Salem, MA

Est. as: Salem Normal School – 1854
NC: Salem Teachers College – 1932
NC: State College at Salem – 1960
NC: Salem State College – 1968

Salisbury University
Salisbury, MD

Est. as: Maryland State Normal School at Salisbury – 1925
NC: Maryland State Teachers College at Salisbury – 1934
NC: Salisbury State College – 1963
NC: Salisbury State University – 1988
NC: Salisbury University – 2001

By MO: By merger (of) *DM:* Dissolved merger (with) *MW:* Merged with *NC:* Name change (to)

Salve Regina University
Newport, RI

Est. as: Salve Regina College – 1934
NC: Salve Regina-The Newport School – 1976
NC: Salve Regina University – 1992

Sam Houston State University
Huntsville, TX

Est. as: Sam Houston Normal Institute – 1879
NC: Sam Houston State Teachers College – 1923
NC: Sam Houston State College – 1965
NC: Sam Houston State University – 1969

Samford University
Birmingham, AL

Est. as: Howard College – 1841
MW: Cumberland School of Law – 1961
NC: Howard University – 1965
NC: Samford University – 1965
MW: Ida V Moffett School of Nursing – 1973

Location changes
Marion, AL – 1841
East Lake, AL – 1887
Birmingham, AL – 1957

San Diego State University
San Diego, CA

Est. as: San Diego State Normal School – 1897
NC: San Diego State Teachers College – 1921
NC: San Diego State College – 1935
NC: California State University, San Diego – 1972
NC: San Diego State University – 1974

San Diego, University of
San Diego, CA

Est. as: San Diego College for Men – 1949
MW: San Diego College for Women – 1972
MW: San Diego School of Law – 1972
NC: University of San Diego – 1972

By MO: By merger (of) *DM:* Dissolved merger (with) *MW:* Merged with *NC:* Name change (to)

San Francisco State University
San Francisco, CA

Est. as: San Francisco State Normal School – 1899
NC: San Francisco State Teachers College – 1921
NC: San Francisco State College – 1935
NC: California State University: San Francisco – 1972
NC: San Francisco State University – 1974

Girls High & Normal School, founding date unknown, became San Francisco State Normal School in 1899.

San Francisco, University of
San Francisco, CA

Est. as: Saint Ignatius Academy – 1855
NC: Saint Ignatius College – 1859
NC: University of San Francisco – 1930

San Jose State University
San Jose, CA

Est. as: Minn's Evening Normal School – 1857
NC: California State Normal School – 1862
NC: San Jose State Normal School – 1887
NC: San Jose State Teachers College – 1921
NC: San Jose State College – 1935
NC: California State University: San Jose – 1972
NC: San Jose State University – 1974

Location changes
San Francisco, CA – 1857
San Jose, CA – 1871

Santa Clara University
Santa Clara, CA

Est. as: Santa Clara College – 1851
NC: University of Santa Clara – 1912
NC: Santa Clara University – 1986

Santa Fe, The College of
Santa Fe, NM

Est. as: Saint Michael's College – 1859*
NC: College of Santa Fe, The – 1966
MW: University of Albuquerque – 1986

*Recognizes 1947, when college-level courses were re-instituted, as official established year.

Chartered in 1874 as College of Christian Brothers of New Mexico, a DBA name only. From shortly after World War I until 1947, college level courses were discontinued.

Sarah Lawrence College
Bronxville, NY

Est. as: Sarah Lawrence College for Women – 1926
NC: Sarah Lawrence College – 1947

Savannah State University
Savannah, GA

Est. as: Georgia State Industrial School for Colored Youth – 1890
NC: Georgia State College – c1936
NC: Savannah State College – 1950
NC: Savannah State University – 1996

Location changes
Athens, GA – 1890
Savannah, GA – 1891

Schreiner University
Kerrville, TX

Est. as: Schreiner Institute – 1917*
NC: Schreiner College – 1973
NC: Schreiner University – 2001

*Recognizes 1923, when institution opened, as official established year.

Science & Arts of Oklahoma, University of
Chickasha, OK

Est. as: Oklahoma Industrial Institute & College for Girls – 1908
NC: Oklahoma College for Women – 1916
NC: Oklahoma College of Liberal Arts – 1965
NC: University of Science & Arts of Oklahoma – 1974

Scranton, University of
Scranton, PA

Est. as: Saint Thomas College – 1888
NC: University of Scranton – 1938

"The" is not official but is used.

Scripps College
Claremont, CA

Est. as: Scripps College for Women – 1926
NC: Scripps College – 1927

Seattle Pacific University
Seattle, WA

Est. as: Seattle Seminary – 1891
NC: Seattle Seminary & College – 1913
NC: Seattle Pacific College – 1915
NC: Seattle Pacific University – 1977

Seattle University
Seattle, WA

Est. as: School of the Immaculate Conception – 1891
NC: Seattle College – 1898
NC: Seattle University – 1948

Seton Hall University

South Orange, NJ

Est. as: Seton Hall College – 1856
NC: Seton Hall University – 1950
MW: John Marshall Law School – 1950

Location changes
Madison, NJ – 1856
South Orange, NJ – 1860

John Marshall Law School closed; library, etc., given to Seton Hall which opened its law school at Marshall site and agreed to maintain and administer records of Marshall alumni.

Seton Hill University

Greensburg, PA

Est. as: Saint Joseph Academy – 1883*
NC: Seton Junior College – 1914
NC: Seton Hill College – 1918
NC: Seton Hill University – 2002

*Recognizes 1918, when institution was re-chartered, as official established year.

Shaw University

Raleigh, NC

Est. as: Raleigh Institute – 1865
NC: Shaw Collegiate Institute – 1870
NC: Shaw University – 1875

Shawnee State University

Portsmouth, OH

Est. as: Ohio University: Portsmouth – 1945*
MW: Scioto Technical College – 1975
NC: Shawnee State General & Technical College – 1975
NC: Shawnee State Community College – 1977
NC: Shawnee State University – 1986

*Recognizes 1986 as official established year.

Shenandoah University
Winchester, VA

Est. as: Shenandoah High School – 1875
NC: Shenandoah Seminary – 1876
NC: Shenandoah Institute – 1884
NC: Shenandoah Collegiate Institute & School of Music – 1902
NC: Shenandoah College & School of Music – 1925
NC: Shenandoah College – 1937
NC: Shenandoah College & Conservatory of Music – 1974
NC: Shenandoah University – 1991

Location changes
Dayton, VA – 1875
Winchester, VA – 1960

1937, Conservatory is separately incorporated to be able to offer music degrees; 1974, college and conservatory again become a single institution.

Shepherd College
Shepherdstown, WV

Est. as: Shepherd College – 1871
NC: Shepherd College State Normal School – 1873
NC: Shepherd State Teachers College – 1931
NC: Shepherd College – 1943

State established a normal school in the existing institution and took over the then-private school.

Shimer College
Waukegan, IL

Est. as: Mount Carroll Seminary – 1853
NC: Frances Shimer Academy of the University of Chicago – 1896
NC: Frances Shimer Junior College & Preparatory School – 1910
NC: Shimer College – 1950

Location changes
Mount Carroll, IL – 1853
Waukegan, IL – 1979

Shippensburg University of Pennsylvania of the State System of Higher Education
Shippensburg, PA

Est. as: Cumberland Valley State Normal School – 1871
NC: State Teachers College at Shippensburg – 1927
NC: Shippensburg State College – 1960
NC: Shippensburg University of Pennsylvania of the State System of Higher Education – 1983

Shorter College
Rome, GA

Est. as: Cherokee Baptist Female Academy – 1873
NC: Shorter Female College – 1877
NC: Shorter College – 1923

Siena College
Loudonville, NY

Est. as: Saint Bernardine of Siena College – 1937
NC: Siena College – 1968

Originally operated as an extension of Saint Bonaventure University.

Siena Heights University
Adrian, MI

Est. as: Saint Joseph Academy – 1893*
NC: Saint Joseph College – 1919
NC: Siena Heights College – 1938
NC: Siena Heights University – 1998

*Recognizes 1919 as official established year.

Sierra Nevada College
Incline Village, NV

Est. as: Sierra Nevada College – 1969

Silver Lake College

Manitowoc, WI

Est. as: Holy Family Normal School – 1869*
NC: Holy Family College – 1935
NC: Silver Lake College of the Holy Family – 1972
NC: Silver Lake College – 1975

*Recognizes 1935 as official established year.

Simmons College

Boston, MA

Est. as: Simmons Female College – 1899
NC: Simmons College – 1915
MW: Garland Junior College – 1976

Simpson College

Indianola, IA

Est. as: Indianola Male & Female Seminary – 1860
NC: Simpson Centenary College – 1866
NC: Simpson College – 1885

Simpson College

Redding, CA

Est. as: Simpson Bible Institute – 1921
NC: Simpson Bible College – 1955
NC: Simpson College – 1971

Location changes
Seattle, WA – 1921
San Francisco, CA – 1955
Redding, CA – 1989

By MO: By merger (of) *DM:* Dissolved merger (with) *MW:* Merged with *NC:* Name change (to)

Sioux Falls, University of
Sioux Falls, SD

Est. as: Dakota Collegiate Institute – 1883
NC: Sioux Falls University – 1885
MW: Parker College – c1929
MW: Des Moines University – c1929
MW: Cedar Valley Seminary – c1929
MW: Grand Island College – 1931
NC: Sioux Falls College – 1931
NC: University of Sioux Falls – 1995

1929 mergers occurred between 1929 and 1931; dates unknown. The schools had closed; records and students were absorbed. 1931 merger with Grand Island College was a true merger.

Skidmore College
Saratoga Springs, NY

Est. as: Young Women's Industrial Club of Saratoga – 1903
NC: Skidmore College of Arts of Saratoga Springs – 1911
NC: Skidmore College – 1922

Slippery Rock University of Pennsylvania of the State System of Higher Education
Slippery Rock, PA

Est. as: Slippery Rock State Normal School – 1889
NC: Slippery Rock State Teachers College – 1927
NC: Slippery Rock State College – 1960
NC: Slippery Rock University of Pennsylvania of the State System of Higher Education – 1983

Smith College
Northampton, MA

Est. as: Smith College – 1871

Sonoma State University
Rohnert Park, CA

Est. as: Sonoma State College – 1960
NC: California State College: Sonoma – 1972
NC: Sonoma State College – 1976
NC: Sonoma State University – 1978

By MO: By merger (of) *DM:* Dissolved merger (with) *MW:* Merged with *NC:* Name change (to)

South Alabama, University of
Mobile, AL

Est. as: University of South Alabama – 1963

South Carolina Aiken, University of
Aiken, SC

Est. as: University of South Carolina at Aiken Center – 1961
NC: University of South Carolina at Aiken – 1968
NC: University of South Carolina Aiken – 1976

South Carolina Spartanburg, University of
Spartanburg, SC

Est. as: Spartanburg Regional Campus – 1967
NC: University of South Carolina Spartanburg – 1975

South Carolina State University
Orangeburg, SC

Est. as: South Carolina Agricultural College & Mechanics Institute – 1872*
NC: Claflin College – 1878
DM: Claflin University – 1896
NC: Normal Industrial, Agricultural, & Mechanical College for the Colored Race – 1896
NC: South Carolina State College – 1954
NC: South Carolina State University – 1992

*Recognizes 1896 as official established year.

State College of Agriculture & Mechanics was established in 1872 by the state legislature as a co-ordinate college of Claflin University.

South Carolina, University of
Columbia, SC

Est. as: South Carolina College – 1801
NC: University of South Carolina – 1866
NC: South Carolina College of Agriculture & Mechanical Arts – 1880
NC: South Carolina College – 1882
NC: University of South Carolina – 1887
NC: South Carolina College – 1890
NC: University of South Carolina – 1906

May have been known as College of South Carolina while closed from 1877-1880.

South Dakota State University
Brookings, SD

Est. as: Dakota Agricultural College – 1881
NC: South Dakota State College of Agriculture & Mechanic Arts – 1907
NC: South Dakota State University – 1964

South Dakota, The University of
Vermillion, SD

Est. as: University of Dakota – 1862
NC: University of South Dakota – 1891
NC: State University of South Dakota – 1959
NC: University of South Dakota, The – 1964

South Florida, University of
Tampa, FL

Est. as: University of South Florida – 1956
MW: New College – 1975

South, The University of the
Sewanee, TN

Est. as: University of the South, The – 1857

Frequently known as Sewanee.

242

Southeast Missouri State University
Cape Girardeau, MO

Est. as: Third District Normal School of Southeast Missouri – 1873
NC: Southeast Missouri State Teachers College – 1919
NC: Southeast Missouri State College – 1945
NC: Southeast Missouri State University – 1973

Southeastern Louisiana University
Hammond, LA

Est. as: Hammond Junior College – 1925
NC: Southeastern Louisiana College – 1928
NC: Southeastern Louisiana University – 1970

Southeastern Oklahoma State University
Durant, OK

Est. as: Southeastern Normal School – 1909
NC: Southeastern Teachers College – 1920
NC: Southeastern State College – 1939
NC: Southeastern Oklahoma State University – 1974

Southeastern University
Washington, DC

Est. as: Unknown name; sponsored by the YMCA of The District of Columbia – 1879
NC: Southeastern University of the YMCA of The District of Columbia – 1923
NC: Southeastern University – 1937

Southern Adventist University
Collegedale, TN

Est. as: Graysville Academy – 1892
NC: Southern Industrial School – 1896
NC: Southern Training School – 1901
NC: Southern Junior College – 1916
NC: Southern Missionary College – 1944
NC: Southern College of Seventh-day Adventists – 1983
NC: Southern Adventist University – 1996

Location changes
Graysville, TN – 1892
Collegedale, TN – 1916

Southern Arkansas University
Magnolia, AR

Est. as: Third District Agricultural School – 1909
NC: State Agricultural & Mechanical College: Third District – 1925
NC: Southern State College – 1951
NC: Southern Arkansas University – 1976

Known in early years as Magnolia A&M.

Southern California, University of
Los Angeles, CA

Est. as: University of Southern California – 1880

Southern Colorado, University of
Pueblo, CO

Est. as: San Isabel Junior College – 1933
NC: Southern Colorado Junior College, The – 1934
NC: Pueblo Junior College – 1937
NC: Southern Colorado State College – 1964
NC: University of Southern Colorado – 1975

Legislation for name change to Colorado State University-Pueblo enacted in mid-2002 with effective date of July 1, 2003.

Southern Connecticut State University
New Haven, CT

Est. as: New Haven Normal School – 1893
NC: New Haven State Teachers College – 1937
NC: Southern Connecticut State College – 1959
NC: Southern Connecticut State University – 1983

Southern Illinois University Carbondale
Carbondale, IL

Est. as: Southern Illinois Normal University – 1869
NC: Southern Illinois University – 1947
NC: Southern Illinois University Carbondale – c1998

By MO: By merger (of) ***DM:*** Dissolved merger (with) ***MW:*** Merged with ***NC:*** Name change (to)

244

Southern Illinois University Edwardsville
Edwardsville, IL

Est. as: Southern Illinois University at Edwardsville – 1957
NC: Southern Illinois University Edwardsville – c1998

Southern Indiana, University of
Evansville, IN

Est. as: Indiana State University: Evansville – 1965
NC: University of Southern Indiana – 1985

Southern Maine, University of
Gorham, ME

Est. as: Western Maine Normal School – 1878
NC: Gorham State Teachers College – 1945
MW: University of Maine at Portland – 1970
NC: University of Maine at Portland-Gorham – 1970
NC: University of Southern Maine – 1978

Southern Methodist University
Dallas, TX

Est. as: Southern Methodist University – 1911

Southern Mississippi, The University of
Hattiesburg, MS

Est. as: Mississippi Normal College – 1910
NC: Mississippi State Teachers College – 1924
NC: Mississippi Southern College – 1940
NC: University of Southern Mississippi, The – 1962

Southern Nazarene University
Bethany, OK

Est. as: Texas Holiness College – 1899
NC: Peniel University – 1911
MW: Oklahoma Holiness College – 1920
NC: Bentany-Peniel College – 1920
MW: Central Nazarene University – 1929
MW: Arkansas Holiness College – 1930
MW: Bresee College – 1940
NC: Bethany Nazarene College – 1955
NC: Southern Nazarene University – 1986

Location changes
Peniel, TX – 1899
Bethany, OK – 1920

1911-1920 known as Peniel College.

Southern Oregon University
Ashland, OR

Est. as: Ashland Academy – 1869*
NC: Ashland College & Normal School – 1882
NC: Southern Oregon State Normal School – 1926
NC: Southern Oregon College of Education – 1939
NC: Southern Oregon College – 1956
NC: Southern Oregon State College – 1975
NC: Southern Oregon University – 1997

*Recognizes 1926 as official established year.

Southern University & Agricultural & Mechanical College
Baton Rouge, LA

Est. as: Southern University – 1880
NC: Southern University & Agricultural & Mechanical College – 1914

Location changes
New Orleans, LA – 1880
Baton Rouge, LA – 1914

Southern Utah State University
Cedar City, UT

Est. as: Branch Normal School of the University of Utah – 1897
NC: Branch Agricultural College of Utah – 1913
NC: College of Southern Utah – 1953
NC: Southern Utah State College – 1969
NC: Southern Utah State University – 1991

Southern Vermont College
Bennington, VT

Est. as: Saint Joseph Business School – 1926
NC: Saint Joseph College – 1962
NC: Southern Vermont College – 1974

Southern Wesleyan University
Central, SC

Est. as: Wesleyan Methodist Bible Institute – 1906
NC: Wesleyan Methodist College – 1909
NC: Central Wesleyan College – 1959
NC: Southern Wesleyan University – 1995

Southwest Baptist University
Bolivar, MO

Est. as: Southwest Baptist College – 1878
NC: Southwest Baptist College – 1964
NC: Southwest Baptist University – 1980

Location changes
Lebanon, MO – 1878
Bolivar, MO – 1879

Southwest Missouri State University
Springfield, MO

Est. as: Missouri State Normal School of the Fourth District – 1905
NC: Southwest Missouri State Teachers College – 1919
NC: Southwest Missouri State College – 1945
NC: Southwest Missouri State University – 1972

By MO: By merger (of) *DM:* Dissolved merger (with) *MW:* Merged with *NC:* Name change (to)

Southwest State University
Marshall, MN

Est. as: Southwest Minnesota State College – 1963
NC: Southwest State University – 1975

Southwest Texas State University
San Marcos, TX

Est. as: Southwest Texas State Normal School – 1899
NC: Southwest Texas State Normal College – 1918
NC: Southwest Texas State Teachers College – 1923
NC: Southwest Texas State College – 1959
NC: Southwest Texas State University – 1969

Pending name change to Texas State University tabled until new president is selected in late 2002.

Southwest, College of the
Hobbs, NM

Est. as: Hobbs Baptist College – 1956*
NC: New Mexico Baptist College – 1958
NC: College of the Southwest – 1962

*Recognizes 1962 as official established year.

Southwestern Adventist University
Keene, TX

Est. as: Keene Independent Academy – 1893
NC: Southwestern Junior College – 1916
NC: Southwestern Union College – 1963
NC: Southwestern Adventist College – 1976
NC: Southwestern Adventist University – 1989

May also have been known at establishment as Keene Industrial Academy.

248

Southwestern College
Winfield, KS

Est. as: Southwest Kansas Conference College – 1886
MW: Southern Kansas Normal & Business School – 1896
NC: Southwestern College – 1908
MW: Winfield College of Music – 1926

Known at establishment as Southwest Kansas Conference College of the Methodist Episcopal Church.

Southwestern Oklahoma State University
Weatherford, OK

Est. as: Southwestern Normal School – 1901
NC: Southwestern State Teachers College – 1920
NC: Southwestern State College of Diversified Occupations – 1939
NC: Southwestern Institute of Technology – 1941
NC: Southwestern State College – 1949
NC: Southwestern Oklahoma State University – 1974
MW: Sayre Junior College – 1987

Southwestern University
Georgetown, TX

Est. as: Rutersville College – 1840
MW: University of Eastern Texas – 1873
MW: McKenzie College – 1873
MW: Soule College – 1873
NC: Texas University – 1873
NC: Southwestern University – 1875
MW: Westminster College – 1942
MW: Weatherford College – 1944
MW: Daniel Baker College – 1946
DM: Weatherford College – 1949
DM: Westminster College – 1950
DM: Daniel Baker College – 1950

All of the schools involved in the 1873 merger had closed; merger was of charters. Technically only Eastern Texas, which had merged with Wesleyan, was involved in the merger. Weatherford and Westminster became junior college branches; Daniel Baker became a four-year branch. Westminster College (merged in 1942; merger dissolved in 1950) was in Tehucana.

By MO: By merger (of) *DM:* Dissolved merger (with) *MW:* Merged with *NC:* Name change (to)

Spalding University
Louisville, KY

Est. as: Nazareth College – 1920
NC: Catherine Spalding College – 1963
NC: Spalding College – 1969
MW: Nazareth College – 1969
NC: Spalding University – 1984

Nazareth College (1969 merger) was in Bardstown, KY, and was closed in 1971. It is not the existing Nazareth College in Rochester, NY.

Spelman College
Atlanta, GA

Est. as: Atlanta Baptist Female Seminary – 1881
NC: Spelman Seminary – 1884
NC: Spelman College – 1924

Spring Arbor University
Spring Arbor, MI

Est. as: Spring Arbor Seminary – 1873
NC: Spring Arbor Seminary & Junior College – 1929
NC: Spring Arbor College – 1960
NC: Spring Arbor University – 2001

Spring Hill College
Mobile, AL

Est. as: Spring Hill College – 1830

Springfield College
Springfield, MA

Est. as: School for Christian Workers – 1885
NC: International YMCA Training School – 1890
NC: International YMCA College – 1912
NC: Springfield College – 1953

By MO: By merger (of) *DM:* Dissolved merger (with) *MW:* Merged with *NC:* Name change (to)

Stanford, Junior, University, Leland
Palo Alto, CA

Est. as: Leland Stanford, Junior, University – 1891
MW: Cooper Medical College – 1908

Recognizes Stanford University as official name. Merger with Cooper Medical College was completed in 1912.

Staten Island of the City University of New York, The College of
Staten Island, NY

Est. as: Staten Island Community College – 1955
MW: Richmond College of the City University of New York – 1976
NC: College of Staten Island of the City University of New York, The – 1976

Stephen F Austin State University
Nacogdoches, TX

Est. as: Stephen F Austin State Teachers College – 1923
NC: Stephen F Austin State College – 1948
NC: Stephen F Austin State University – 1969

Stephens College
Columbia, MO

Est. as: Columbia Female Academy – 1833
NC: Columbia Female Baptist Academy – 1856
NC: Stephens College – 1870

Sterling College
Sterling, KS

Est. as: Cooper Memorial College – 1887
NC: Cooper College – 1914
NC: Sterling College – 1919

Stetson University
DeLand, FL

Est. as: DeLand Academy – 1883
NC: DeLand Academy & College – 1885
NC: DeLand University – 1887
NC: John B Stetson University – 1889
NC: Stetson University – 1993

Stevens Institute of Technology
Hoboken, NJ
Est. as: Stevens Institute of Technology – 1870

Stillman College
Tuscaloosa, AL
Est. as: Tuscaloosa Institute – 1876
NC: Stillman Institute – 1894
NC: Stillman College – 1948

Stonehill College
Easton, MA
Est. as: Stonehill College – 1948

Strayer University
Washington, DC
Est. as: Strayer's Business College – 1892
NC: Strayer College of Accountancy – 1928
NC: Strayer Junior College of Finance – 1958
NC: Strayer College – 1969
NC: Strayer University – 1998
Location changes
Baltimore, MD – 1892
Washington, DC – 1904

Suffolk University
Boston, MA
Est. as: Suffolk Law School – 1906
NC: Suffolk University – 1937

Sul Ross State University
Alpine, TX
Est. as: Sul Ross Normal College – 1920
NC: Sul Ross State Teachers College – 1923
NC: Sul Ross State College – 1949
NC: Sul Ross State University – 1969

Is successor to Alpine Summer Normal School, 1910, where students studied in summer for teacher certificates; operated by Alpine Public School System which petitioned state for what became the university.

By MO: By merger (of) *DM:* Dissolved merger (with) *MW:* Merged with *NC:* Name change (to)

252

Sullivan University

Louisville, KY

Est. as: Sullivan Business College – 1962
MW: Bryant & Stratton: Louisville – c1972
NC: Sullivan Junior College of Business – 1976
NC: Sullivan College – 1990
NC: Sullivan University – 2000

Susquehanna University

Selinsgrove, PA

Est. as: Missionary Institute of the Evangelical Lutheran Church –
1858
MW: Susquehanna Female Academy – 1873
NC: Susquehanna University – 1895

Swarthmore College

Swarthmore, PA

Est. as: Swarthmore College – 1864

Sweet Briar College

Sweet Briar, VA

Est. as: Sweet Briar Institute – 1901
NC: Sweet Briar College – 1906

First president said "institute" sounded like a "penal institution in the Blue Ridge Mountains."

Syracuse University

Syracuse, NY

Est. as: Syracuse University – 1870
MW: Geneva Medical School – 1872

Geneva Medical School eventually became State University of New York Upstate Medical University.

By MO: By merger (of) *DM:* Dissolved merger (with) *MW:* Merged with *NC:* Name change (to)

Tabor College
Hillsboro, KS
Est. as: Tabor College – 1908

Talladega College
Talladega, AL
Est. as: Swayne School – 1867
NC: Talladega College – 1869

Tampa, The University of
Tampa, FL
Est. as: Tampa Junior College – 1931
NC: University of Tampa, The – 1933

Tarleton State University
Stephenville, TX
Est. as: Stephenville College – 1893*
NC: John Tarleton College – 1899
NC: John Tarleton Agricultural College – 1917
NC: Tarleton State College – 1949
NC: Tarleton State University – 1973

*Recognizes 1899, when charter of Steubenville College, a private institution, was transferred to newly-formed John Tarleton College, as official established year.

254

Taylor University
Upland, IN

Est. as: Fort Wayne Female College – 1846
MW: Fort Wayne Collegiate Institute – 1855
NC: Fort Wayne College – 1855
MW: Fort Wayne College of Medicine – 1890
NC: Taylor University – 1890
MW: Summit Christian College – 1992

Location changes
Fort Wayne, IN – 1846
Upland, IN – 1893

Teikyo Post University
Waterbury, CT

Est. as: Mattoon School of Shorthand – 1890
NC: Bliss & Harrington's Business College & School of Shorthand – 1893
NC: Waterbury Business College – 1897
NC: Post College – 1931
NC: Post Junior College of Commerce – 1939
NC: Post Junior College – 1962
NC: Post College – 1976
MW: Teikyo Yamanashi Education & Welfare Foundation – 1990
NC: Teikyo Post University – 1990

Temple University
Philadelphia, PA

Est. as: Temple College – 1884
NC: Temple University – 1907
MW: Philadelphia Dental College – 1907
MW: Ambler Junior College – 1958
MW: New School of Music, The – 1986
MW: Pennsylvania College of Podiatric Medicine – 1998

Official name apparently includes "... of the Commonwealth System of Higher Education," effective 1965 or 1966. Pennsylvania School of Horticulture for Women had changed its name to Ambler Junior College early in 1958 in preparation for the merger later in the year. After the merger, it was Ambler Junior College of Temple University until 1961 when it became The Ambler Campus of Temple University.

By MO: By merger (of) *DM:* Dissolved merger (with) *MW:* Merged with *NC:* Name change (to)

Tennessee at Chattanooga, The University of
Chattanooga, TN

Est. as: Chattanooga University – 1886
MW: Grant Memorial University – 1889
NC: U S Grant Memorial University – 1889
NC: University of Chattanooga – 1907
MW: Chattanooga City College – 1969
MW: University of Tennessee, The – 1969
NC: University of Tennesseee at Chattanooga, The – 1969

Location changes
Chattanooga, TN – 1886
Athens, TN – 1889
Chattanooga, TN – 1904

Tennessee State University
Nashville, TN

Est. as: Tennessee Agricultural & Industrial State Normal School –
1912
NC: Tennessee Agricultural & Industrial State Normal College –
1924
NC: Tennessee Agricultural & Industrial State College – 1927
NC: Tennessee Agricultural & Industrial State University – 1951
NC: Tennessee State University – 1969
MW: University of Tennessee: Nashville – 1979

Proposed merger with Nashville School of Law for 2002 still in discussion stage as of February 2002.

Tennessee Technological University
Cookeville, TN

Est. as: University of Dixie – 1909*
NC: Tennessee Polytechnic Institute – 1915
NC: Tennessee Technological University – 1965

*Recognizes 1915 as official established year.

By MO: By merger (of) *DM:* Dissolved merger (with) *MW:* Merged with *NC:* Name change (to)

256

Tennessee Wesleyan College
Athens, TN

Est. as: Athens Female College – 1857
NC: East Tennessee Wesleyan College – 1866
NC: East Tennessee Wesleyan University – 1867
NC: Grant Memorial University – 1886
MW: Chattanooga University – 1889
NC: U S Grant Memorial University – 1889
NC: Athens School of the University of Chattanooga – 1907
DM: University of Chattanooga – 1925
NC: Tennessee Wesleyan College – 1925

Tennessee, The University of
Knoxville, TN

Est. as: Blount College – 1794
NC: East Tennessee College – 1807
NC: East Tennessee University – 1840
NC: University of Tennessee, The – 1879

"The" was not in enabling legislation but subsequently was adopted by trustees.

Tennessee: Martin, The University of
Martin, TN

Est. as: Tennessee Junior College – 1927
NC: University of Tennessee, Martin Branch – 1951
NC: University of Tennessee: Martin, The – 1967

Hall-Moody Junior College merged with Union University in 1927; state took over Hall-Moody campus and established Tennessee Junior College thereon.

By MO: By merger (of) ***DM:*** Dissolved merger (with) ***MW:*** Merged with ***NC:*** Name change (to)

Texas at Arlington, The University of
Arlington, TX

Est. as: Arlington College – 1895
NC: Carlisle Military Academy – 1901
NC: Arlington Training School – 1913
NC: Grubbs Vocational College – 1917
NC: North Texas Junior Agricultural College – 1923
NC: North Texas Agricultural College – UNK
NC: Arlington State College – 1949
NC: University of Texas at Arlington, The – 1967

North Texas Agricultural College may have been unofficial name, c1945.

Texas at Austin, The University of
Austin, TX

Est. as: University of Texas, The – 1883
NC: University of Texas at Austin, The – 1967

Texas at Dallas, The University of
Richardson, TX

Est. as: University of Texas at Dallas, The – 1969

Established when founders of Texas Instruments gave Southwest Center for Advanced Study to the State of Texas. Founded in 1961, Center originally named Graduate Research Center of the Southwest; name changed in 1967.

Texas at El Paso, The University of
El Paso, TX

Est. as: Texas State School of Mines & Metallurgy – 1913
NC: University of Texas, Department of Mines & Metallurgy – 1919
NC: Texas College of Mines & Metallurgy – 1920
MW: El Paso Junior College – 1927
NC: Texas Western College – 1949
NC: University of Texas at El Paso, The – 1967

Property of El Paso Military Institute was transferred to The University of Texas for the new institution.

Texas at San Antonio, The University of
San Antonio, TX

Est. as: University of Texas at San Antonio, The – 1969

Texas A&M International University
Laredo, TX

Est. as: Texas A&M University at Laredo – 1970
NC: Laredo State University – 1977
NC: Texas A&M International University – 1993

Texas A&M University
College Station, TX

Est. as: Agricultural & Mechanical College of Texas – 1876
NC: Texas A&M University – 1963

Texas A&M University-Commerce
Commerce, TX

Est. as: East Texas Normal College – 1889
NC: East Texas State Normal College – 1917
NC: East Texas State Teachers College – 1923
NC: East Texas State College – 1957
NC: East Texas State University – 1965
NC: Texas A&M University-Commerce – 1996

Location changes
Cooper, TX – 1889
Commerce, TX – 1894

Texas A&M University-Corpus Christi
Corpus Christi, TX

Est. as: Arts & Technological College – 1947
NC: University of Corpus Christi – 1947
NC: Texas A&I University at Corpus Christi – 1973
NC: Corpus Christi State University – 1977
NC: Texas A&M University-Corpus Christi – 1993

259

Texas A&M University-Kingsville
Kingsville, TX

Est. as: South Texas State Teachers College – 1925
NC: Texas College of Arts & Industries – 1929
NC: Texas A & I University – 1967
NC: Texas A&M University-Kingsville – 1993

Texas Christian University
Fort Worth, TX

Est. as: AddRan Male & Female Academy – 1873
NC: AddRan Christian University – 1889
NC: Texas Christian University – 1902

Location changes
Thorp Springs, TX – 1873
Waco, TX – 1895
Fort Worth, TX – 1911

Founders moved their private school, begun in 1869, from Fort Worth to Thorp Springs in 1873.

Texas Lutheran University
Seguin, TX

Est. as: Evangelical Lutheran College – 1891
NC: Evangelical Lutheran Proseminary – 1909
NC: Lutheran College – 1912
MW: Trinity College – 1929
NC: Texas Lutheran College – 1934
MW: Clifton College – 1954
NC: Texas Lutheran University – 1996

Location changes
Brenham, TX – 1891
Seguin, TX – 1912

Trinity College of the 1934 merger was in Round Rock; it is not the existing Trinity College in San Antonio.

Texas of the Permian Basin, The University of
Odessa, TX

Est. as: University of Texas of the Permian Basin, The – 1969

By MO: By merger (of) *DM:* Dissolved merger (with) *MW:* Merged with *NC:* Name change (to)

260

Texas Southern University
Houston, TX

Est. as: Texas State University for Negroes – 1947
NC: Texas Southern University – 1951

In 1947, state acquired campus of Houston College for Negroes which apparently was established in 1927 as Houston Colored Junior College.

Texas Tech University
Lubbock, TX

Est. as: Texas Technological College – 1923
NC: Texas Tech University – 1969

Texas Woman's University
Denton, TX

Est. as: Girl's Industrial College – 1901
NC: College of Industrial Arts – 1905
NC: Texas State College for Women – 1934
NC: Texas Woman's University – 1957

Texas-Pan American, The University of
Edinburg, TX

Est. as: Edinburg College – 1927
NC: Edinburg Junior College – 1933
NC: Edinburg Regional College – 1948
NC: Pan American College – 1952
NC: Pan American University – 1971
NC: University of Texas-Pan American, The – 1989

Thiel College
Greenville, PA

Est. as: Thiel Hall – 1866
NC: Thiel College – 1870

Location changes
Phillipsburg (now Monaca), PA – 1866
Greenville, PA – 1870
Greensburg, PA – 1903
Greenville, PA – 1907

Thomas Aquinas College
Santa Paula, CA

Est. as: Thomas Aquinas College – 1971

Location changes
San Rafael, CA – 1969
Calabasas, CA – 1971
Santa Paula, CA – 1978

Thomas University
Thomasville, GA

Est. as: Birdwood Junior College – 1950
NC: Thomas County Community College – 1976
NC: Thomas College – 1986
NC: Thomas University – 2000

Toledo, The University of
Toledo, OH

Est. as: Toledo University of Arts & Trades – 1872
NC: Toledo University – 1884
MW: Toledo Medical College – 1904
MW: Toldeo YMCA College of Law – 1909
NC: University of the City of Toledo – 1940
NC: University of Toledo, The – 1967

Touro College
New York, NY

Est. as: Touro College – 1970

Towson University
Towson, MD

Est. as: Maryland State Normal School – 1866
NC: Maryland State Teachers College at Towson – 1935
NC: Towson State College – 1963
NC: Towson State University – 1976
NC: Towson University – 1997

By MO: By merger (of) *DM:* Dissolved merger (with) *MW:* Merged with *NC:* Name change (to)

Transylvania University
Lexington, KY

Est. as: Transylvania Seminary – 1780
MW: Kentucky Academy – 1799
NC: Transylvania University – 1799
MW: Kentucky University – 1865
NC: Kentucky University – 1865
NC: Transylvania University – 1908
NC: Transylvania College – 1915
NC: Transylvania University – 1969

Trevecca Nazarene University
Nashville, TN

Est. as: Pentacostal Literary and Bible Training School – 1901
NC: Trevecca College – 1910
NC: Trevecca Nazarene College – 1917
MW: Southeastern Nazarene College – 1918
NC: Trevecca Nazarene University – 1995

Known at establishment as Pentacostal Literary & Bible Training School for Christian Workers.

Tri-State University
Angola, IN

Est. as: Tri-State Normal College – 1884
NC: Tri-State College – 1906
NC: Tri-State University – 1975

Trinity Christian College
Palos Heights, IL

Est. as: Trinity Christian College – 1959

Trinity College
Hartford, CT

Est. as: Washington College – 1823
NC: Trinity College – 1845

Trinity College
Washington, DC

Est. as: Trinity College – 1897

By MO: By merger (of) *DM:* Dissolved merger (with) *MW:* Merged with *NC:* Name change (to)

Trinity University
San Antonio, TX

Est. as: Trinity University – 1869

Location changes
Tehuacana, TX – 1869
Waxahachie, TX – 1902
San Antonio, TX – 1942

University of San Antonio closed; campus was turned over to Trinity for its move to San Antonio. While in Waxahachie, accepted graduates of defunct Fairemont Female Seminary, Weatherford, as alumnae.

Troy State University
Troy, AL

Est. as: Troy State Normal School – 1887
NC: Troy State Teachers College – 1929
NC: Troy State College – 1957
NC: Troy State University – 1967

Truman State University
Kirksville, MO

Est. as: North Missouri Normal School & Commercial College – 1867
NC: First District Normal School – 1870
NC: Northeast Missouri State Teachers College – 1919
NC: Northeast Missouri State College – 1968
NC: Northeast Missouri State University – 1972
NC: Truman State University – 1996

Known as Kirksville State Normal School (1870-1919) and as Kirksville State Teachers College (1919-1967).

Tufts University
Medford, MA

Est. as: Tufts College – 1852
NC: Tufts University – 1955
MW: Jackson College – 1963

Jackson College, 1910, was a co-ordinate institution for women. Separate classes were held until 1913. In 1963, Jackson was put on Tufts diploma.

264

Tulane University of Louisiana
New Orleans, LA

Est. as: Medical College of Louisiana – 1834
MW: University of Louisiana – 1847
NC: University of Louisiana – 1847
NC: Tulane University of Louisiana – 1884
MW: H Sophie Newcomb Memorial College for Women – 1988

H Sophie Newcomb Memorial College was a co-ordinate college for women.

Tulsa, The University of
Tulsa, OK

Est. as: Presbyterian School for Indian Girls – 1882*
NC: Henry Kendall College – 1894
NC: University of Tulsa, The – 1920

Location changes
Muskogee, OK – 1882
Tulsa, OK – 1907

*Recognizes 1894 as official established year.

Tuskegee University
Tuskegee, AL

Est. as: Normal School for Colored Teachers – 1881
NC: Tuskegee State Normal School – 1881
NC: Tuskegee Normal School – 1887
NC: Tuskegee Normal & Industrial Institute – 1891
NC: Tuskegee Institute – 1937
NC: Tuskegee University – 1985

Union College
Lincoln, NE
Est. as: Union College – 1891

Union College
Schenectady, NY
Est. as: Union College – 1795

Schenectady Academy (1785) was a loose predecessor. In 1870s a consortium known as Union University was formed with Union College, Albany Medical College, Albany Law School, Dudley Observatory, Albany College of Pharmacy; all are autonomous.

Union Institute & University
Cincinnati, OH
Est. as: Union for Experimenting Colleges & Universities, The – 1964
NC: Union Institute, The – 1989
MW: Vermont College – 2001
NC: Union Institute & University – 2001

Union University
Jackson, TN
Est. as: Jackson Male Academy – 1823
NC: West Tennessee College – 1844
NC: Unnamed academy – 1874
NC: Southwestern Baptist University – 1875
NC: Union University – c1907
MW: Hall-Moody Junior College – 1927

Unity College
Unity, ME

Est. as: Unity Institute of Liberal Arts & Sciences – 1965
NC: Unity College – 1967

Upper Iowa University
Fayette, IA

Est. as: Fayette Seminary of the Upper Iowa Conference, The – 1857
NC: Upper Iowa University – 1858

Urbana University
Urbana, OH

Est. as: Urbana University – 1850
NC: Urbana Junior College – 1920
NC: Urbana College – 1962
NC: Urbana University – 1985

Ursinus College
Collegeville, PA

Est. as: Ursinus College – 1869

Todd's School, 1832, and Freeland Seminary, 1848, were previously in area and were sold to or taken over by Ursinus; not part of history.

Ursuline College
Pepper Pike, OH

Est. as: Ursuline College – 1871
NC: Ursuline College for Women – 1922
NC: Ursuline College – 1968
MW: Saint John College School of Nursing – 1975

Location changes
Cleveland, OH – 1871
Pepper Pike, OH – 1966

Utah State University of Agriculture & Applied Science
Logan, UT

Est. as: Agricultural College of Utah – 1888
NC: Utah State Agricultural College – 1929
NC: Utah State University of Agriculture & Applied Science – 1957

By MO: By merger (of) *DM:* Dissolved merger (with) *MW:* Merged with *NC:* Name change (to)

Utah, University of
Salt Lake City, UT

Est. as: University of Deseret – 1850
NC: University of Utah – 1892

Utica College
Utica, NY

Est. as: Utica College of Syracuse University – 1946
NC: Utica College – 1995

V

Valdosta State University
Valdosta, GA

Est. as: South Georgia State Normal College – 1906
NC: Georgia State Woman's College – 1922
NC: Valdosta State College – 1950
NC: Valdosta State University – 1993

Valley City State University
Valley City, ND

Est. as: State Normal School, Valley City – 1890
NC: Valley City State Teachers College – 1921
NC: Valley City State College – 1963
NC: State University of North Dakota-Valley City – 1987
NC: Valley City State University – 1987

Valparaiso University
Valparaiso, IN

Est. as: Valparaiso Male & Female College – 1859
NC: Northern Indiana Normal School & Business Institute – 1873
NC: Valparaiso College – 1900
NC: Valparaiso University – 1907

Vanderbilt University
Nashville, TN

Est. as: Central University of the Methodist Episcopal Church, South, The – 1872*
NC: Vanderbilt University – 1873
MW: Marvin University School – 1907
MW: George Peabody College for Teachers – 1979

*Recognizes 1873 as official established year.

Central University charter was granted to a group of Methodist conferences; it never opened.

Vanguard University of Southern California
Costa Mesa, CA

Est. as: Southern California Bible School – 1920
NC: Southern California Bible College – 1939
NC: Southern California College – 1959
NC: Vanguard University of Southern California – 1999

Vassar College
Poughkeepsie, NY

Est. as: Vassar Female College – 1861
NC: Vassar College – 1867

Vermont, University of & State Agricultural College
Burlington, VT

Est. as: University of Vermont – 1791
MW: State Agricultural College – 1865
NC: University of Vermont & State Agricultural College – 1865

State Agricultural College was established in 1864 adjacent to University of Vermont; the two institutions then merged.

Villa Julie College
Stevenson, MD

Est. as: Villa Julie College – 1947

270

Villanova University
Villanova#, PA

Est. as: Saint Augustine's Academy – 1811*
NC: Augustinian College of Villanova – 1842
NC: Villanova University – 1953

*Recognizes 1842 as official established year.

Known as Villanova College until 1953.

Virginia Commonwealth University
Richmond, VA

Est. as: Medical College of Virginia – 1838
MW: Richmond Professional Institute – 1968
NC: Virginia Commonwealth University – 1968

Medical College of Virginia was established as part of Hampden-Sydney College; became independent in 1854.

Virginia Intermont College
Bristol, VA

Est. as: Southwest Virginia Institute – 1884
NC: Virginia Institute – 1893
NC: Virginia Intermont College – 1910

Location changes
Glade Spring, VA – 1884
Bristol, VA – 1893

Virginia Military Institute
Lexington, VA

Est. as: Virginia Military Institute – 1839

Virginia Polytechnic Institute & State University
Blacksburg, VA

Est. as: Virginia Agricultural & Mechanical College – 1872
NC: Virginia Agricultural & Mechanical College & Polytechnic Institute – 1896
MW: Radford College – 1944
DM: Radford College – 1970
NC: Virginia Polytechnic Institute & State University – 1970

Virginia State University
Petersburg, VA

Est. as: Virginia Normal & Collegiate Institute – 1882
NC: Virginia Normal & Industrial Institute – 1902
NC: Virginia State College for Negroes – 1930
NC: Virginia State College – 1946
NC: Virginia State University – 1979

Virginia Union University
Richmond, VA

Est. as: Richmond Theological School for Freedmen – 1865
NC: Richmond Institute – 1876
MW: Richmond Theological Seminary – 1899
MW: Wayland Seminary – 1899
NC: Virginia Union University – 1899
MW: Hartshorn Memorial College – 1932
MW: Storer College – 1964

Hartshorn Memorial College was a women's institution adjacent to Virginia Union. Virginia Union was primarily men only until 1920s when Hartshorn began to curtail college level courses and women came to Virginia Union. Storer College, in Harpers Ferry, also operated by Baptist Mission Association, closed; endowment and students transferred to Virginia Union.

Virginia Wesleyan College
Norfolk, VA

Est. as: Virginia Wesleyan College – 1961

Virginia, University of
Charlottesville, VA

Est. as: University of Virginia – 1819

Charter College, an academy, was reconstituted as a college in 1816; it was re-chartered in 1819 as the University of Virginia.

Viterbo University
La Crosse, WI

Est. as: Saint Rose Normal School – 1890
NC: Saint Rose Junior College – 1934
NC: Viterbo College – 1937
NC: Viterbo University – 2000

Wabash College
Crawfordsville, IN

Est. as: Wabash Manual Labor College & Teachers Seminary – 1832
NC: Wabash College – 1851

Wagner College
Staten Island, NY

Est. as: Rochester Lutheran Proseminary – 1883
NC: Wagner Memorial Lutheran College – 1886
NC: Wagner Lutheran College – 1952
NC: Wagner College – 1959

Location changes
Rochester, NY – 1883
Staten Island, NY – 1918

Wake Forest University
Winston-Salem, NC

Est. as: Wake Forest Institute – 1834
NC: Wake Forest College – 1838
NC: Wake Forest University – 1967

Location changes
Wake Forest, NC – 1834
Winston-Salem, NC – 1956

Walla Walla College
College Place, WA

Est. as: Walla Walla College – 1892

Walsh University
North Canton, OH

Est. as: Canton College – 1958
NC: Walsh College – c1959
NC: Walsh University – 1995

Warner Pacific College
Portland, OR

Est. as: Pacific Bible College – 1937
NC: Warner Pacific College – 1959

Location changes
Spokane, WA – 1937
Portland, OR – 1940

Warner Southern College
Lake Wales, FL

Est. as: Warner Southern College – 1968

Warren Wilson College
Swannanoa, NC

Est. as: Asheville Farm School – 1894
MW: Dorland-Bell School – 1942
NC: Warren Wilson Vocational Junior College – 1942
NC: Warren Wilson College – 1966

By MO: By merger (of) *DM:* Dissolved merger (with) *MW:* Merged with *NC:* Name change (to)

Wartburg College
Waverly, IA

Est. as: Unnamed teachers seminary – 1852
MW: Unnamed teachers seminary in Waverly – 1885
NC: Wartburg College – 1885
MW: Wartburg Normal College – 1933
MW: Saint Paul-Luther College – 1935

Location changes
Saginaw, MI – 1852
Dubuque, IA – 1853
Saint Sebald, IA – 1857
Galena, IL – 1868
Mendota, IL – 1875
Waverly, IA – 1885
Clinton, IA – 1894
Waverly, IA – 1935

The teachers seminary became a theological seminary, with no formal name, in 1854 and became a theological and teachers seminary, known as Wartburg,, in 1857. In 1868, a collegiate program known as "the college" was established. In 1878, synod opened a teachers seminary in Andrew; moved it to Waverly 1879. It was then merged with the teachers seminary in Mendota in 1885. In 1894, programs separated: college to Clinton, teacher training remained in Waverly as Wartburg Teachers (1920 name change to Wartburg Normal College).

Washburn University of Topeka
Topeka, KS

Est. as: Lincoln College – 1865
NC: Washburn College – 1868
NC: Washburn University of Topeka – 1952

Washington College
Chestertown, MD

Est. as: Kent County School – 1718*
NC: Washington College – 1782

*Recognizes 1782 as official established year.

Washington State University
Pullman, WA

Est. as: Washington Agricultural College & School of Science – 1890
NC: State College of Washington, The – 1905
NC: Washington State University – 1959

Washington University in Saint Louis
Saint Louis, MO

Est. as: Eliot Seminary – 1853
NC: Washington Institute in Saint Louis – 1854
MW: Washington University – 1857
MW: Saint Louis Medical College – 1891
MW: Missouri Medical College – 1899
NC: Washington University in Saint Louis – 1976

Washington & Jefferson College
Washington, PA

Est. as: Washington Academy – 1781
NC: Washington College – 1806
MW: Jefferson College – 1865
NC: Washington & Jefferson College – 1865

After merger, classes were held at both sites until 1869.

Washington & Lee University
Lexington, VA

Est. as: Augusta Academy – 1749
NC: Liberty Hall – 1776
NC: Liberty Hall Academy – 1782
NC: Washington Academy – 1798
NC: Washington College – 1813
NC: Washington & Lee University – 1871

Location changes
Twenty miles north of Lexington, VA – 1749
Lexington, VA – 1780

Washington, University of
Seattle, WA

Est. as: Territorial University of Washington – 1861
NC: University of Washington – 1889

Wayland Baptist University
Plainview, TX

Est. as: Wayland Literary & Technical Institution – 1908
NC: Wayland Baptist College – 1910
NC: Wayland Baptist University – 1981

Wayne State College
Wayne, NE

Est. as: Nebraska Normal College – 1891*
NC: Wayne Normal School – 1910
NC: State Normal School & State Teachers College at Wayne – 1921
NC: Nebraska State Teachers College at Wayne – 1949
NC: Wayne State College – 1963

*Recognizes 1910 as official established year.

Wayne State University
Detroit, MI

Est. as: Detroit Medical College – 1868
MW: Detroit Teachers College – 1933
MW: College of the City of Detroit – 1933
NC: Colleges of the City of Detroit – 1933
NC: Wayne University – 1934
MW: Detroit City Law School – 1937
NC: Wayne State University – 1956

Waynesburg College
Waynesburg, PA

Est. as: Waynesburg College – 1849*
By MO: Greene Academy – 1849
By MO: Madison College – 1849

*Recognizes merger year, 1849, as official established year; does not recognize histories of merged institutions.

By MO: By merger (of) **DM:** Dissolved merger (with) **MW:** Merged with **NC:** Name change (to)

Weber State University
Ogden, UT

Est. as: Weber Stake Academy – 1889
NC: Weber Academy – 1908
NC: Weber Normal School – 1918
NC: Weber College – 1922
NC: Weber State College – 1959
NC: Weber State University – 1991

It was Weber STAKE Academy!

Webster University
Webster Groves, MO

Est. as: Loretto College – 1915
NC: Webster College – 1924
NC: Webster University – 1983

Wellesley College
Wellesley, MA

Est. as: Wellesley Female Seminary – 1870
NC: Wellesley College – 1873

Wells College
Aurora, NY

Est. as: Wells Seminary for the Higher Education of Young Women – 1868
NC: Wells College – 1870

Wesley College
Dover, DE

Est. as: Wilmington Conference Collegiate Institute – 1873
NC: Wesley Collegiate Institute – 1917
NC: Wesley Junior College – 1950
NC: Wesley College – 1958

Wesleyan College
Macon, GA

Est. as: Georgia Female College, The – 1836
NC: Wesleyan Female College – 1843
NC: Wesleyan College – 1917

By MO: By merger (of) **DM:** Dissolved merger (with) **MW:** Merged with **NC:** Name change (to)

278

Wesleyan University

Middletown, CT

Est. as: Wesleyan University – 1831

West Alabama, University of

Livingston, AL

Est. as: Livingston Female Academy – 1835
NC: Livingston Collegiate Institute – 1840
NC: Alabama Normal College – 1882
NC: State Teachers College, Livingston – 1929
NC: Livingston State College – 1957
NC: Livingston University – 1967
NC: University of West Alabama – 1995

West Chester University of Pennsylvania of the State System of Higher Education

West Chester, PA

Est. as: West Chester Academy – 1812*
NC: West Chester State Normal School – 1871
NC: West Chester State Teachers College – 1927
NC: West Chester State College – 1960
NC: West Chester University of Pennsylvania of the State System of Higher Education – 1983

*Recognizes 1871 as official established year.

West Florida, The University of

Pensacola, FL

Est. as: University of West Florida, The – 1963

West Georgia, State University of

Carrollton, GA

Est. as: West Georgia College – 1933
NC: State University of West Georgia – 1996

Fourth District A&M College was closed and replaced by the new institution. Bowden college also was closed when the new institution opened.

By MO: By merger (of) ***DM:*** Dissolved merger (with) ***MW:*** Merged with ***NC:*** Name change (to)

West Liberty State College
West Liberty, WV

Est. as: West Liberty Academy – 1837
NC: West Liberty State Normal School – 1870
NC: West Liberty State Teachers College – 1931
NC: West Liberty State College – 1943

West Texas A&M University
Canyon, TX

Est. as: West Texas State Normal College – 1910
NC: West Texas State Teachers College – 1923
NC: West Texas State College – 1949
NC: West Texas State University – 1963
NC: West Texas A&M University – 1993

West Virginia State College
Institute, WV

Est. as: West Virginia Colored Institute – 1891
NC: West Virginia Collegiate Institute – 1915
NC: West Virginia State College – 1929

West Virginia University
Morgantown, WV

Est. as: Monogalia Academy – 1814*
NC: Agricultural College of West Virginia – 1867
NC: West Virginia University – 1868

*Recognizes 1867 as official established year.

West Virginia University Institute of Technology
Montgomery, WV

Est. as: West Virginia University: Montgomery Preparatory Branch – 1895
NC: West Virginia Trades School – 1917
NC: New River State School – 1921
NC: New River State College – 1931
NC: West Virginia Institute of Technology – 1941
NC: West Virginia University Institute of Technology – 1996

West Virginia Wesleyan College
Buckhannon, WV

Est. as: West Virginia Conference Seminary – 1890
NC: Wesleyan University of West Virginia – 1905
NC: West Virginia Wesleyan College – 1906

Western Baptist College
Salem, OR

Est. as: Arizona Bible Institute – 1935
NC: Western Baptist Bible College & Theological Seminary – 1946
NC: Western Baptist College – 1973
Location changes
Phoenix, AZ – 1935
Oakland, CA – 1946
El Cerrito, CA – 1956
Salem, OR – 1969

Western Carolina University
Cullowhee, NC

Est. as: Cullowhee High School – 1889
NC: Cullowhee Normal & Industrial School – 1905
NC: Cullowhee State Normal School – 1925
NC: Western Carolina Teachers College – 1929
NC: Western Carolina College – 1953
NC: Western Carolina University – 1967

Western Connecticut State University
Danbury, CT

Est. as: Danbury Normal School – 1903
NC: Danbury State Teachers College – 1937
NC: Danbury State College – 1959
NC: Western Connecticut State College – 1967
NC: Western Connecticut State University – 1983

Western Illinois University
Macomb, IL

Est. as: Western Illinois State Normal School – 1899
NC: Western Illinois State Teachers College – 1921
NC: Western Illinois State College – 1947
NC: Western Illinois University – 1957

Western International University
Phoenix, AZ

Est. as: Western International University – 1978

Western Kentucky University
Bowling Green, KY

Est. as: Western Kentucky State Normal School – 1906
NC: Western Kentucky State Normal School & Teachers College – 1922
MW: Ogden College – 1928
NC: Western Kentucky State Teachers College – 1930
NC: Western Kentucky State College – 1948
MW: Bowling Green College of Commerce – 1963
NC: Western Kentucky University – 1966

Western Michigan University
Kalamazoo, MI

Est. as: Western State Normal School – 1903
NC: Western State Teachers College – 1927
NC: Western Michigan College of Education – 1941
NC: Western Michigan College – 1955
NC: Western Michigan University – 1957

Western New England College
Springfield, MA

Est. as: Northeastern University: Springfield Division – 1919
NC: Western New England College – 1951

Western New Mexico University
Silver City, NM

Est. as: Territorial Normal School – 1893
NC: New Mexico Normal School – 1912
NC: New Mexico State Teachers College – 1923
NC: New Mexico Western College – 1950
NC: Western New Mexico University – 1963

282

Western Oregon University
Monmouth, OR

Est. as: Monmouth University – 1856
MW: Bethel College – 1865
NC: Christian College – 1865
NC: Oregon State Normal School – 1882
NC: Oregon Normal School – 1911
NC: Oregon College of Education – 1937
NC: Western Oregon State College – 1981
NC: Western Oregon University – 1997

Western State College of Colorado, The
Gunnison, CO

Est. as: State Normal School – 1901
NC: Western State College of Colorado, The – 1923

Original legislation does not specify an actual name; "at Gunnison" referred to.

Western Washington University
Bellingham, WA

Est. as: State Normal School at New Watcom – 1893
NC: State Normal School at Watcom – 1901
NC: Washington State Normal School at Bellingham – 1904
NC: Western Washington College of Education – 1937
NC: Western Washington State College – 1961
NC: Western Washington University – 1977

Westfield State College
Westfield, MA

Est. as: Barre Normal School – 1838
NC: Normal School at Westfield – 1844
NC: State Teachers College at Westfield – 1932
NC: State College at Westfield – 1960
NC: Westfield State College – 1968

Location changes
Barre, MA – 1838
Westfield, MA – 1844

By MO: By merger (of) **DM:** Dissolved merger (with) **MW:** Merged with **NC:** Name change (to)

Westminster College
Fulton, MO

Est. as: Fulton College – 1851
NC: Westminster College – 1852

Westminster College
New Wilmington, PA

Est. as: Westminster Collegiate Institute – 1852
NC: Westminster College – 1897

Westminster College
Salt Lake City, UT

Est. as: Salt Lake Collegiate Institute – 1875
NC: Sheldon Jackson College – 1895
NC: Westminster College – 1903
NC: Westminster College of Salt Lake City – 1983
NC: Westminster College – 1998

Westmont College
Santa Barbara, CA

Est. as: Bible Missionary College – 1937
NC: Western Bible College – 1939
NC: Westmont College – 1940

Location changes
Los Angeles, CA – 1937
Santa Barbara, CA – 1945

Wheaton College
Norton, MA

Est. as: Wheaton Female Academy – 1834
NC: Wheaton College – 1912

Wheaton College
Wheaton, IL

Est. as: Illinois Institute – 1854*
NC: Wheaton College – 1860

*Recognizes 1860 as official established year.

Wheeling Jesuit University
Wheeling, WV

Est. as: Wheeling College – 1954
NC: Wheeling Jesuit College – 1987
NC: Wheeling Jesuit University – 1996

Wheelock College
Boston, MA

Est. as: Wheelock School – 1888
NC: Wheelock College – 1941

Whitman College
Walla Walla, WA

Est. as: Whitman Seminary – 1859
NC: Whitman College – 1889

Whittier College
Whittier, CA

Est. as: Whittier College – 1887

Whitworth College
Spokane, WA

Est. as: Sumner Academy – 1883*
NC: Whitworth College – 1890
Location changes
Sumner, WA – 1883
Tacoma, WA – 1889
Spokane, WA – 1914

*Recognizes 1890 as official established year.

Wichita State University
Wichita, KS

Est. as: Fairmount Institute, The – 1892*
NC: Fairmount College – 1895
NC: Municipal University of Wichita – 1926
NC: University of Wichita – 1956
NC: Wichita State University – 1964

*Recognizes 1895 as official established year.

By MO: By merger (of) *DM:* Dissolved merger (with) *MW:* Merged with *NC:* Name change (to)

Widener University
Chester, PA

Est. as: Bullock School – 1821
NC: Alsop School – 1846
NC: Hyatt's Select School for Boys – 1853
NC: Delaware Military Academy – 1859
NC: West Chester Military Academy – 1862
NC: Pennsylvania Military Academy – 1862
NC: Pennsylvania Military College – 1892
MW: Morton College – 1966
NC: PMC Colleges – 1966
NC: Widener College – 1972
MW: Delaware Law School – 1975
MW: Brandywine Junior College – 1976
NC: Widener University – 1979

Location changes
Wilmington, DE – 1821
West Chester, PA – 1862
Upland, PA – 1866
Chester, PA – 1868

PMC Colleges was acronym for Pennsylvania Military College and Morton College.

Wilberforce University
Wilberforce, OH

Est. as: Wilberforce University – 1856
MW: Union Seminary – 1863

Wiley College
Marshall, TX

Est. as: Wiley University – 1873
NC: Wiley College – 1929

Wilkes University
Wilkes-Barre, PA

Est. as: Bucknell University Junior College – 1933
NC: Wilkes College – 1947
NC: Wilkes University – 1993

By MO: By merger (of) ***DM:*** Dissolved merger (with) ***MW:*** Merged with ***NC:*** Name change (to)

Willamette University
Salem, OR

Est. as: Oregon Institute – 1842
NC: Willamette University – 1854

Charter is for "Willamet" University.

William Carey College
Hattiesburg, MS

Est. as: South Mississippi College – 1906
NC: Mississippi Woman's College – 1911
NC: William Carey College – 1954

William Jewell College
Liberty, MO

Est. as: William Jewell College – 1849

William Paterson University of New Jersey, The
Wayne, NJ

Est. as: Patterson City Normal School – 1855
NC: New Jersey State Normal School at Paterson – 1923
NC: New Jersey State Teachers College at Paterson – 1937
NC: Paterson State College – 1958
NC: William Paterson College of New Jersey, The – 1971
NC: William Paterson University of New Jersey, The – 1997

Location changes
Paterson, NJ – 1855
Wayne, NJ – 1951

William Penn University
Oskaloosa, IA

Est. as: Penn College – 1873
NC: William Penn College – 1933
NC: William Penn University – 2000

By MO: By merger (of) *DM:* Dissolved merger (with) *MW:* Merged with *NC:* Name change (to)

William Smith College
Geneva, NY

Est. as: William Smith College – 1908

Co-ordinate college with Hobart (men); the official name, The Colleges of the Seneca, was adopted in 1943. Originally a department of Hobart; became independent in 1943.

William Tyndale College
Farmington Hills, MI

Est. as: Detroit Bible Institute – 1945
NC: Detroit Bible College – 1960
NC: William Tyndale College – 1981

Location changes
Detroit, MI – 1945
Farmington Hills, MI – 1976

William Woods University
Fulton, MO

Est. as: Orphan School of the Christian Church of Missouri, The – 1870
NC: Daughters College – 1899
NC: William Woods College for Girls of the Christian Church of Missouri – 1901
NC: William Woods College – 1950's
NC: William Woods University – 1993

Location changes
Camden Point, MO – 1870
Fulton, MO – 1890

William & Mary, The College of
Williamsburg, VA

Est. as: College of William & Mary, The – 1693

Williams Baptist College
Walnut Ridge, AR

Est. as: Southern Baptist College – 1941
NC: Williams Baptist College – 1991

Williams College
Williamstown, MA

Est. as: Free School – 1791*
NC: Williams College – 1793

*Recognizes 1793 as official established year.

Wilmington College
New Castle, DE

Est. as: Wilmington College – 1967

Wilmington College
Wilmington, OH

Est. as: Wilmington College – 1870
MW: National Normal University – 1917

Wilson College
Chambersburg, PA

Est. as: Wilson Female College – 1869
NC: Wilson College – 1920

Wingate University
Wingate, NC

Est. as: Wingate Academy – 1896
NC: Wingate College – 1923
NC: Wingate University – 1995

Winona State University
Winona, MN

Est. as: First State Normal School of Minnesota – 1858
NC: Winona State Normal School – 1873
NC: Winona State Teachers College – 1921
NC: Winona State College – 1957
NC: Winona State University – 1975

By MO: By merger (of) *DM:* Dissolved merger (with) *MW:* Merged with *NC:* Name change (to)

Winston-Salem State University
Winston-Salem, NC

Est. as: Slater Industrial Academy – 1892
NC: Slater Industrial & State Normal School – 1897
NC: Winston-Salem Teachers College – 1925
NC: Winston-Salem State College – 1963
NC: Winston-Salem State University – 1969

Winthrop University
Rock Hill, SC

Est. as: Winthrop Training School for Teachers – 1886
NC: South Carolina Industrial & Winthrop Normal College – 1891
NC: Winthrop Normal & Industrial College of South Carolina – 1893
NC: Winthrop College – 1920
NC: Winthrop University – 1992

Location changes
Columbia, SC – 1886
Rock Hill, SC – 1895

Wisconsin Lutheran College
Milwaukee, WI

Est. as: Wisconsin Lutheran College – 1973

Wisconsin-Eau Claire, University of
Eau Claire, WI

Est. as: Eau Claire State Normal School – 1916
NC: Eau Claire State Teachers College – 1927
NC: Wisconsin State College at Eau Claire – 1951
NC: Wisconsin State University at Eau Claire – 1964
NC: University of Wisconsin-Eau Claire – 1971

Wisconsin-Green Bay, University of
Green Bay, WI

Est. as: University of Wisconsin-Green Bay – 1965

Wisconsin-La Crosse, University of
La Crosse, WI

Est. as: La Crosse State Normal School – 1909
NC: La Crosse State Teachers College – 1927
NC: Wisconsin State College at La Crosse – 1951
NC: Wisconsin State University at La Crosse – 1964
NC: University of Wisconsin-La Crosse – 1971

Wisconsin-Madison, University of
Madison, WI

Est. as: University of Wisconsin – 1849
NC: University of Wisconsin-Madison – 1968

Wisconsin-Milwaukee, University of
Milwaukee, WI

Est. as: Milwaukee Normal School – 1885
NC: Milwaukee State Teachers College – 1927
NC: Wisconsin State College at Milwaukee – 1951
MW: Wisconsin University Extension – 1955
NC: University of Wisconsin-Milwaukee – 1955

Wisconsin-Oshkosh, University of
Oshkosh, WI

Est. as: Oshkosh State Normal School – 1871
NC: Oshkosh State Teachers College – 1927
NC: Wisconsin State College at Oshkosh – 1951
NC: Wisconsin State University at Oshkosh – 1964
NC: University of Wisconsin-Oshkosh – 1971

Wisconsin-Parkside, University of
Kenosha, WI

Est. as: University of Wisconsin-Parkside – 1968

Formed by replacing University of Wisconsin Centers in Kenosa and Racine.

By MO: By merger (of) *DM:* Dissolved merger (with) *MW:* Merged with *NC:* Name change (to)

Wisconsin-Platteville, University of
Platteville, WI

Est. as: Wisconsin State Normal School, Platteville – 1866
NC: Platteville State Teachers College – 1927
NC: Wisconsin State College at Platteville – 1951
MW: Wisconsin Institute of Technology – 1959
NC: Wisconsin State College & Institute of Technology at Platteville –
  1959
NC: Wisconsin State University at Platteville – 1964
NC: University of Wisconsin-Platteville – 1971

Wisconsin-River Falls, University of
River Falls, WI

Est. as: River Falls State Normal School – 1874
NC: River Falls State Teachers College – 1927
NC: Wisconsin State College at River Falls – 1951
NC: Wisconsin State University at River Falls – 1964
NC: University of Wisconsin-River Falls – 1971

Wisconsin-Stevens Point, University of
Stevens Point, WI

Est. as: Stevens Point State Normal School – 1894
NC: Central State Teachers College – 1927
NC: Wisconsin State College at Stevens Point – 1951
NC: Wisconsin State University at Stevens Point – 1964
NC: University of Wisconsin-Stevens Point – 1971

Wisconsin-Stout, University of
Menomonie, WI

Est. as: Stout Manual Training & Domestic Science School – 1891
NC: Stout Institute – 1908
NC: Stout State College – 1955
NC: Stout State University – 1964
NC: University of Wisconsin-Stout – 1971

Wisconsin-Superior, University of
Superior, WI

Est. as: Superior Normal School – 1893
NC: Superior State Teachers College – 1927
NC: Wisconsin State College at Superior – 1951
NC: Wisconsin State University at Superior – 1964
NC: University of Wisconsin-Superior – 1971

Wisconsin-Whitewater, University of
Whitewater, WI

Est. as: Whitewater Normal School – 1868
NC: Whitewater State Teachers College – 1927
NC: Wisconsin State College at Whitewater – 1951
NC: Wisconsin State University at Whitewater – 1964
NC: University of Wisconsin-Whitewater – 1971

Wise, The University of Virginia's College at
Wise, VA

Est. as: Clinch Valley College of The University of Virginia – 1954
NC: University of Virginia's College at Wise, The – 1999

Wittenberg University
Springfield, OH

Est. as: Wittenberg College – 1845
NC: Wittenberg University – 1959

Wofford College
Spartanburg, SC

Est. as: Wofford College – 1854

Administrative merger with Columbia College, 1948-1951.

Woodbury University
Burbank, CA

Est. as: Woodbury College – 1884
NC: Isaacs-Woodbury College – 1903
NC: Woodbury College – 1922
NC: Woodbury University – 1974

Location changes
Los Angeles, CA – 1884
Burbank, CA – 1987

Wooster, The College of
Wooster, OH

Est. as: University of Wooster – 1866
NC: College of Wooster, The – 1914

Worcester Polytechnic Institute
Worcester, MA

Est. as: Worcester County Free Institute of Industrial Science – 1865
NC: Worcester Polytechnic Institute – 1887

Worcester State College
Worcester, MA

Est. as: State Normal School at Worcester – 1874
NC: Worcester State Teachers College – 1932
NC: State College at Worcester – 1960
NC: Worcester State College – 1963

Wright State University
Dayton, OH

Est. as: Dayton Campus of Miami University & Ohio State University – 1964
NC: Wright State University – 1965

Wyoming, University of
Laramie, WY

Est. as: University of Wyoming – 1886

By MO: By merger (of) *DM:* Dissolved merger (with) *MW:* Merged with *NC:* Name change (to)

Xavier University
Cincinnati, OH

Est. as: Athenaeum, The – 1831
NC: Saint Xavier College – 1840
NC: Xavier University – 1930
MW: Edgecliff College – 1980

Xavier University of Louisiana
New Orleans, LA

Est. as: Xavier University – 1925
NC: Xavier University of Louisiana – 1966

Began as a high school in 1915; college of arts & sciences established in 1925.

Y

Yale University
New Haven, CT

Est. as: Collegiate School, The – 1701
NC: Yale College – 1717
NC: Yale University – 1887

Location changes
Branford CT – 1701
Killingsworth (now Clinton), CT – 1702
Saybrook (now Old Saybrook), CT – 1707
New Haven, CT – 1716

Yeshiva University
New York, NY

Est. as: Yeshiva Eitz Chaim – 1886
MW: Rabbi Isaac Elchanan Theological Seminary – 1915
NC: Rabbi Isaac Elchanan Theological Seminary – 1915
NC: Rabbi Isaac Elchanan Theological Seminary & Yeshiva College – 1928
NC: Yeshiva University – 1945

York College
York, NE

Est. as: Franklin Academy – 1886*
NC: York College – 1890
MW: York Business College – 1916
MW: Kansas City University – 1931

Location changes
Gibbon, NE – 1886
York, NE – 1890

*Recognizes 1890 as official established year.

Closed in 1954 after Evangelical United Brethren Church trans-ferred its financial support to Westmar College; re-opened in 1956 under United Church of Christ. In 1928, received part of assets of Philomath (IL) College. Franklin Academy was also known as Gib-bon Collegiate Institute.

York College of Pennsylvania
York, PA

Est. as: York Academy – 1787
NC: York County Academy – 1797
MW: York Collegiate Institute – 1929
NC: York Collegiate Institute – 1929
NC: Junior College of the York Collegiate Institute, The – 1941
NC: York Junior College – 1947
NC: York College of Pennsylvania – 1968

College level courses added to York Collegiate Institute in 1941; the institute closed in 1947.

York College of the City University of New York
Jamaica, NY

Est. as: York College of the City University of New York – 1966

By MO: By merger (of) *DM:* Dissolved merger (with) *MW:* Merged with *NC:* Name change (to)

Youngstown State University

Youngstown, OH

Est. as: School of Law of the Youngstown Association School – 1908

NC: Youngstown Institute of Technology – 1921

NC: Youngstown College – 1928

NC: Youngstown University – 1955

NC: Youngstown State University – 1967

Former Names

Former Name	Current Name
A M Chesbrough Seminary	Roberts Wesleyan College
Abilene Baptist College	Hardin-Simmons University
Abilene Christian College	Abilene Christian University
Adams State Normal School	Adams State College
Adams State Teachers College of Southern Colorado	Adams State College
AddRan Christian University	Texas Christian University
AddRan Male & Female Academy	Texas Christian University
Adelbert College of Western Reserve University	Case Western Reserve University
Adelphi College	Adelphi University
Adelphi Suffolk College	Dowling College
African Institute, The	Cheyney University of Pennsylvania of the State System of Higher Education
Agnes Scott Institute	Agnes Scott College
Agricultural College of Colorado	Colorado State University
Agricultural College of Pennsylvania	Pennsylvania State University, The
Agricultural College of the State of Michigan	Michigan State University
Agricultural College of the State of Montana	Montana State University-Bozeman
Agricultural College of the State of Oregon	Oregon State University
Agricultural College of Utah	Utah State University of Agriculture & Applied Science
Agricultural College of West Virginia	West Virginia University
Agricultural & Mechanical College of Alabama	Auburn University
Agricultural & Mechanical College of Texas	Texas A&M University
Agricultural & Mechanical College of the State of Mississippi	Mississippi State University

Former Name	Current Name
Agricultural & Technical College of North Carolina	North Carolina Agricultural & Technical State University
Agriculture & Mechanical Arts, College of	Hawaii at Manoa, University of
Akron, The Municipal University of	Akron, The University of
Alabama Agricultural & Mechanical College	Alabama Agricultural & Mechanical University
Alabama Bible & Manual Training Institute	Albany State University
Alabama Christian College	Faulkner University
Alabama College	Montevallo, University of
Alabama Colored Peoples University	Alabama State University
Alabama Conference Female College	Huntingdon College
Alabama Girls Industrial School	Montevallo, University of
Alabama Girls Technical Institute	Montevallo, University of
Alabama in Birmingham, The University of	Alabama at Birmingham, The University of
Alabama Lutheran Academy & College	Concordia College
Alabama Normal College	West Alabama, University of
Alabama Polytechnic Institute	Auburn University
Alabama State College	Alabama State University
Alabama State College for Negroes	Alabama State University
Alabama's Huntsville Campus, The University of	Alabama in Huntsville, The University of
Alabama's Huntsville Center, The University of	Alabama in Huntsville, The University of
Alabama: Birmingham Extension Center, The University of	Alabama at Birmingham, The University of
Alameda County State College	California State University, Hayward
Alaska Agricultural College & School of Mines, The	Alaska Fairbanks, University of
Alaska Methodist University	Alaska Pacific University
Alaska, Anchorage, University of	Alaska Anchorage, University of
Alaska, Fairbanks, University of	Alaska Fairbanks, University of
Alaska, Juneau, University of	Alaska Southeast, University of
Alaska, University of	Alaska Fairbanks, University of
Albany Collegiate Institute	Lewis & Clark College
Albany State College	Albany State University
Albright College of the Evangelical Church	Albright College
Alcorn Agricultural & Mechanical College	Alcorn State University

Former Name	Current Name
Alcorn University	Alcorn State University
Alfred Academy	Alfred University
Alison's Academy	Delaware, University of
Allentown College for Women	Cedar Crest College
Allentown College of Saint Francis de Sales	DeSales University
Allentown Collegiate Institute	Muhlenberg College
Allentown Collegiate & Military Institute	Muhlenberg College
Allentown Female College	Cedar Crest College
Allentown Seminary	Muhlenberg College
Almira College	Greenville College
Alsop School	Widener University
Alta Vista Agricultural College	Prairie View A&M University
Alverno Teachers College	Alverno College
American Literary, Scientific, & Military Academy	Norwich University
American University, The	American University
Anderson Bible Training School	Anderson University
Anderson Bible Training School & Seminary	Anderson University
Anderson College	Anderson University
Anderson College & Technological Seminary	Anderson University
Angelo State College	Angelo State University
Anna Maria College for Women	Anna Maria College
Anna S C Blake Manual Training School	California, Santa Barbara, University of
Antioch College	Antioch University
Appalachian State Normal School	Appalachian State University
Appalachian State Teachers College	Appalachian State University
Appalachian Training School for Teachers	Appalachian State University
Arizona Bible Institute	Western Baptist College
Arizona Normal School	Arizona State University
Arizona State College at Flagstaff	Northern Arizona University
Arizona State College at Tempe	Arizona State University
Arizona State Teachers College at Flagstaff	Northern Arizona University
Arizona State Teachers College at Tempe	Arizona State University
Arizona Territorial Normal School at Tempe	Arizona State University

Former Name	Current Name
Arkadelphia Methodist College	Henderson State University
Arkansas Agricultural & Mechanical College	Arkansas at Monticello, University of
Arkansas Agricultural, Mechanical & Normal College	Arkansas at Pine Bluff, University of
Arkansas College	Lyon College
Arkansas Cumberland College	Ozarks, University of the
Arkansas Industrial University	Arkansas, University of
Arkansas Polytechnic College	Arkansas Tech University
Arkansas State College	Arkansas State University
Arkansas State Normal School	Central Arkansas, University of
Arkansas State Teachers College	Central Arkansas, University of
Arlington College	Texas at Arlington, The University of
Arlington State College	Texas at Arlington, The University of
Arlington Training School	Texas at Arlington, The University of
Armour Institute	Illinois Institute of Technology
Armour Institute of Technology	Illinois Institute of Technology
Armstrong College	Armstrong Atlantic State University
Armstrong Junior College of Savannah	Armstrong Atlantic State University
Armstrong State College	Armstrong Atlantic State University
Aroostook State College	Maine at Presque Isle, University of
Aroostook State College of the University of Maine	Maine at Presque Isle, University of
Aroostook State Normal School	Maine at Presque Isle, University of
Aroostook State Teachers College	Maine at Presque Isle, University of
Arts & Technological College	Texas A&M University-Corpus Christi
Asheville Farm School	Warren Wilson College
Asheville-Biltmore College	North Carolina at Asheville, The University of
Ashland Academy	Southern Oregon University
Ashland College	Ashland University
Ashland College & Normal School	Southern Oregon University
Ashmum Institute	Lincoln University
Assissi Junior College	Saint Francis, University of
Athenaeum, The	Rochester Institute of Technology
Athenaeum, The	Xavier University
Athens Female College	Tennessee Wesleyan College
Athens School of the University of Chattanooga	Tennessee Wesleyan College
Atlanta Baptist College	Morehouse College

Former Name	Current Name
Atlanta Baptist Female Seminary	Spelman College
Atlanta Baptist Seminary	Morehouse College
Atlantic Christian College	Barton College
Auburndale Female Seminary	Lasell College
Augsburg College & Theological Seminary	Augsburg College
Augsburg Seminarium	Augsburg College
Augusta Academy	Washington & Lee University
Augusta College	Augusta State University
Augusta Female Academy	Mary Baldwin College
Augusta Institute	Morehouse College
Augustana College & Normal School	Augustana College
Augustana College & Seminary	Augustana College
Augustana College & Theological Seminary	Augustana College
Augustana Seminary	Augustana College
Augustana Seminary & Academy	Augustana College
Augustana Seminary & Marshall Academy	Augustana College
Augustinian College of the Merrimack Valley	Merrimack College
Augustinian College of Villanova	Villanova University
Aurora College	Aurora University
Austin Peay Normal School	Austin Peay State University
Austin Peay State College	Austin Peay State University
Averett College	Averett University
Azusa College	Azusa Pacific University
Azusa Pacific College	Azusa Pacific University
A. & M. College for the Colored Race	North Carolina Agricultural & Technical State University

B

Baldwin Institute	Baldwin-Wallace College
Baldwin School	Macalester College
Baldwin University	Baldwin-Wallace College
Baldwin University	Macalester College
Ball Teachers College, Indiana State Normal School, Eastern Division	Ball State University
Baltimore Normal School	Bowie State University
Baltimore Normal School #3	Bowie State University
Baptist Bible Institute	Mid-Continent College

304

Former Name	Current Name
Baptist Bible Institute of Grand Rapids, Michigan	Cornerstone University
Baptist Bible Institute & School of Theology of Grand Rapids Michigan	Cornerstone University
Baptist College at Charleston	Charleston Southern University
Baptist College at McMinnville	Linfield College
Baptist Female Seminary	Averett University
Baptist Female University	Meredith College
Baptist Institute	Arkansas Baptist College
Baptist University for Women	Meredith College
Baptist University of Oklahoma, The	Oklahoma Baptist University, The
Barboursville College	Charleston, University of
Barboursville Seminary	Charleston, University of
Barre Normal School	Westfield State College
Barry College	Barry University
Bartlesville Wesleyan College	Oklahoma Wesleyan University
Battle Creek College	Andrews University
Bay Path Institute	Bay Path College
Bay Path Junior College	Bay Path College
Bay Path Secretarial School	Bay Path College
Baylor College for Women	Mary Hardin-Baylor, The University of
Baylor Female College	Mary Hardin-Baylor, The University of
Baylor University	Mary Hardin-Baylor, The University of
Beaver College	Arcadia University
Beaver College & Musical Institute	Arcadia University
Beaver Female Seminary	Arcadia University
Beckley College	Mountain State University
Belhaven College for Young Ladies	Belhaven College
Belhaven College & Industrial Institute	Belhaven College
Bellarmine College	Bellarmine University
Bellarmine College	Fairfield University
Bellevue College	Bellevue University
Belmont College	Belmont University
Belmont Junior College	Belmont University
Bemidji State College	Bemidji State University
Bemidji State Normal School	Bemidji State University
Benedict Institute	Benedict College
Benedictine High School	Saint Leo University
Benjamin P Cheney Academy	Eastern Washington University
Bentany-Peniel College	Southern Nazarene University

Former Name	Current Name
Bentley College of Accounting & Finance	Bentley College
Bentley School of Accounting & Finance	Bentley College
Berkeley Bible Seminary	Chapman University
Bernard M Baruch School of Business & Public Administration of the City College of New York	Bernard M Baruch College of the City University of New York
Berry School	Berry College
Berry Schools, The	Berry College
Bethany Academy	Bethany College
Bethany Bible College	Bethany College of the Assemblies of God
Bethany Nazarene College	Southern Nazarene University
Bethel Academy & Theological Seminary	Bethel College
Bethel College of the Mennonite Church of North America, The	Bethel College
Bethel College & Seminary	Bethel College
Bethel Institute	Bethel College
Bethel Seminary	Bethel College
Bethlehem Female Seminary	Moravian College & Moravian Theological Seminary
Bible Institute of Los Angeles	Biola University
Bible Missionary College	Westmont College
Biddle Memorial Institute	Johnson C Smith University
Biddle University	Johnson C Smith University
Big Rapids Industrial School	Ferris State University
Biltmore Junior College	North Carolina at Asheville, The University of
Bimidji State Teachers College	Bemidji State University
Biola College	Biola University
Birdwood Junior College	Thomas University
Biscayne College	Saint Thomas University
Black Hills State College	Black Hills State University
Black Hills Teachers College	Black Hills State University
Blackburn Theological Seminary	Blackburn University, The
Bliss & Harrington's Business College & School of Shorthand	Teikyo Post University
Bloomfield College & Seminary	Bloomfield College
Bloomfield Theological Seminary	Bloomfield College
Bloomsburg Academy	Bloomsburg University of Pennsylvania of the State System of Higher Education

Former Name	Current Name
Bloomsburg Literary Institute	Bloomsburg University of Pennsylvania of the State System of Higher Education
Bloomsburg Literary Institute & State Normal School	Bloomsburg University of Pennsylvania of the State System of Higher Education
Bloomsburg State College	Bloomsburg University of Pennsylvania of the State System of Higher Education
Bloomsburg State Normal School	Bloomsburg University of Pennsylvania of the State System of Higher Education
Bloomsburg State Teachers College	Bloomsburg University of Pennsylvania of the State System of Higher Education
Blount College	Tennessee, The University of
Blue Mountain Female College	Blue Mountain College
Blue Mountain Female Institute	Blue Mountain College
Bluefield Colored Institute	Bluefield State College
Bluefield State Teachers College	Bluefield State College
Boca Raton, College of	Lynn University
Boiling Springs High School	Gardner-Webb University
Boise College	Boise State University
Boise Junior College	Boise State University
Boise State College	Boise State University
Boston Conservatory of Oratory	Emerson College
Boston Missionary Training Institute	Gordon College, The United College of Gordon & Barrington
Boston Missionary Training School	Gordon College, The United College of Gordon & Barrington
Boston Theological School	Boston University
Boulder, University at	Colorado at Boulder, University of
Bowie State College	Bowie State University
Bowling Green State College	Bowling Green State University
Bowling Green State Normal College	Bowling Green State University
Boy's Industrial School	Berry College
Bradley Polytechnic Institute	Bradley University
Branch Agricultural College of Utah	Southern Utah State University
Branch Normal College	Arkansas at Pine Bluff, University of
Branch Normal School of the University of Utah	Southern Utah State University
Brenau College	Brenau University
Brescia College	Brescia University
Brevard Engineering College	Florida Institute of Technology

Former Name	Current Name
Brewton-Parker Institute	Brewton-Parker College
Brewton-Parker Junior College	Brewton-Parker College
Briar Cliff College	Briar Cliff University
Bridgewater Normal School	Bridgewater State College
Bridgewater State Normal School	Bridgewater State College
Bridgewater State Teachers College	Bridgewater State College
Brigham Young Academy	Brigham Young University
Bristol High School	King College
Brockport Collegiate Institute	New York College at Brockport, State University of
Brockport State Normal School	New York College at Brockport, State University of
Brockway College	Ripon College
Brooklyn College	Brooklyn College of the City University of New York
Brooklyn Collegiate & Polytechnic Institute	Polytechnic University
Brown Theological Institute	Edward Waters College
Brown University	Edward Waters College
Brown's Schoolhouse	Duke University
Buchtel College	Akron, The University of
Bucknell University Junior College	Wilkes University
Buena Vista College	Buena Vista University
Buffalo Male & Female Institute	Milligan College
Buffalo Normal School	New York College at Buffalo, State University of
Buffalo, University of	New York University Center at Buffalo, State University of
Buie's Creek Academy	Campbell University
Bullock School	Widener University
Buncombe County Junior College	North Carolina at Asheville, The University of
Burlington Business College	Champlain College
Burlington Collegiate Institute	Champlain College

C

Caldwell College for Women	Caldwell College
California Academy	California University of Pennsylvania of the State System of Higher Education
California at Los Angeles, University of	California, Los Angeles, University of
California Baptist College	California Baptist University

Former Name	Current Name
California Christian College	Chapman University
California Lutheran College	California Lutheran University
California Polytechnic School	California Polytechnic State University, San Luis Obispo
California State College	California University of Pennsylvania of the State System of Higher Education
California State College at Fullerton	California State University, Fullerton
California State College at Hayward	California State University, Hayward
California State College at Los Angeles	California State University, Los Angeles
California State College, Bakersfield	California State University, Bakersfield
California State College, Chico	California State University, Chico
California State College, Dominquez Hills	California State University, Dominquez Hills
California State College, Fresno	California State University, Fresno
California State College, Fullerton	California State University, Fullerton
California State College, Long Beach	California State University, Long Beach
California State College, Los Angeles	California State University, Los Angeles
California State College, San Bernardino	California State University, San Bernardino
California State College, Sonoma	Sonoma State University
California State College, Stanislaus	California State University, Stanislaus
California State Normal School	California University of Pennsylvania of the State System of Higher Education
California State Normal School	San Jose State University
California State Polytechnic College	California Polytechnic State University, San Luis Obispo
California State Polytechnic School	California Polytechnic State University, San Luis Obispo
California State Teachers College	California University of Pennsylvania of the State System of Higher Education
California State University at Humboldt	Humboldt State University
California State University, San Diego	San Diego State University
California State University, San Francisco	San Francisco State University
California State University, San Jose	San Jose State University
California Wesleyan University	Pacific, University of the
California Western University	Alliant International University
California, Riverside Campus, University of	California, Riverside, University of
California, Scripps Institition of Oceanography, University of	California, San Diego, University of
California, Southern Branch, University of	California, Los Angeles, University of

Former Name	Current Name
California, University of	California, Berkeley, University of
Calumet College	Calumet College of Saint Joseph
Cameron College	Cameron University
Cameron State Agricultural College	Cameron University
Cameron State School of Agriculture	Cameron University
Campbell College	Campbell University
Campbell Junior College	Campbell University
Campbellsville College	Campbellsville University
Cane Hill College	Ozarks, University of the
Caney Creek Community Center	Alice Lloyd College
Caney Junior College	Alice Lloyd College
Canton College	Walsh University
Cardinal Stritch College	Cardinal Stritch University
Carlisle Grammar School	Dickinson College
Carlisle Military Academy	Texas at Arlington, The University of
Carnegie Institute of Technology	Carnegie Mellon University
Carnegie Technical Schools	Carnegie Mellon University
Carrier Seminary of Western Pennsylvania	Clarion University of Pennsylvania of the State System of Higher Education
Carson College	Carson-Newman College
Cass County University	Nebraska Wesleyan University, The
Castleton Normal School	Castleton State College
Castleton Seminary	Castleton State College
Castleton Seminary & State Normal School	Castleton State College
Castleton Teachers College	Castleton State College
Catawba High School	Catawba College
Cathedral College	Gannon University
Catherine Spalding College	Spalding University
Catholepistemiad (Universitstis Michigania)	Michigan, University of
Catholic Junior College	Aquinas College
Cazenovia Junior College for Women	Cazenovia College
Cazenovia Seminary Junior College	Cazenovia College
Cazenovia Seminary, The	Cazenovia College
Cedar Rapids Collegiate Institute	Coe College
Cedarville College	Cedarville University
Centenary Biblical Institute	Morgan State University
Centenary College for Women	Centenary College
Centenary Collegiate Institute	Centenary College

310

Former Name	Current Name
Centenary Junior College	Centenary College
Central Christian College	Oklahoma Christian University
Central College	Central Methodist College
Central College	Huntington College
Central Collegiate Institute	Hendrix College
Central Connecticut State College	Central Connecticut State University
Central High School of Needle Trade	New York Fashion Institute of Technology, State University of
Central Institute	Hendrix College
Central Mennonite College	Bluffton College
Central Michigan College	Central Michigan University
Central Michigan College of Education	Central Michigan University
Central Michigan Normal School	Central Michigan University
Central Michigan Normal School & Business Institute	Central Michigan University
Central Missouri State College	Central Missouri State University
Central Missouri State Teachers College	Central Missouri State University
Central Pennsylvania College	Albright College
Central Pilgrim College	Oklahoma Wesleyan University
Central State College	Central Oklahoma, University of
Central State College	Central State University
Central State Normal School	Central Oklahoma, University of
Central State Normal School	Lock Haven University of Pennsylvania of the State System of Higher Education
Central State Teachers College	Central Michigan University
Central State Teachers College	Wisconsin-Stevens Point, University of
Central State Teachers College	Central Oklahoma, University of
Central State University	Central Oklahoma, University of
Central University of Iowa	Central College
Central University of Kentucky	Centre College
Central University of the Methodist Episcopal Church, South, The	Vanderbilt University
Central Washington College of Education	Central Washington University
Central Washington State College	Central Washington University
Central Wesleyan College	Southern Wesleyan University
Chaminade College of Honolulu	Chaminade University of Honolulu
Champlain College of Commerce	Champlain College
Chapman College	Chapman University

Former Name	Current Name
Charlotte College	North Carolina at Charlotte, The University of
Charlotte Female Institute	Queens College
Chattanooga University	Tennessee at Chattanooga, The University of
Chattanooga, University of	Tennessee at Chattanooga, The University of
Cherokee Baptist Female Academy	Shorter College
Cherokee Indian Normal School of Robeson County, The	North Carolina at Pembroke, The University of
Cherokee National Female Seminary	Northeastern State University
Chestnut Hill College of the Sisters of Saint Joseph	Chestnut Hill College
Cheyney State College	Cheyney University of Pennsylvania of the State System of Higher Education
Cheyney State Normal School	Cheyney University of Pennsylvania of the State System of Higher Education
Cheyney State Teachers College	Cheyney University of Pennsylvania of the State System of Higher Education
Cheyney Training School for Teachers	Cheyney University of Pennsylvania of the State System of Higher Education
Chicago Kindergarten College	National-Louis University
Chicago Kindergarten Training School	National-Louis University
Chicago Normal College	Chicago State University
Chicago Normal School Chicago Board of Education	Chicago State University
Chicago State College	Chicago State University
Chicago Teachers College	Chicago State University
Chicago Teachers College, North Side	Northeastern Illinois University
Chicago Teachers College, South	Chicago State University
Chicago Undergraduate Division of the University of Illinois	Illinois at Chicago, University of
Chico State Normal School	California State University, Chico
Childers Classical Institute	Abilene Christian University
Chili Seminary	Roberts Wesleyan College
Chowan Baptist Female Institute	Chowan College
Christ College Irvine	Concordia University
Christian College	Columbia College
Christian College	Western Oregon University
Christian Female College	Columbia College

Former Name	Current Name
Christian Normal Institute	Kentucky Christian College
Christian University	Culver-Stockton College
Christian Workers Training School	Malone College
Christopher Newport College	Christopher Newport University
Church College of Hawaii, The	Brigham Young University-Hawaii
Citrus Experiment Station	California, Riverside, University of
City College, The	City College of the City University of New York
Claflin College	Claflin University
Claflin College	South Carolina State University
Claremont College Undergraduate School for Men	Claremont McKenna College
Claremont Men's College	Claremont McKenna College
Clarion State College	Clarion University of Pennsylvania of the State System of Higher Education
Clarion State Normal School	Clarion University of Pennsylvania of the State System of Higher Education
Clarion State Teachers College	Clarion University of Pennsylvania of the State System of Higher Education
Clark & Erskine Seminary	Erskine College
Clayton State College	Clayton College & State University
Clemson Agricultural College of South Carolina	Clemson University
Cleveland Bible College	Malone College
Cleveland Bible Institute	Malone College
Cleveland Bible Institute & Training School	Malone College
Cleveland University	John Carroll University
Cleveland YMCA School of Technology	Cleveland State University
Clinch Valley College of The University of Virginia	Wise, The University of Virginia's College at
Clinton College	Presbyterian College
Coastal Carolina Junior College	Coastal Carolina University
Coastal Carolina Junior College of the College of Charleston	Coastal Carolina University
Coe Collegiate Institute	Coe College
Coker College for Women	Coker College
Colby Academy, The	Colby-Sawyer College
Colby College-New Hampshire	Colby-Sawyer College
Colby Junior College for Women	Colby-Sawyer College
Colby School for Girls	Colby-Sawyer College

Former Name	Current Name
Colby University	Colby College
Colby-Sawyer College	Colby-Sawyer College
College of Agriculture at Davis	California, Davis, University of
College of Industrial Arts	Texas Woman's University
College Seraphique	New England, University of
College & Academy & Charitable School in the Province of Philadelphia	Pennsylvania, University of
Collegiate School, The	Yale University
Colorado Agricultural & Mechanical College	Colorado State University
Colorado Christian College	Colorado Christian University
Colorado Electronic Technical College	Colorado Technical University
Colorado Electronic Training, Inc.	Colorado Technical University
Colorado Seminary	Denver, University of
Colorado Springs Bible College	Oklahoma Wesleyan University
Colorado Springs Bible Training School	Oklahoma Wesleyan University
Colorado State College	Northern Colorado, University of
Colorado State College of Agriculture & Mechanic Arts, The	Colorado State University
Colorado State College of Education	Northern Colorado, University of
Colorado State Teachers College	Northern Colorado, University of
Colorado Technical College	Colorado Technical University
Colorado-Colorado Springs Center, University of	Colorado at Colorado Springs, University of
Colorado-Denver Center, University of	Colorado at Denver, University of
Colored Agricultural & Normal University	Langston University
Colored Industrial & Agricultural School	Grambling State University
Colored Methodist Episcopal High School	Lane College
Columbia College	Loras College
Columbia College in the City of New York	Columbia University in the City of New York
Columbia College of Chicago	Columbia College Chicago
Columbia College of Expression	Columbia College Chicago
Columbia College of Oratory	Columbia College Chicago
Columbia Female Academy	Stephens College
Columbia Female Baptist Academy	Stephens College
Columbia Female College, The	Columbia College
Columbia Institution for the Instruction of the Deaf & Dumb & Blind	Gallaudet University

Former Name	Current Name
Columbia University	Portland, University of
Columbian College in the District of Columbia, The	George Washington University, The
Columbian University	George Washington University, The
Columbus College	Columbus State University
Combined Normal & Industrial Department at Wilberforce University	Central State University
Concord State Normal School	Concord College
Concord State Teachers College	Concord College
Concordia College	Concordia University
Concordia College	Concordia University Wisconsin
Concordia College	Concordia University, Saint Paul
Concordia College Wisconsin	Concordia University Wisconsin
Concordia Gymnasium	Concordia College
Concordia Junior College	Concordia University
Concordia Lutheran College	Concordia University at Austin
Concordia Lutheran Junior College	Concordia University
Concordia Teachers College	Concordia University
Connecticut Agricultural College	Connecticut, University of
Connecticut College for Women	Connecticut College
Connecticut College of Commerce	Quinnipiac University
Connecticut State College	Connecticut, University of
Cook County Normal School	Chicago State University
Cooper College	Sterling College
Cooper Memorial College	Sterling College
Cooper-Limestone Institute	Limestone College
Coppin State Teachers College	Coppin State College
Coppin Teachers College	Coppin State College
Cornerstone College & Grand Rapids Baptist Seminary	Cornerstone University
Corpus Christi State University	Texas A&M University-Corpus Christi
Corpus Christi, University of	Texas A&M University-Corpus Christi
Cortland State Normal School	New York College at Cortland, State University of
Corvallis Academy	Oregon State University
Corvallis Agricultural College	Oregon State University
Corvallis College	Oregon State University
Corvallis College & Agricultural College of Oregon	Oregon State University
Corvallis College & Oregon Agricultural College	Oregon State University

Former Name	Current Name
Corvallis College & Oregon State Agricultural College	Oregon State University
Corvallis College & State Agricultural College	Oregon State University
Corvallis State Agricultural College	Oregon State University
Croatan Normal School	North Carolina at Pembroke, The University of
Cullowhee High School	Western Carolina University
Cullowhee Normal & Industrial School	Western Carolina University
Cullowhee State Normal School	Western Carolina University
Cumberland College	Cumberland University
Cumberland Valley State Normal School	Shippensburg University of Pennsylvania of the State System of Higher Education

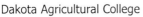

D

Former Name	Current Name
Dakota Agricultural College	South Dakota State University
Dakota Collegiate Institute	Sioux Falls, University of
Dakota Normal School	Dakota State University
Dakota Northwestern University	Minot State University
Dakota State College	Dakota State University
Dakota University	Dakota Wesleyan University
Dakota, University of	South Dakota, The University of
Dallas Baptist College	Dallas Baptist University
Dana College & Trinity Seminary	Dana College
Dana Hall School, Post-secondary division of	Pine Manor College
Danbury Normal School	Western Connecticut State University
Danbury State College	Western Connecticut State University
Danbury State Teachers College	Western Connecticut State University
Danville College for Young Women	Averett University
Danville Female Institute	Averett University
Daughters College	William Woods University
David Lipscomb College	David Lipscomb University
Dayton Campus of Miami University & Ohio State University	Wright State University
Daytona Literary & Industrial School for Training Negro Girls	Bethune-Cookman College
Daytona-Cookman Collegiate Institute	Bethune-Cookman College
Decatur Baptist College	Dallas Baptist University

Former Name	Current Name
Decatur College & Industrial School of the James Millikin University	Millikin University
Decatur Female Seminary	Agnes Scott College
Defiance Female Seminary	Defiance College, The
Deforest Training School	DeVry University
DeLand Academy	Stetson University
DeLand Academy & College	Stetson University
DeLand University	Stetson University
Delaware College	Delaware, University of
Delaware Conference Academy	Maryland Eastern Shore, University of
Delaware Military Academy	Widener University
Delaware State College	Delaware State University
Delaware Valley College of Science & Agriculture	Delaware Valley College
Delta State College	Delta State University
Delta State Teachers College	Delta State University
Denver Bible College	Colorado Christian University
Denver Bible Institute	Colorado Christian University
Department of Correspondence & Extension in Denver	Colorado at Denver, University of
Department of Eastern Baptist Theological Seminary	Eastern University
Deseret, University of	Utah, University of
Detroit Bible College	William Tyndale College
Detroit Bible Institute	William Tyndale College
Detroit Medical College	Wayne State University
Detroit, Colleges of the City of	Wayne State University
DeVry Institute of Technology	DeVry University
DeVry Technical Institute	DeVry University
Dickinson Junior College	Lycoming College
Dickinson Normal School	Dickinson State University
Dickinson Seminary	Lycoming College
Dickinson State College	Dickinson State University
Dickinson State Teachers College	Dickinson State University
District of Columbia Teachers College	District of Columbia, University of the
Dixie, University of	Tennessee Technological University
Dominican College of San Rafael	Dominican University of California
Dominican Junior College of Blauvelt	Dominican College
Drew Theological Seminary	Drew University
Drexel Institute of Arts, Sciences, & Industry	Drexel University

Former Name	Current Name
Drexel Institute of Technology	Drexel University
Drury College	Drury University
Dubuque College	Loras College
Dubuque German College & Seminary	Dubuque, University of
Due West, The Academy at	Erskine College
Duluth State Normal School	Minnesota, Duluth, University of
Duluth State Teachers College	Minnesota, Duluth, University of
Dunlora Academy	Richmond, University of
Duquesne University	Duquesne University of the Holy Ghost
Durham State Normal School	North Carolina Central University

E

Former Name	Current Name
East Alabama Male College	Auburn University
East Carolina College	East Carolina University
East Carolina Teacher Training School	East Carolina University
East Carolina Teachers College	East Carolina University
East Central Oklahoma State University	East Central University
East Central State College	East Central University
East Central State Normal School	East Central University
East Central State Teachers College	East Central University
East Florida Seminary	Florida, University of
East Stroudsburg Normal School	East Stroudsburg University of Pennsylvania of the State System of Higher Education
East Stroudsburg State College	East Stroudsburg University of Pennsylvania of the State System of Higher Education
East Stroudsburg State Normal School	East Stroudsburg University of Pennsylvania of the State System of Higher Education
East Stroudsburg State Teachers College	East Stroudsburg University of Pennsylvania of the State System of Higher Education
East Tennessee College	Tennessee, The University of
East Tennessee State College	East Tennessee State University
East Tennessee State Normal School	East Tennessee State University
East Tennessee State Teachers College	East Tennessee State University
East Tennessee University	Tennessee, The University of
East Tennessee Wesleyan College	Tennessee Wesleyan College

Former Name	Current Name
East Tennessee Wesleyan University	Tennessee Wesleyan College
East Texas Baptist College	East Texas Baptist University
East Texas Normal College	Texas A&M University-Commerce
East Texas State College	Texas A&M University-Commerce
East Texas State Normal College	Texas A&M University-Commerce
East Texas State Teachers College	Texas A&M University-Commerce
East Texas State University	Texas A&M University-Commerce
Eastern Baptist College	Eastern University
Eastern College	Eastern University
Eastern Connecticut State College	Eastern Connecticut State University
Eastern Illinois State College	Eastern Illinois University
Eastern Illinois State Normal School	Eastern Illinois University
Eastern Illinois State Teachers College	Eastern Illinois University
Eastern Indiana Normal University	Ball State University
Eastern Kentucky State College	Eastern Kentucky University
Eastern Kentucky State Normal School	Eastern Kentucky University
Eastern Kentucky State Normal School & Teachers College	Eastern Kentucky University
Eastern Kentucky State Teachers College	Eastern Kentucky University
Eastern Mennonite College and Seminary	Eastern Mennonite University
Eastern Mennonite School	Eastern Mennonite University
Eastern Michigan College	Eastern Michigan University
Eastern Montana College	Montana State University-Billings
Eastern Montana College of Education	Montana State University-Billings
Eastern Montana State Normal School	Montana State University-Billings
Eastern New Mexico College	Eastern New Mexico University
Eastern New Mexico Junior College	Eastern New Mexico University
Eastern Oregon College	Eastern Oregon University
Eastern Oregon College of Education	Eastern Oregon University
Eastern Oregon Normal School	Eastern Oregon University
Eastern Oregon State College	Eastern Oregon University
Eastern State Normal School	Dakota State University
Eastern State Teachers College	Dakota State University
Eastern Washington College of Education	Eastern Washington University
Eastern Washington State College	Eastern Washington University

Former Name	Current Name
Eau Claire State Normal School	Wisconsin-Eau Claire, University of
Eau Claire State Teachers College	Wisconsin-Eau Claire, University of
Ebenezer Mitchell Home & School	Pfeiffer University
Edgewood College of the Sacred Heart	Edgewood College
Edinboro Academy	Edinboro University of Pennsylvania of the State System of Higher Education
Edinboro Normal School	Edinboro University of Pennsylvania of the State System of Higher Education
Edinboro State College	Edinboro University of Pennsylvania of the State System of Higher Education
Edinboro State Normal School	Edinboro University of Pennsylvania of the State System of Higher Education
Edinboro State Teachers College	Edinboro University of Pennsylvania of the State System of Higher Education
Edinburg College	Texas-Pan American, The University of
Edinburg Junior College	Texas-Pan American, The University of
Edinburg Regional College	Texas-Pan American, The University of
Education & Industrial Arts, College of	Central State University
Eliot Seminary	Washington University in Saint Louis
Elizabeth City State College	Elizabeth City State University
Elizabeth City State Colored Normal School	Elizabeth City State University
Elizabeth City State Teachers College	Elizabeth City State University
Elkhart Institute of Science, Industry, & the Arts	Goshen College
Elmhurst Academy & Junior College	Elmhurst College
Elmhurst Pro-Seminary & Academy	Elmhurst College
Elmira Female College	Elmira College
Elon College	Elon University
Embry-Riddle Aeronautical Institute	Embry-Riddle Aeronautical University
Embry-Riddle Company, The	Embry-Riddle Aeronautical University
Embry-Riddle International School of Aviation	Embry-Riddle Aeronautical University
Emerson College of Oratory	Emerson College
Emmanuel College & School of Christian Ministry	Emmanuel College
Emmanuel Missionary College	Andrews University
Emory College	Emory University
Emporia Kansas State College	Emporia State University
Endicott Junior College	Endicott College
Epworth University	Oklahoma City University

320

Former Name	Current Name
Eugene Bible College	Northwest Christian College
Eugene Bible University	Northwest Christian College
Eugene Divinity School	Northwest Christian College
Evangel College	Evangel University of the Assemblies of God
Evangelical Lutheran College	Texas Lutheran University
Evangelical Lutheran College at Portland, Oregon, The	Concordia University
Evangelical Lutheran Proseminary	Texas Lutheran University
Evanston Collegiate Institute	Kendall College
Evansville College	Evansville, University of
Evening Institute for Young Men	Northeastern University
Expression & Elocution, School of	Curry College
Extension Campus of the College of Saint Teresa	Lourdes College
Extension Center of Hannibal-LaGrange College	Missouri Baptist College

F

Former Name	Current Name
Fairfield University of Saint Robert Bellarmine	Fairfield University
Fairleigh Dickinson College	Fairleigh Dickinson University
Fairleigh Dickinson Junior College	Fairleigh Dickinson University
Fairmont State Normal School	Fairmont State College
Fairmont State Teachers College	Fairmont State College
Fairmount College	Wichita State University
Fairmount Institute, The	Wichita State University
Fannie Jackson Coppin Normal School	Coppin State College
Farmer's High School	Pennsylvania State University, The
Farmington State College	Maine at Farmington, University of
Farmington State College of the University of Maine	Maine at Farmington, University of
Farmington State Normal School	Maine at Farmington, University of
Farmington State Teachers College	Maine at Farmington, University of
Farmville Female Seminary	Longwood College
Fayette Seminary of the Upper Iowa Conference, The	Upper Iowa University
Fayetteville State College	Fayetteville State University
Fayetteville State Teachers College	Fayetteville State University
Female Normal & High School	Hunter College of the City University of New York

Former Name	Current Name
Fenn College	Cleveland State University
Ferris Industrial School	Ferris State University
Ferris Institute	Ferris State University
Ferris State College	Ferris State University
Ferrum Junior College	Ferrum College
Ferrum Training School	Ferrum College
Ferrum Training School-Ferrum Junior College	Ferrum College
Fifth District Normal School	Northwest Missouri State University
Findlay College	Findlay, The University of
First District Agricultural School	Arkansas State University
First District Agricultural & Mechanical College	Arkansas State University
First District Agricultural & Mechanical High School	Georgia Southern University
First District Normal School	Truman State University
First Pennsylvania State Normal School of the Second District	Millersville University of Pennsylvania of the State System of Higher Education
First State Normal School of Minnesota	Winona State University
Fisk School	Fisk University
Florence Normal School	North Alabama, University of
Florence State College	North Alabama, University of
Florence State Teachers College	North Alabama, University of
Florence State University	North Alabama, University of
Florida Agricultural & Mechanical College for Negroes	Florida Agricultural & Mechanical University
Florida Baptist Institute	Florida Memorial College
Florida Conference College	Florida Southern College
Florida Normal & Industrial College	Florida Memorial College
Florida Normal & Industrial Memorial College	Florida Memorial College
Florida Normal & Industrial Memorial Institute	Florida Memorial College
Florida Presbyterian College	Eckerd College
Florida Seminary	Florida Southern College
Florida State College for Women, The	Florida State University, The
Florida State College, The	Florida State University, The
Florida Technological University	Central Florida, University of
Florida, University of the State of	Florida, University of
Fontbonne College	Fontbonne University
Fort Hays Kansas State College	Fort Hays State University

Former Name	Current Name
Fort Hays Kansas State Normal School	Fort Hays State University
Fort Kent State College	Maine at Fort Kent, University of
Fort Kent State College of the University of Maine	Maine at Fort Kent, University of
Fort Kent State Normal School	Maine at Fort Kent, University of
Fort Kent State Teachers College	Maine at Fort Kent, University of
Fort Lewis Agricultural & Mechanical College	Fort Lewis College
Fort Lewis School	Fort Lewis College
Fort Valley High & Industrial School	Fort Valley State University
Fort Valley Normal & Industrial School	Fort Valley State University
Fort Valley State College	Fort Valley State University
Fort Wayne College	Taylor University
Fort Wayne Female College	Taylor University
Fort Wright College	Heritage College
Fourth District Agricultural School	Arkansas at Monticello, University of
Framingham State Teachers College	Framingham State College
Frances Shimer Academy of the University of Chicago	Shimer College
Frances Shimer Junior College & Preparatory School	Shimer College
Francis Marion College	Francis Marion University
Francis T Nicholls Junior College of Louisiana State University	Nicholls State University
Francis T Nicholls State College	Nicholls State University
Franklin Academy	York College
Franklin College	Franklin College of Indiana
Franklin College	Franklin & Marshall College
Franklin Springs Institute	Emmanuel College
Fredonia Academy	New York College at Fredonia, State University of
Free School	Williams College
Freed-Hardeman College	Freed-Hardeman University
Frence Broad Baptist Institute	Mars Hill College
French-American College	American International College
French-Protestant College	American International College
Fresno Pacific College	Fresno Pacific University
Fresno State Normal School	California State University, Fresno
Friends Bible Institute & Training School, The	Malone College

Former Name	Current Name
Friends Boarding School	Earlham College
Friends Pacific Academy	George Fox University
Friends School at New Garden, The	Guilford College
Frostburg State College	Frostburg State University
Fulton College	Westminster College
Furman Academy & Theological Institution	Furman University, The
Furman Institution	Furman University, The
Furman Theological Institution	Furman University, The

G

Former Name	Current Name
Gallaudet College	Gallaudet University
Gannon College	Gannon University
Gannon School of Arts & Sciences	Gannon University
Gardner-Webb College	Gardner-Webb University
Gardner-Webb Junior College	Gardner-Webb University
General Beadle State College	Dakota State University
General Beadle State Teachers College	Dakota State University
Genesee Conference, The Seminary of the	Cazenovia College
Genesee & Oneida Conferences, The Seminary of the	Cazenovia College
Geneseo Normal & Training School	New York College at Geneseo, State University of
Geneva Academy	Hobart College
Geneva College	Hobart College
Geneva Hall	Geneva College
George Fox College	George Fox University
George Mason College	George Mason University
George Pepperdine College	Pepperdine University
Georgetown College	Georgetown University
Georgetown College in the District of Columbia	Georgetown University
Georgetown in the District of Columbia, College of	Georgetown University
Georgia Baptist Female Seminary	Brenau University
Georgia College	Georgia College & State University
Georgia College at Milledgeville	Georgia College & State University
Georgia Evening School, University System of	Georgia State University
Georgia Extension Center in Atlanta, University of	Georgia State University

324

Former Name	Current Name
Georgia Female College, The	Wesleyan College
Georgia Normal School	Georgia Southern University
Georgia Normal & Agricultural College	Albany State University
Georgia Normal & Industrial College for Girls	Georgia College & State University
Georgia School of Technology	Georgia Institute of Technology
Georgia School of Technology Evening School of Commerce	Georgia State University
Georgia Southern College	Georgia Southern University
Georgia Southwestern College	Georgia Southwestern State University
Georgia State College	Georgia State University
Georgia State College	Savannah State University
Georgia State College for Women	Georgia College & State University
Georgia State College of Business Administration	Georgia State University
Georgia State Industrial School for Colored Youth	Savannah State University
Georgia State Woman's College	Valdosta State University
Georgia Teachers College	Georgia Southern University
Georgia: Atlanta Division, University of	Georgia State University
Georgie Robertson Christian College	Freed-Hardeman University
German Presbyterian Theological School of the Northwest	Dubuque, University of
German Theological School	Bloomfield College
German Theological School of the Northwest	Dubuque, University of
Girl's Industrial College	Texas Woman's University
Glad Tidings Bible Institute	Bethany College of the Assemblies of God
Glassboro State College	Rowan University
Glenville State Normal School	Glenville State College
Glenville State Teachers College	Glenville State College
Goddard School for Girls	Goddard College
Goddard Seminary	Goddard College
Gonzaga College	Gonzaga University
Gordon Bible College	Gordon College, The United College of Gordon & Barrington
Gordon Bible Institute	Gordon College, The United College of Gordon & Barrington
Gordon Bible & Missionary Training School	Gordon College, The United College of Gordon & Barrington
Gordon College	Gordon College, The United College of Gordon & Barrington

Former Name	Current Name
Gordon College of Theology & Missions	Gordon College, The United College of Gordon & Barrington
Gordon College & Gordon Divinity School	Gordon College, The United College of Gordon & Barrington
Gordon School of the Newton Theological Institution	Gordon College, The United College of Gordon & Barrington
Gorham State Teachers College	Southern Maine, University of
Grace Bible Institute	Grace University
Grace College of the Bible	Grace University
Grace Theological Seminary, Collegiate Division	Grace College & Seminary
Graceland College	Graceland University
Grambling College	Grambling State University
Grand Canyon College	Grand Canyon University
Grand Junction State Junior College	Mesa State College
Grand Rapids Baptist Bible College & Seminary	Cornerstone University
Grand Rapids Baptist College & Seminary	Cornerstone University
Grand Rapids Baptist Theological Seminary & Bible Institute	Cornerstone University
Grand Valley State College	Grand Valley State University
Grant Memorial University	Tennessee Wesleyan College
Granville College	Denison University
Granville Literary & Theological Institution	Denison University
Graysville Academy	Southern Adventist University
Great Falls College of Education	Great Falls, University of
Great Falls Normal College	Great Falls, University of
Great Falls, College of	Great Falls, University of
Green Mountain Central Institute	Goddard College
Green Mountain Junior College	Green Mountain College
Greensboro College for Women	Greensboro College
Greensboro Female College	Greensboro College
Grubbs Vocational College	Texas at Arlington, The University of
Gwynedd-Mercy Junior College	Gwynedd-Mercy College

H

Hamilton Literary & Theological Institution	Colgate University
Hamilton-Oneida Academy	Hamilton College
Hammond Junior College	Southeastern Louisiana University

Former Name	Current Name
Hampden-Sydney Academy	Hampden-Sydney College
Hampstead Academy	Mississippi College
Hampton Institute	Hampton University
Hampton Normal & Agricultural Institute	Hampton University
Hanover Academy	Hanover College
Hardin College	Midwestern State University
Hardin Junior College	Midwestern State University
Harding College	Harding University
Harpur College	New York University Center at Binghamton, State University of
Hartford Art School	Hartford, University of
Hartford Society for Decorative Art	Hartford, University of
Hartsville Academy	Huntington College
Hartsville College	Huntington College
Hartsville University	Huntington College
Hartwick Seminary	Hartwick College
Harvard College	Harvard University
Haverford School	Haverford College
Hawaii Extension Division, University of	Hawaii at Hilo, University of
Hawaii Pacific College	Hawaii Pacific University
Hawaii, College of	Hawaii at Manoa, University of
Hawaii, Hilo College, University of	Hawaii at Hilo, University of
Hawaii, University of	Hawaii at Manoa, University of
Heidelberg University	Heidelberg College
Henderson College	Henderson State University
Henderson Male & Female Institute	Freed-Hardeman University
Henderson Masonic Male & Female Institute	Freed-Hardeman University
Henderson State College	Henderson State University
Henderson State Teachers College	Henderson State University
Henderson-Brown College	Henderson State University
Hendrix-Henderson College	Hendrix College
Henry Kendall College	Tulsa, The University of
Heraldsburg Academy	Pacific Union College
Heraldsburg College	Pacific Union College
Hesperian College	Chapman University
High Point College	High Point University
High School for Needle Trade	New York Fashion Institute of Technology, State University of

Former Name	Current Name
High School & College of the Florida Conference	Florida Southern College
High & Training School	Coppin State College
Highland Academy	Lenoir-Rhyne College
Hillsboro College	Carthage College
Hobart Free College	Hobart College
Hobbs Baptist College	Southwest, College of the
Hofstra College	Hofstra University
Hofstra College of New York University	Hofstra University
Holland Academy, The	Hope College
Hollins College	Hollins University
Hollins Institute	Hollins University
Holy Angels College Department, Academy of the	Our Lady of Holy Cross College
Holy Angels Normal School, Academy of the	Our Lady of Holy Cross College
Holy Cross Normal College	Our Lady of Holy Cross College
Holy Family College	Silver Lake College
Holy Family Normal School	Silver Lake College
Holy Ghost, University of the	Duquesne University of the Holy Ghost
Holy Infancy, Academy of the	Manhattan College
Holy Name Technical School	Lewis University
Holy Names Junior College	Holy Names College
Holy Names, College of the	Heritage College
Holy Names, College of the	Holy Names College
Holy Names, Convent & College of the	Holy Names College
Houghton Wesleyan Methodist Seminary	Houghton College
Houston Baptist College	Houston Baptist University
Houston Central Campus, University of	Houston, University of
Houston Junior College	Houston, University of
Houston-University Park, University of	Houston, University of
Howard College	Samford University
Howard Payne College	Howard Payne University
Howard School	Fayetteville State University
Howard University	Samford University
Humboldt State College	Humboldt State University
Humboldt State Normal School	Humboldt State University
Humboldt State Teachers College	Humboldt State University

Former Name	Current Name
Hunter College	Hunter College of the City University of New York
Hunter College in the Bronx	Herbert H Lehman College of the City University of New York
Huntingdon Normal School	Juniata College
Huntsville Normal School	Alabama Agricultural & Mechanical University
Huntsville, State Normal & Industrial School at	Alabama Agricultural & Mechanical University
Huron College	Huron University
Hyatt's Select School for Boys	Widener University

Former Name	Current Name
Idaho Holiness College	Northwest Nazarene University
Idaho Holiness School	Northwest Nazarene University
Idaho State College	Idaho State University
Idaho Technical Institute, The	Idaho State University
Idaho, The Academy of	Idaho State University
Idaho, The College of	Albertson College of Idaho
Idaho-Southern Branch, University of	Idaho State University
Illinois Benedictine College	Benedictine University
Illinois Conference Female Academy	MacMurray College
Illinois Female Academy	MacMurray College
Illinois Female College	MacMurray College
Illinois Holiness University	Olivet Nazarene University
Illinois Industrial University	Illinois at Urbana-Champaign, University of
Illinois Institute	Wheaton College
Illinois State Normal University	Illinois State University
Illinois State University	Carthage College
Illinois Teachers College: Chicago North	Northeastern Illinois University
Illinois Teachers College: Chicago South	Chicago State University
Illinois University	Illinois Wesleyan University
Illinois Women's College	MacMurray College
Illinois, Chicago Circle, University of	Illinois at Chicago, University of
Illinois, University of	Illinois at Urbana-Champaign, University of
Immaculata College	Hilbert College
Immaculata College	Immaculata University

Former Name	Current Name
Immaculate Conception Junior College	Felician College
Immaculate Conception Normal School	Felician College
Immaculate Conception, College of	Loyola University New Orleans
Immaculate Conception, School of the	Seattle University
Incarnate Word School	Incarnate Word, University of the
Incarnate Word, College & Academy of the	Incarnate Word, University of the
Indian Normal School of Robeson County, The	North Carolina at Pembroke, The University of
Indiana Asbury University	DePauw University
Indiana Baptist Manual Labor Institute	Franklin College of Indiana
Indiana Central College	Indianapolis, University of
Indiana Central University	Indianapolis, University of
Indiana College	Indiana University
Indiana Normal School	Indiana University of Pennsylvania
Indiana Normal School & College of Applied Science	Ball State University
Indiana State College	Indiana State University
Indiana State College	Indiana University of Pennsylvania
Indiana State Normal School	Indiana State University
Indiana State Normal School	Indiana University of Pennsylvania
Indiana State Normal School, Eastern Division	Ball State University
Indiana State Seminary	Indiana University
Indiana State Teachers College	Indiana State University
Indiana State Teachers College	Indiana University of Pennsylvania
Indiana State University: Evansville	Southern Indiana, University of
Indiana University at Indianapolis	Indiana University-Purdue University Indianapolis
Indianapolis Downtown Campus	Indiana University-Purdue University Indianapolis
Indianola Male & Female Seminary	Simpson College
Industrial Branch of Morgan State College	Maryland Eastern Shore, University of
Industrial Institute of South Dakota	Northern State University
Industrial Institute & College of Louisiana	Louisiana Tech University
Institute for Coloured Youth	Cheyney University of Pennsylvania of the State System of Higher Education

330

Former Name	Current Name
Institute of Education	Marietta College, The
Institute of the Sisters of Saint Joseph	Medaille College
Institution for the Education of Colored Youth, The	District of Columbia, University of the
Intermountain Union College	Rocky Mountain College
International YMCA College	Springfield College
International YMCA Training School	Springfield College
Iowa Agricultural College & Model Farm	Iowa State University
Iowa College	Grinnell College
Iowa Conference Seminary	Cornell College
Iowa State College of Agriculture & Mechanical Arts	Iowa State University
Iowa State Normal School	Northern Iowa, University of
Iowa State Teachers College	Northern Iowa, University of
Iowa State University of Science & Technology	Iowa State University
Iowa Wesleyan University	Iowa Wesleyan College
Isaacs-Woodbury College	Woodbury University
Ithaca Conservatory of Music	Ithaca College
Ithaca Conservatory & Affiliated Schools	Ithaca College
J S Green College	Piedmont College
J & S Green Collegiate Institute	Piedmont College
Jackson College	Jackson State University
Jackson College for Negro Teachers	Jackson State University
Jackson Male Academy	Union University
Jackson State College	Jackson State University
Jackson State College for Negro Teachers	Jackson State University
Jacksonville Junior College	Jacksonville University
Jacksonville State College	Jacksonville State University
Jacksonville State Normal School	Jacksonville State University
Jacksonville State Teachers College	Jacksonville State University
Jarvis Christian Institute	Jarvis Christian College
Jasper County Junior College	Missouri Southern State College
Jefferson Seminary	Louisville, University of
Jersey City State College	New Jersey City University
Jersey City State Teachers College	New Jersey City University

Former Name	Current Name
Jesus College	Macalester College
John B Stetson University	Stetson University
John Calvin Junior College	Calvin College
John E Brown College	John Brown University
John McNeese Junior College	McNeese State University
John Tarleton Agricultural College	Tarleton State University
John Tarleton College	Tarleton State University
Johnson Academy	Johnson State College
Johnson Normal School	Johnson State College
Johnson Teachers College	Johnson State College
Johnson & Wales College	Johnson & Wales University
Johnson & Wales College of Business	Johnson & Wales University
Johnson & Wales Junior College of Business	Johnson & Wales University
Joplin Junior College	Missouri Southern State College
Judson Female Institute	Judson College
Junior College of Augusta	Augusta State University
Junior College of Commerce	Quinnipiac University
Junior College of Connecticut	Bridgeport, University of

K

Kalamazoo Literary Institute	Kalamazoo College
Kalamazoo Literary Institute	Kalamazoo College
Kansas City, University of	Missouri-Kansas City, University of
Kansas Newman College	Newman University
Kansas Normal School of Emporia, Western Branch	Fort Hays State University
Kansas State Agricultural College	Kansas State University
Kansas State College of Agriculture & Applied Science	Kansas State University
Kansas State College of Pittsburg	Pittsburg State University
Kansas State Manual Training Normal School	Pittsburg State University
Kansas State Manual Training Normal School Auxiliary	Pittsburg State University
Kansas State Normal School	Emporia State University
Kansas State Teachers College	Emporia State University
Kansas State Teachers College of Hays	Fort Hays State University
Kansas State Teachers College of Pittsburg	Pittsburg State University
Kansas Wesleyan	Kansas Wesleyan University
Kean College of New Jersey	Kean University

Former Name	Current Name
Kearney State College	Nebraska at Kearney, University of
Keene Independent Academy	Southwestern Adventist University
Keene Normal School	Keene State College
Keene Teachers College	Keene State College
Kennesaw College	Kennesaw State University
Kennesaw Junior College	Kennesaw State University
Kennesaw State College	Kennesaw State University
Kent County School	Washington College
Kent State College	Kent State University
Kent State Normal College	Kent State University
Kent State Normal School	Kent State University
Kentucky Female Orphans School	Midway College
Kentucky Holiness College	Asbury College
Kentucky Normal & Industrial Institute	Kentucky State University
Kentucky State College	Kentucky State University
Kentucky State College for Negroes	Kentucky State University
Kentucky State Industrial College for Colored Persons	Kentucky State University
Kentucky University	Transylvania University
Kentucky University Agricultural & Mechanical College	Kentucky, University of
Kentucky, Agricultural & Mechanical College of	Kentucky, University of
Kentucky, State University of	Kentucky, University of
Keuka College for Women	Keuka College
Keuka Institute	Keuka College
Keystone Normal School	Kutztown University of Pennsylvania of the State System of Higher Education
King William's School	Saint John's College
King's College of the Province of New York	Columbia University in the City of New York
Knox Manual Labor College	Knox College
Kutztown State College	Kutztown University of Pennsylvania of the State System of Higher Education
Kutztown State Teachers College	Kutztown University of Pennsylvania of the State System of Higher Education
La Crosse State Normal School	Wisconsin-La Crosse, University of
La Crosse State Teachers College	Wisconsin-La Crosse, University of
La Salle College	La Salle University

Former Name	Current Name
La Sierra Academy	La Sierra University
La Sierra College	La Sierra University
La Verne College	La Verne, University of
Ladies Literary Society	Ohio Dominican College
LaGrange College	Hannibal-LaGrange College
LaGrange College	North Alabama, University of
LaGrange Female Academy	LaGrange College
LaGrange Female College	LaGrange College
LaGrange Female Institute	LaGrange College
LaGrange Male & Female Seminary	Hannibal-LaGrange College
Lake Charles Junior College	McNeese State University
Lake Erie Female Seminary	Lake Erie College
Lake Erie Seminary & College	Lake Erie College
Lake Forest University	Lake Forest College
Lake Superior State College	Lake Superior State University
Lamar College	Lamar University
Lamar State College of Technology	Lamar University
Lamar University-Beaumont	Lamar University
Lambuth College	Lambuth University
Lamoille County Grammar School	Johnson State College
Lancaster County Normal Institute	Millersville University of Pennsylvania of the State System of Higher Education
Lancaster County Normal School	Millersville University of Pennsylvania of the State System of Higher Education
Lancaster Junior College	Atlantic Union College
Lander College	Lander University
Lane Institute	Lane College
Laredo State University	Texas A&M International University
Las Vegas College	Regis University
Lasell Female Seminary	Lasell College
Lasell Junior College	Lasell College
Lasell Seminary for Young Women	Lasell College
Lawrence College	Lawrence University
Lawrence Institute of Technology	Lawrence Technological University
Lawrence Institute of Wisconsin	Lawrence University
Lawrence University of Wisconsin	Lawrence University
Lebanon Seminary	McKendree College
Lee College	Lee University
Lenoir College	Lenoir-Rhyne College

Former Name	Current Name
Lesley College	Lesley University
Lesley Normal School	Lesley University
Lesley School, The	Lesley University
LeTourneau College	LeTourneau University
LeTourneau Technical Institute of Texas	LeTourneau University
Lewis College	Lewis University
Lewis College	Norwich University
Lewis College of Science & Technology	Lewis University
Lewis Holy Name School of Aeronautics	Lewis University
Lewis Holy Name Technical School	Lewis University
Lewis School of Aeronautics	Lewis University
Lewisburg, The University at	Bucknell University
Lewiston State Normal School	Lewis-Clark State College
Lewis-Clark Normal School	Lewis-Clark State College
Liberty Baptist College	Liberty University
Liberty Hall	Washington & Lee University
Liberty Hall Academy	Washington & Lee University
Limestone Springs School	Limestone College
Lincoln College	Washburn University of Topeka
Lincoln Institute	Lincoln University
Lincoln Normal School	Alabama State University
Lincoln Parish Training School	Grambling State University
Lind University	Lake Forest College
Lindenwood	Lindenwood University
Lindenwood College	Lindenwood University
Lindenwood Female College	Lindenwood University
Lindsey Wilson Training School	Lindsey Wilson College
Literary & Theological Institute of the Lutheran Church in the Far West	Carthage College
Little Rock Junior College	Arkansas at Little Rock, University of
Little Rock University	Arkansas at Little Rock, University of
Livingston Collegiate Institute	West Alabama, University of
Livingston Female Academy	West Alabama, University of
Livingston State College	West Alabama, University of
Livingston University	West Alabama, University of
Lock Haven State College	Lock Haven University of Pennsylvania of the State System of Higher Education

Former Name	Current Name
Lock Haven State Teachers College	Lock Haven University of Pennsylvania of the State System of Higher Education
Loma Linda University, Riverside	La Sierra University
Long Beach State College	California State University, Long Beach
Long Island University	Long Island University: Brooklyn Campus
Long Island University: Brooklyn Center	Long Island University: Brooklyn Campus
Long Island University: The Zeckendorf Campus	Long Island University: Brooklyn Campus
Lordsburg College	La Verne, University of
Loretto College	Webster University
Los Angeles Baptist College	Master's College, The
Los Angeles Baptist Theological Seminary	Master's College, The
Los Angeles College	Loyola Marymount University
Los Angeles State College	California State University, Los Angeles
Los Angeles State College of Applied Arts & Sciences	California State University, Los Angeles
Los Angeles-Orange County State College	California State University, Long Beach
Louisiana Normal & Industrial Institute	Grambling State University
Louisiana Polytechnic Institute	Louisiana Tech University
Louisiana State House of Education	Louisiana State University & Agricultural & Mechanical College
Louisiana State Normal College	Northwestern State University of Louisiana
Louisiana State Normal School	Northwestern State University of Louisiana
Louisiana State School of Education	Louisiana State University & Agricultural & Mechanical College
Louisiana State Seminary of Learning & Military Academy	Louisiana State University & Agricultural & Mechanical College
Louisiana State University in New Orleans	New Orleans, University of
Louisiana State University, The	Louisiana State University & Agricultural & Mechanical College
Louisiana State University: Northeast Center	Louisiana at Monroe, University of
Louisiana State University: Northeast Junior College	Louisiana at Monroe, University of

336

Former Name	Current Name
Louisiana, College of	Centenary College of Louisiana
Louisiana, Seminary of Learning of the State of	Louisiana State University & Agricultural & Mechanical College
Louisiana, University of	Louisiana at Lafayette, University of
Louisiana, University of	Tulane University of Louisiana
Lourdes Junior College	Lourdes College
Lowell State College	Massachusetts Lowell, University of
Lowell, University of	Massachusetts Lowell, University of
Loyola College	Loyola College in Maryland
Loyola College of Los Angeles	Loyola Marymount University
Loyola University	Loyola University New Orleans
Loyola University Chicago	Loyola University of Chicago
Loyola University of Los Angeles	Loyola Marymount University
Lubbock Christian College	Lubbock Christian University
Lutheran College	Texas Lutheran University
Lutheran Concordia College	Concordia University at Austin
Lutheran Seminary, The	Concordia University
Lyceum of Ripon	Ripon College
Lynchburg Baptist College	Liberty University
Lyndon Institute	Lyndon State College
Lyndon Teachers College	Lyndon State College

M

MacMurray College for Women	MacMurray College
Madawaska Training School	Maine at Fort Kent, University of
Madison College	James Madison University
Madison State Normal School	Dakota State University
Madison University	Colgate University
Madonna College	Madonna University
Maharishi International University	Maharishi University of Management
Maine at Orono, University of	Maine, University of
Maine at Portland-Gorham, University of	Southern Maine, University of
Maine Literary & Theological Institution	Colby College
Maine School of Commerce	Husson College
Maine State Seminary	Bates College
Manhattan Academy	Manhattan College
Manhattanville College of the Sacred Heart	Manhattanville College

Former Name	Current Name
Mankato State College	Minnesota State University, Mankato
Mankato State Normal School	Minnesota State University, Mankato
Mankato State Teachers College	Minnesota State University, Mankato
Mankato State University	Minnesota State University, Mankato
Mansfield Classical Seminary	Mansfield University of Pennsylvania of the State System of Higher Education
Mansfield State College	Mansfield University of Pennsylvania of the State System of Higher Education
Mansfield State Normal School	Mansfield University of Pennsylvania of the State System of Higher Education
Mansfield State Teachers College	Mansfield University of Pennsylvania of the State System of Higher Education
Marian College	Marian College of Fond du Lac
Marian College	Marist College
Marietta Collegiate Institute & Western Teachers Seminary	Marietta College, The
Marine Biological Station of San Diego	California, San Diego, University of
Marion College	Indiana Wesleyan University
Marist Training School	Marist College
Marquette College	Marquette University
Marrimack Valley Branch of the University of New Hampshire	New Hampshire at Manchester, University of
Marshall Academy	Marshall University
Marshall College	Marshall University
Marshall, College of	East Texas Baptist University
Martin Center College	Martin University
Martin College	Martin Methodist College
Martin Female College	Martin Methodist College
Mary Baldwin Junior College	Mary Baldwin College
Mary Baldwin Seminary	Mary Baldwin College
Mary College	Mary, University of
Mary Hardin-Baylor College	Mary Hardin-Baylor, The University of
Mary Washington College of the University of Virginia	Mary Washington College
Maryland Agricultural College	Maryland, College Park, University of
Maryland Agricultural College, Eastern Branch of	Maryland Eastern Shore, University of
Maryland Baltimore County, University of	Maryland, Baltimore County, University of
Maryland Normal & Industrial School at Bowie	Bowie State University
Maryland State College	Maryland Eastern Shore, University of

Former Name	Current Name
Maryland State College of Agriculture	Maryland, College Park, University of
Maryland State Normal School	Towson University
Maryland State Normal School at Salisbury	Salisbury University
Maryland State Teachers College at Salisbury	Salisbury University
Maryland State Teachers College at Towson	Towson University
Maryland Teachers College at Bowie	Bowie State University
Maryland: Eastern Shore, University of	Maryland Eastern Shore, University of
Marylhurst College	Marylhurst University
Marylhurst College for Lifelong Learning	Marylhurst University
Marylhurst Education Center	Marylhurst University
Marymount College	Lynn University
Marymount College of Virginia	Marymount University
Marymount Junior College	Marymount Manhattan College
Marymount Junior College	Marymount University
Maryville College	Maryville University of Saint Louis
Maryville College of the Sacred Heart	Maryville University of Saint Louis
Maryville College & Academy of the Sacred Heart	Maryville University of Saint Louis
Marywood College	Marywood University
Masonic University of Tennessee	Rhodes College
Massachusetts Agricultural College	Massachusetts Amherst, University of
Massachusetts at Boston, University of	Massachusetts Boston, University of
Massachusetts State College	Massachusetts Amherst, University of
Massachusetts State College at Lowell	Massachusetts Lowell, University of
Massachusetts State Normal School at Lowell	Massachusetts Lowell, University of
Massachusetts, University of	Massachusetts Amherst, University of
Mattoon School of Shorthand	Teikyo Post University
Mayville Normal School	Mayville State University
Mayville State College	Mayville State University
Mayville State Teachers College	Mayville State University
McKendrian College	McKendree College
McMinnville College	Linfield College
McMurry College	McMurry University
McNeese State College	McNeese State University
McPherson College & Industrial Institute	McPherson College

Former Name	Current Name
Medical College of Louisiana	Tulane University of Louisiana
Medical College of Virginia	Virginia Commonwealth University
Memphis Conference Female Institute	Lambuth University
Memphis State College	Memphis, The University of
Mendota College	Aurora University
Mendota Seminary	Aurora University
Menlo School & College	Menlo College
Menlo School & Junior College	Menlo College
Mercer Institute	Mercer University
Mercy Junior College	Maryville University of Saint Louis
Mercy Junior College	Mercy College
Merrimack Valley College	New Hampshire at Manchester, University of
Mesa College	Mesa State College
Messiah Bible College	Messiah College
Messiah Bible School & Missionary Training Home	Messiah College
Methodist General Biblical Institute	Boston University
Methodist University of Oklahoma, The	Oklahoma City University
Metropolitan State College	Metropolitan State College of Denver
Michigan Agricultural College	Michigan State University
Michigan Central College	Hillsdale College
Michigan Christian College	Rochester College
Michigan Christian Junior College	Rochester College
Michigan College of Mines	Michigan Technological University
Michigan College of Mining & Technology	Michigan Technological University
Michigan College of Mining & Technology, Sault Saint Marie Branch	Lake Superior State University
Michigan Mining School	Michigan Technological University
Michigan State College of Agriculture & Applied Science	Michigan State University
Michigan State Normal College	Eastern Michigan University
Michigan State Normal School	Eastern Michigan University
Michigan State University of Agriculture & Applied Science	Michigan State University
Michigan State University-Oakland	Oakland University
Michigan & Huron Institute, The	Kalamazoo College
Michigan: Kalamazoo Branch, University of	Kalamazoo College

Former Name	Current Name
MidAmerica Nazarene College	MidAmerica Nazarene University
Middle Tennessee State College	Middle Tennessee State University
Middle Tennessee State Normal School	Middle Tennessee State University
Middle Tennessee State Teachers College	Middle Tennessee State University
Midland College	Midland Lutheran College
Midway Junior College	Midway College
Midwest Christian Junior College	Dordt College
Midwestern University	Midwestern State University
Mid-Continent Baptist Bible College	Mid-Continent College
Mid-South Bible College	Crichton College
Mid-South Bible Institute	Crichton College
Mid-South Bible Training Center	Crichton College
Miles Memorial College	Miles College
Millersville State College	Millersville University of Pennsylvania of the State System of Higher Education
Millersville State Teachers College	Millersville University of Pennsylvania of the State System of Higher Education
Mills Seminary	Mills College
Mills Seminary & College	Mills College
Milwaukee Normal School	Wisconsin-Milwaukee, University of
Milwaukee State Teachers College	Wisconsin-Milwaukee, University of
Miner Normal School	District of Columbia, University of the
Miner Teachers College	District of Columbia, University of the
Minister's Institute	Arkansas Baptist College
Minnesota Elementary School	Gustavus Adolphus College
Minnesota Metropolitan State College	Metropolitan State University
Minn's Evening Normal School	San Jose State University
Minot Normal School	Minot State University
Minot State College	Minot State University
Minot State Teachers College	Minot State University
Miss Harrison's Training School	National-Louis University
Mission House	Lakeland College
Missionary Institute of the Evangelical Lutheran Church	Susquehanna University
Missionary Training Institute	Nyack College
Mississippi Academy	Mississippi College
Mississippi Industrial Institute & College	Mississippi University for Women

Former Name	Current Name
Mississippi Negro Training School	Jackson State University
Mississippi Normal College	Southern Mississippi, The University of
Mississippi Southern College	Southern Mississippi, The University of
Mississippi State College	Mississippi State University
Mississippi State College for Women	Mississippi University for Women
Mississippi State Teachers College	Southern Mississippi, The University of
Mississippi Valley State College	Mississippi Valley State University
Mississippi Vocational College	Mississippi Valley State University
Mississippi Woman's College	William Carey College
Missouri Baptist College-Hannibal	Hannibal-LaGrange College
Missouri Baptist College-Saint Louis	Missouri Baptist College
Missouri School of Mines & Metalurgy, University of	Missouri-Rolla, University of
Missouri Southern College	Missouri Southern State College
Missouri State Normal School of the Fourth District	Southwest Missouri State University
Missouri State University	Missouri-Columbia, University of
Missouri, University of	Missouri-Columbia, University of
Mitchell Junior College	Pfeiffer University
Mobile College	Mobile, University of
Molloy Catholic College for Women	Molloy College
Mommouth Junior College	Monmouth University
Monmouth Academy, The	Monmouth College, The
Monmouth College	Monmouth University
Monmouth University	Western Oregon University
Monogalia Academy	West Virginia University
Monroe College of Oratory	Emerson College
Montana Collegiate Institute	Rocky Mountain College
Montana State College	Montana State University-Bozeman
Montana State College of Agriculture & Mechanic Arts	Montana State University-Bozeman
Montana State Normal College	Montana-Western, The University of
Montana State Normal School	Montana-Western, The University of
Montana State University	Montana State University-Bozeman
Montana State University	Montana-Missoula, The University of
Montana, College of	Rocky Mountain College
Montana, State University of	Montana-Missoula, The University of
Montana, University of	Montana-Missoula, The University of
Montclair State College	Montclair State University
Montclair State Teachers College	Montclair State University

Former Name	Current Name
Montgomery Bible School	Faulkner University
Montgomery Masonic College	Rhodes College
Moores Hill College	Evansville, University of
Moores Hill Male & Female Collegiate Institute	Evansville, University of
Moorhead State College	Minnesota State University, Moorhead
Moorhead State Normal School	Minnesota State University, Moorhead
Moorhead State Teachers College	Minnesota State University, Moorhead
Moorhead State University	Minnesota State University, Moorhead
Moravian Seminary for Young Ladies	Moravian College & Moravian Theological Seminary
Moravian Seminary & College for Women	Moravian College & Moravian Theological Seminary
Morehead State College	Morehead State University
Morehead State Normal School	Morehead State University
Morehead State Normal School & Teachers College	Morehead State University
Morehead State Teachers College	Morehead State University
Morgan College	Morgan State University
Morgan State College	Morgan State University
Morris Brown University	Morris Brown College
Morris Harvey College	Charleston, University of
Mossy Creek Baptist College	Carson-Newman College
Mossy Creek Baptist Seminary	Carson-Newman College
Mount Allen Junior College	Mount Olive College
Mount Aloysius Academy	Mount Aloysius College
Mount Aloysius Junior College	Mount Aloysius College
Mount Carroll Seminary	Shimer College
Mount Holyoke Female Seminary	Mount Holyoke College
Mount Holyoke Seminary & College	Mount Holyoke College
Mount Marty Academy	Mount Marty College
Mount Marty Junior College	Mount Marty College
Mount Mary College	Mount Mary College
Mount Mercy Academy	Mount Mercy College
Mount Mercy College	Carlow College
Mount Mercy Junior College	Mount Mercy College
Mount Olive Junior College	Mount Olive College
Mount Pleasant Collegiate Institute	Iowa Wesleyan College
Mount Pleasant Literary Institute	Iowa Wesleyan College
Mount Saint Bernard	Loras College
Mount Saint Charles College	Carroll College

Former Name	Current Name
Mount Saint Clare Academy	Mount Saint Clare College
Mount Saint Joseph Academy	Chestnut Hill College
Mount Saint Joseph Academy	Mount Saint Joseph, College of
Mount Saint Joseph Academy and College	Clarke College
Mount Saint Joseph College	Chestnut Hill College
Mount Saint Joseph College	Saint Joseph College
Mount Saint Joseph College	Medaille College
Mount Saint Joseph Collegiate Institute	Chestnut Hill College
Mount Saint Joseph Teachers College	Medaille College
Mount Saint Joseph-on-the-Ohio, College of	Mount Saint Joseph, College of
Mount Saint Mary College & Academy	Georgian Court College
Mount Saint Mary Normal & Training School	Mount Saint Mary College
Mount Saint Vincent, Academy of	Mount Saint Vincent, College of
Mount Union Seminary	Mount Union College
Mount Vernon College	Peru State College
Mount Vernon Nazarene College	Mount Vernon Nazarene University
Muncie Ball State Teachers College	Ball State University
Muncie National Institute	Ball State University
Muncie Normal Institute	Ball State University
Murray State College	Murray State University
Murray State Normal School	Murray State University
Murray State Normal School & Teachers College	Murray State University
Murray State Teachers College	Murray State University

Former Name	Current Name
Nashville Bible School	David Lipscomb University
Nassau College-Hofstra Memorial New York University	Hofstra University
Natchez Seminary	Jackson State University
National Agricultural College	Delaware Valley College
National College	National American University
National College for the Deaf & Dumb	Gallaudet University
National College of Business	National American University
National College of Education	National-Louis University
National Deaf-Mute College	Gallaudet University

Former Name	Current Name
National Farm School & Junior College, The	Delaware Valley College
National Farm School, The	Delaware Valley College
National Kindergarten College	National-Louis University
National Kindergarten & Elementary College	National-Louis University
National Religious Training School & Chatauqua	North Carolina Central University
National School of Business	National American University
National Teachers Normal & Business College	Freed-Hardeman University
National Training School	North Carolina Central University
Nazarene University	Point Loma Nazarene University
Nazareth College	Spalding University
Nebraska Normal College	Wayne State College
Nebraska State Normal College at Chadron	Chadron State College
Nebraska State Normal School	Peru State College
Nebraska State Normal School at Kearney	Nebraska at Kearney, University of
Nebraska State Teachers College at Chadron	Chadron State College
Nebraska State Teachers College at Kearney	Nebraska at Kearney, University of
Nebraska State Teachers College at Peru	Peru State College
Nebraska State Teachers College at Wayne	Wayne State College
Nebraska Wesleyan University, The	Nebraska Wesleyan University, The
Nebraska, University of	Nebraska-Lincoln, University of
Nevada Southern University	Nevada: Las Vegas, University of
Nevada State University	Nevada: Reno, University of
Nevada, Southern Regional Branch, University of	Nevada: Las Vegas, University of
Nevada, University of	Nevada: Reno, University of
New Bedford Institute of Technology	Massachusetts Dartmouth, University of
New Bedford Institute of Textiles & Technology	Massachusetts Dartmouth, University of
New Bedford Technical Institute	Massachusetts Dartmouth, University of
New Bedford Textile School	Massachusetts Dartmouth, University of
New Britain Normal School	Central Connecticut State University

Former Name	Current Name
New Church College, Academy of the	Bryn Athyn College of the New Church
New College	New College of Florida
New College of the University of South Florida	New College of Florida
New College, The	Saint Francis, University of
New England Aeronautical Institute	Daniel Webster College
New Garden Boarding School	Guilford College
New Hampshire College of Agriculture & Mechanical Arts	New Hampshire, University of
New Haven College	New Haven, University of
New Haven Normal School	Southern Connecticut State University
New Haven State Teachers College	Southern Connecticut State University
New Haven YMCA Junior College	New Haven, University of
New Jersey Normal School at Montclair	Montclair State University
New Jersey Normal School of Jersey City	New Jersey City University
New Jersey State Normal School	New Jersey, The College of
New Jersey State Normal School at Glassboro	Rowan University
New Jersey State Normal School at Newark	Kean University
New Jersey State Normal School at Paterson	William Paterson University of New Jersey, The
New Jersey State Normal School at Trenton	New Jersey, The College of
New Jersey State Teachers College at Glassboro	Rowan University
New Jersey State Teachers College at Paterson	William Paterson University of New Jersey, The
New Jersey State Teachers College at Trenton	New Jersey, The College of
New Jersey State Teachers College & State Normal School at Trenton	New Jersey, The College of
New Jersey, College of	Princeton University
New London Literary & Scientific Institution	Colby-Sawyer College
New London Seminary	Colby-Sawyer College
New Mexico Baptist College	Southwest, College of the
New Mexico College of Agriculture & Mechanical Arts	New Mexico State University

Former Name	Current Name
New Mexico Institute of Mining & Technology	New Mexico Institute of Mining & Technology
New Mexico Normal School	New Mexico Highlands University
New Mexico Normal School	Western New Mexico University
New Mexico School of Mines	New Mexico Institute of Mining & Technology
New Mexico State Normal University	New Mexico Highlands University
New Mexico State Teachers College	Western New Mexico University
New Mexico State University of Agriculture, Engineering, & Science	New Mexico State University
New Mexico Western College	Western New Mexico University
New Paltz Academy	New York College at New Paltz, State University of
New Paltz Classical School	New York College at New Paltz, State University of
New Paltz Normal School	New York College at New Paltz, State University of
New River State College	West Virginia University Institute of Technology
New River State School	West Virginia University Institute of Technology
New School for Social Research	New School University
New York Agricultural & Technical Institute, State University of	New York College of Technology at Farmingdale, State University of
New York City Community College of Applied Arts & Sciences	New York City College of Technology
New York City Technical College of the City University of New York	New York City College of Technology
New York College of Education at Oneonta, State University of	New York College at Oneonta, State University of
New York Conference Seminary, The Seminary of the	Cazenovia College
New York Free Academy	City College of the City University of New York
New York Progymnasium	Concordia College
New York State College for Teachers	New York University Center at Albany, State University of
New York State College for Teachers at Buffalo	New York College at Buffalo, State University of
New York State College of Forestry at Syracuse	New York College of Environmental Science & Forestry at Syracuse, State University of
New York State Institute of Applied Arts & Sciences	New York City College of Technology
New York State Normal College	New York University Center at Albany, State University of

Former Name	Current Name
New York State Normal School	New York University Center at Albany, State University of
New York State Normal & Training School at Plattsburgh	New York College at Plattsburgh, State University of
New York, The College of the City of	City College of the City University of New York
New York, University of the City of	New York University
Newark College of Engineering	New Jersey Institute of Technology
Newark Normal School	Kean University
Newark State College	Kean University
Newark State Teachers College	Kean University
Newark Technical School	New Jersey Institute of Technology
Newark, The Academy of	Delaware, University of
Newbury Biblical Institute	Boston University
Norfolk College of the College of William & Mary of the Colleges of William & Mary	Old Dominion University
Norfolk Division of the College of William & Mary	Old Dominion University
Norfolk Polytechnic College	Norfolk State University
Norfolk State College	Norfolk State University
Normal College	Duke University
Normal Industrial, Agricultural, & Mechanical College for the Colored Race	South Carolina State University
Normal School at Duluth	Minnesota, Duluth, University of
Normal School at Westfield	Westfield State College
Normal School for Colored Girls in the City of Washington	District of Columbia, University of the
Normal School for Colored Teachers	Tuskegee University
Normal School of Arizona	Arizona State University
Normal & Industrial School for Women at Harrisonburg	James Madison University
Normandy Residence Center of the University of Missouri	Missouri-Saint Louis, University of
North Adams Normal School	Massachusetts College of Liberal Arts
North Adams State College	Massachusetts College of Liberal Arts
North American Indian Boarding School	Minnesota, Morris, University of
North Carolina Agricultural & Technical State University	North Carolina Agricultural & Technical State University
North Carolina College at Durham	North Carolina Central University
North Carolina College Conference Center	North Carolina at Wilmington, The University of

Former Name	Current Name
North Carolina College for Negroes	North Carolina Central University
North Carolina College for Women	North Carolina at Greensboro, The University of
North Carolina College of Agriculture & Mechanic Arts	North Carolina State University at Raleigh
North Carolina State College of Agriculture & Engineering	North Carolina State University at Raleigh
North Carolina State College of Agriculture & Engineering of the University of North Carolina	North Carolina State University at Raleigh
North Carolina State College of the University of North Carolina at Raleigh	North Carolina State University at Raleigh
North Carolina, The University of	North Carolina at Chapel Hill, The University of
North Carolina: Charlotte Center, University of	North Carolina at Charlotte, The University of
North Central Christian College	Rochester College
North Dakota Agricultural College	North Dakota State University
North Dakota-Dickinson, State University of	Dickinson State University
North Dakota-Mayville, State University of	Mayville State University
North Dakota-Minot, State University of	Minot State University
North Dakota-Valley City, State University of	Valley City State University
North Georgia Agricultural College	North Georgia College & State University
North Georgia College	North Georgia College & State University
North Greenville Baptist Academy	North Greenville College
North Greenville High School	North Greenville College
North Greenville Junior College	North Greenville College
North Louisiana Agricultural & Industrial School	Grambling State University
North Missouri Normal School & Commercial College	Truman State University
North Park College & Theological Seminary	North Park University
North Texas Agricultural College	Texas at Arlington, The University of
North Texas Junior Agricultural College	Texas at Arlington, The University of
North Texas Normal College	North Texas, University of
North Texas State College	North Texas, University of

Former Name	Current Name
North Texas State Normal College	North Texas, University of
North Texas State Teachers College	North Texas, University of
North Texas State University	North Texas, University of
North Western Christian University	Butler University
North Western University	Northwestern University
North Wisconsin Academy	Northland College
Northeast Louisiana State College	Louisiana at Monroe, University of
Northeast Louisiana University	Louisiana at Monroe, University of
Northeast Missouri State College	Truman State University
Northeast Missouri State Teachers College	Truman State University
Northeast Missouri State University	Truman State University
Northeastern College	Northeastern University
Northeastern Illinois State College	Northeastern Illinois University
Northeastern Oklahoma State University	Northeastern State University
Northeastern State College	Northeastern State University
Northeastern State Normal School	Northeastern State University
Northeastern State Teachers College	Northeastern State University
Northeastern University of the Boston Young Men's Christian Association	Northeastern University
Northeastern University School of Commerce & Finance: Providence Branch	Roger Williams University
Northeastern University: Springfield Division	Western New England College
Northern Arizona Normal School	Northern Arizona University
Northern Arizona State Teachers College	Northern Arizona University
Northern Baptist Seminary, College Division	Judson College
Northern Branch of the College of Agriculture, University of California	California, Davis, University of
Northern Idaho College of Education	Lewis-Clark State College
Northern Illinois State College	Northern Illinois University
Northern Illinois State Normal School	Northern Illinois University
Northern Illinois State Teachers College	Northern Illinois University
Northern Indiana Normal School & Business Institute	Valparaiso University
Northern Kentucky State College	Northern Kentucky University
Northern Michigan College	Northern Michigan University
Northern Michigan College of Education	Northern Michigan University

Former Name	Current Name
Northern Montana Agricultural & Manual Training School	Montana State University-Northern
Northern Montana College	Montana State University-Northern
Northern Montana School	Montana State University-Northern
Northern Normal & Industrial School	Northern State University
Northern State College	Northern State University
Northern State Normal School	Maine at Farmington, University of
Northern State Normal School	Northern Michigan University
Northern State Teachers College	Northern Michigan University
Northern State Teachers College	Northern State University
Northern Virginia Branch of the University of Virginia	George Mason University
Northfield College	Carleton College
Northwest Bible College	Northwest College of the Assemblies of God
Northwest Bible Institute	Northwest College of the Assemblies of God
Northwest Missouri State College	Northwest Missouri State University
Northwest Missouri State Teachers College	Northwest Missouri State University
Northwest Nazarene College	Northwest Nazarene University
Northwestern Bible & Missionary Training School	Northwestern College
Northwestern Classical Academy	Northwestern College
Northwestern Junior College	Northwestern College
Northwestern Normal School	Northwestern Oklahoma State University
Northwestern Ohio Normal School	Ohio Northern University
Northwestern Schools	Northwestern College
Northwestern State College	Northwestern Oklahoma State University
Northwestern State College of Louisiana	Northwestern State University of Louisiana
Northwestern State Normal School	Northwestern Oklahoma State University
Northwestern State Teachers College	Northwestern Oklahoma State University
Northwestern Territorial Normal School	Northwestern Oklahoma State University
Northwest, University of the	Morningside College
North-Western College	North Central College
Notre Dame of Maryland Collegiate Institute for Young Ladies	Notre Dame of Maryland, College of
Notre Dame, College of	Notre Dame de Namur University

Former Name	Current Name
Noviate Normal School	Aquinas College
Nuclear Medicine Institute	Findlay, The University of
Nyack Missionary College	Nyack College

Former Name	Current Name
Oak Hollow Academy	Brevard College
Oakland Bible Institute	Patten College
Oakland City College	Oakland City University
Oakwood Industrial School	Oakwood College
Oakwood Junior College	Oakwood College
Oakwood Manual Training School	Oakwood College
Oberlin Collegiate Institute	Oberlin College
Oberlin Home & School	Pfeiffer University
Occidental University of Los Angeles, The	Occidental College
Oglethorpe College	Oglethorpe University
Ohio Agricultural & Mechanical College	Ohio State University, The
Ohio Normal University	Ohio Northern University
Ohio University: Portsmouth	Shawnee State University
Oklahoma Agricultural & Mechanical College	Oklahoma State University
Oklahoma Christian College	Oklahoma Christian University
Oklahoma Christian University of Science & Arts	Oklahoma Christian University
Oklahoma City College	Oklahoma City University
Oklahoma College for Women	Science & Arts of Oklahoma, University of
Oklahoma College of Liberal Arts	Science & Arts of Oklahoma, University of
Oklahoma Industrial Institute & College for Girls	Science & Arts of Oklahoma, University of
Oklahoma Panhandle State College of Agriculture & Applied Science	Oklahoma Panhandle State University
Old Dominion College	Old Dominion University
Olivet College	Olivet Nazarene University
Olivet Institute	Olivet College
Olivet Nazarene College	Olivet Nazarene University
Olivet University	Olivet Nazarene University
Omaha, Municipal University of	Nebraska at Omaha, University of
Omaha, University of	Nebraska at Omaha, University of
Oneida Conference, The Seminary of the	Cazenovia College

352

Former Name	Current Name
Oneonta State Normal School	New York College at Oneonta, State University of
Orange County State College	California State University, Fullerton
Orange State College	California State University, Fullerton
Oregon Agricultural College	Oregon State University
Oregon City College	Linfield College
Oregon City University	Linfield College
Oregon College of Education	Western Oregon University
Oregon Institute	Willamette University
Oregon Normal School	Western Oregon University
Oregon State Agricultural College	Oregon State University
Oregon State College	Oregon State University
Oregon State Normal School	Western Oregon University
Orphan School of the Christian Church of Missouri, The	William Woods University
Oshkosh State Normal School	Wisconsin-Oshkosh, University of
Oshkosh State Teachers College	Wisconsin-Oshkosh, University of
Oswego Primary Teachers Training School	New York College at Oswego, State University of
Oswego State Normal & Training School	New York College at Oswego, State University of
Otterbein University	Otterbein College
Ouachita Baptist College	Ouachita Baptist University
Ouachita Parish Junior College	Louisiana at Monroe, University of
Our Lady of Angels College	Neumann College
Our Lady of Holy Cross College	Our Lady of Holy Cross College
Our Lady of Mercy, College of	Saint Joseph's College
Our Lady of the Angels, College & Seminary of	Niagara University
Our Lady of the Elms, College of	Elms College
Our Lady of the Lake Academy	Our Lady of the Lake University of San Antonio
Our Lady of the Lake College	Our Lady of the Lake University of San Antonio
Our Lady of the Sacred Heart, Convent of	Holy Names College
Ozarks, School of the	Ozarks, College of the
Ozarks, The College of the	Ozarks, University of the

P

| Pace College | Pace University |
| Pace Institute | Pace University |

Former Name	Current Name
Pace School of Accountancy	Pace University
Pacific Bible College	Azusa Pacific University
Pacific Bible College	Point Loma Nazarene University
Pacific Bible College	Warner Pacific College
Pacific Bible Institute	Fresno Pacific University
Pacific Bible Seminary	Hope International University
Pacific Christian College	Hope International University
Pacific College	George Fox University
Pacific College of Fresno	Fresno Pacific University
Pacific Lutheran Academy	Pacific Lutheran University
Pacific Lutheran College	Pacific Lutheran University
Pacific, The College of the	Pacific, University of the
Pacific, The University of the	Pacific, University of the
Paine Institute	Paine College
Palmer University	Ball State University
Pan American College	Texas-Pan American, The University of
Pan American University	Texas-Pan American, The University of
Panhandle Agricultural & Mechanical College	Oklahoma Panhandle State University
Pan-Handle Agricultural Institute	Oklahoma Panhandle State University
Park College	Park University
Parsons Seminary	Coe College
Pasadena College	Point Loma Nazarene University
Paterson State College	William Paterson University of New Jersey, The
Patten Bible College	Patten College
Patten School of Religion	Patten College
Patterson City Normal School	William Paterson University of New Jersey, The
Payne Institute	Allen University
Pembroke State College	North Carolina at Pembroke, The University of
Pembroke State College for Indians	North Carolina at Pembroke, The University of
Pembroke State University	North Carolina at Pembroke, The University of
Peniel University	Southern Nazarene University
Penn College	William Penn University
Pennsylvania College for Women	Chatham College
Pennsylvania College of Gettysburg	Gettysburg College
Pennsylvania Female College	Chatham College
Pennsylvania Military Academy	Widener University

354

Former Name	Current Name
Pennsylvania Military College	Widener University
Pennsylvania State College, The	Pennsylvania State University, The
Pennsylvania, University of the State of	Pennsylvania, University of
Pentacostal Collegiate Institute	Eastern Nazarene College
Pentacostal Literary and Bible Training School	Trevecca Nazarene University
Peru State Teachers College	Peru State College
Pestalozzi-Froebel Teachers College	Columbia College Chicago
Pfeiffer College	Pfeiffer University
Pfeiffer Junior College	Pfeiffer University
Philadelphia College of Textiles & Science	Philadelphia University
Philadelphia Textile Institute	Philadelphia University
Philadelphia Textile School, The	Philadelphia University
Philadelphia, Academy of	Pennsylvania, University of
Pierre University	Huron University
Pikeville Collegiate Institute	Pikeville College
Pine Grove Normal Academy	Grove City College
Pine Manor Junior College	Pine Manor College
Pinkerton High School & Midway Junior College	Midway College
Pioneer School	Hope College
Pittsburgh Academy	Pittsburgh, University of
Pittsburgh Catholic College of the Holy Ghost	Duquesne University of the Holy Ghost
Pittsburgh School of Accountancy	Robert Morris University
Plainfield College	North Central College
Platteville State Teachers College	Wisconsin-Platteville, University of
Plattsburgh Academy	New York College at Plattsburgh, State University of
Plymouth Normal School	Plymouth State College
Plymouth Teachers College	Plymouth State College
PMC Colleges	Widener University
Point Loma College	Point Loma Nazarene University
Point Loma Nazarene College	Point Loma Nazarene University
Point Park Junior College	Point Park College
Polytechnic Institute of Brooklyn	Polytechnic University
Polytechnic Institute of New York	Polytechnic University
Portland State College	Portland State University
Post College	Teikyo Post University
Post Junior College	Teikyo Post University
Post Junior College of Commerce	Teikyo Post University

Former Name	Current Name
Potsdam Normal School	New York College at Potsdam, State University of
Prairie View Agricultural & Mechanical College	Prairie View A&M University
Prairie View State Normal & Industrial College	Prairie View A&M University
Prairie View University	Prairie View A&M University
Prairieville Academy	Carroll College
Presbyterian College for Women	Queens College
Presbyterian College of South Carolina	Presbyterian College
Presbyterian Female College	Queens College
Presbyterian School for Indian Girls	Tulsa, The University of
Presbyterian University of South Dakota	Huron University
Prescott Center College	Prescott College
Presentation Blessed Virgin Mary Junior College	Madonna University
Prince Edward Academy	Hampden-Sydney College
Princess Anne Academy	Maryland Eastern Shore, University of
Princess Anne College	Maryland Eastern Shore, University of
Providence Institute of Engineering & Finance	Roger Williams University
Pueblo Junior College	Southern Colorado, University of
Puget Sound University	Puget Sound, University of
Puget Sound, College of	Puget Sound, University of

Former Name	Current Name
Queen City Business College	Champlain College
Queens College	Queens College
Queens College of the City of New York	Queens College of the City University of New York
Queens-Chicora College	Queens College
Queen's College	Rutgers, The State University of New Jersey
Quincy College	Quincy University
Quincy College & Seminary	Quincy University
Quinnipiac College	Quinnipiac University

Former Name	Current Name
Rabbi Isaac Elchanan Theological Seminary	Yeshiva University
Rabbi Isaac Elchanan Theological Seminary & Yeshiva College	Yeshiva University

Former Name	Current Name
Radford College	Radford University
Raleigh Institute	Shaw University
Red Wing, Academy at	Gustavus Adolphus College
Regency of West Virginia Normal School at Fairmont, The	Fairmont State College
Regional Center of State Continuing Education Division	Maine at Augusta, University of
Regis College	Regis University
Regis College for Women	Regis College
Rensselaer Institute	Rensselaer Polytechnic Institute
Rensselaer School	Rensselaer Polytechnic Institute
Rhode Island College	Brown University
Rhode Island College of Agricultural & Mechanical Arts	Rhode Island, University of
Rhode Island College of Education	Rhode Island College
Rhode Island State College	Rhode Island, University of
Rhode Island State Normal School	Rhode Island College
Richland County, Academy of	Augusta State University
Richmond College	Richmond, University of
Richmond Institute	Virginia Union University
Richmond Theological School for Freedmen	Virginia Union University
Rider Business College, The	Rider University
Rider College	Rider University
Rider-Moore & Stewart School of Business	Rider University
Rio Grande College	Rio Grande, University of
Ripley Female College	Green Mountain College
Rittenhouse Academy	Georgetown College
River Falls State Normal School	Wisconsin-River Falls, University of
River Falls State Teachers College	Wisconsin-River Falls, University of
Roanoke Classical Seminary	Manchester College
Roanoke College	Averett University
Roanoke Female College	Averett University
Roanoke Institute	Averett University
Robert Morris College	Robert Morris University
Robert Morris Junior College	Robert Morris University
Robert Morris School, The	Robert Morris University
Roberts Junior College	Roberts Wesleyan College
Rochester Athenaeum & Mechanics Association	Rochester Institute of Technology

Former Name	Current Name
Rochester Athenaeum & Mechanics Institute	Rochester Institute of Technology
Rochester Athenaeum & Young Men's Association	Rochester Institute of Technology
Rochester Lutheran Proseminary	Wagner College
Rockford Female Seminary	Rockford College
Rockford Seminary	Rockford College
Rockhurst University & High School	Rockhurst University
Rockmont College	Colorado Christian University
Rocky Mountain Missionary & Evangelistic School	Oklahoma Wesleyan University
Roger Williams College	Roger Williams University
Roger Williams Junior College	Roger Williams University
Roosevelt College of Chicago	Roosevelt University
Rosary College	Dominican University
Rosary Hill College	Daemen College
Rowan College of New Jersey	Rowan University
Royal Springs Academy	Georgetown College
Russell Creek Academy	Campbellsville University
Rust University	Rust College
Rutersville College	Southwestern University
Rutgers College	Rutgers, The State University of New Jersey
Rutgers University	Rutgers, The State University of New Jersey
Rutherford Academy	Brevard College
Rutherford College	Brevard College
Rutherford Seminary	Brevard College
Rutland County Grammar School	Castleton State College

S

Sacramento State College	California State University, Sacramento
Sacred Heart Academy	Mount Mercy College
Sacred Heart Academy	Newman University
Sacred Heart Boys School & College	Saint Gregory's University
Sacred Heart College	Aquinas College
Sacred Heart College	Newman University
Sacred Heart College	Regis University
Sacred Heart Junior College	Newman University
Sacred Heart, Academy of the	Manhattanville College

Former Name	Current Name
Sacred Heart, College of the	Manhattanville College
Sacred Heart, College of the	Regis University
Sacred Heart, Convent of the	Maryville University of Saint Louis
Saginaw Bay State College	Saginaw Valley State University
Saginaw Valley College	Saginaw Valley State University
Saginaw Valley State College	Saginaw Valley State University
Saint Aloysius Academy	Mount Aloysius College
Saint Ambrose College	Saint Ambrose University
Saint Ambrose Seminary	Saint Ambrose University
Saint Angela, The College of	New Rochelle, The College of
Saint Anselm's College	Saint Anselm College
Saint Ansgar's Academy	Gustavus Adolphus College
Saint Augustine's Academy	Villanova University
Saint Augustine's Junior College	Saint Augustine's College
Saint Augustine's Normal School & Collegiate Institute	Saint Augustine's College
Saint Augustine's School	Saint Augustine's College
Saint Benedict's Academy	Saint Benedict, College of
Saint Benedict's College	Benedictine College
Saint Benedict's College & Academy	Saint Benedict, College of
Saint Bernardine of Siena College	Siena College
Saint Bonaventure College & Seminary	Saint Bonaventure University
Saint Clara's College	Dominican University
Saint Clare College	Cardinal Stritch University
Saint Cloud State College	Saint Cloud State University
Saint Cloud State Teachers College	Saint Cloud State University
Saint Edward's Academy	Saint Edward's University
Saint Edward's College	Saint Edward's University
Saint Francis Academy	Saint Francis College
Saint Francis Academy	Saint Francis University
Saint Francis Academy for Females	Saint Xavier University
Saint Francis College	New England, University of
Saint Francis College	Saint Francis University
Saint Francis College	Saint Francis, University of
Saint Francis Junior College	New England, University of
Saint Francis Monestary of the City of Brooklyn	Saint Francis College
Saint Francis Normal School	Saint Francis, University of
Saint Francis Normal School for Women	Marian College

Former Name	Current Name
Saint Francis Solano, College of	Quincy University
Saint Francis, College of	Saint Francis, University of
Saint Gregory's College	Saint Gregory's University
Saint Gregory's High School & College	Saint Gregory's University
Saint Ignatius Academy	San Francisco, University of
Saint Ignatius College	John Carroll University
Saint Ignatius College	San Francisco, University of
Saint Ignatius College	Loyola University of Chicago
Saint John's College	Fordham University
Saint John's College	Saint John's University
Saint John's Seminary	Saint John's University
Saint John's University, Brooklyn	Saint John's University
Saint Joseph Academy	Clarke College
Saint Joseph Academy	Seton Hill University
Saint Joseph Academy	Siena Heights University
Saint Joseph Business School	Southern Vermont College
Saint Joseph College	Siena Heights University
Saint Joseph College	Southern Vermont College
Saint Joseph Junior College	Missouri Western State College
Saint Joseph Normal School	Alverno College
Saint Joseph Teachers College	Saint Joseph, College of
Saint Joseph the Provider, The College of	Saint Joseph, College of
Saint Joseph's Calumet College	Calumet College of Saint Joseph
Saint Joseph's College	Loras College
Saint Joseph's College	Saint Joseph's University
Saint Joseph's College Calument Campus	Calumet College of Saint Joseph
Saint Joseph's College Calumet Center	Calumet College of Saint Joseph
Saint Joseph's College for Women	Saint Joseph's College
Saint Joseph's Orphanage	Incarnate Word, University of the
Saint Joseph's School	Mount Mercy College
Saint Lawrence Academy	New York College at Potsdam, State University of
Saint Leo College	Saint Leo University
Saint Leo College Preparatory School	Saint Leo University
Saint Louis Academy	Saint Louis University
Saint Louis College	Saint Louis University
Saint Louis College	Saint Mary's University of San Antonio

Former Name	Current Name
Saint Louis Junior College	Chaminade University of Honolulu
Saint Mary Academy	Marygrove College
Saint Mary College	Marygrove College
Saint Mary Junior College	Saint Mary College
Saint Mary of the Springs, College of	Ohio Dominican College
Saint Mary's	Saint Mary's College of California
Saint Mary's Academy	Clarke College
Saint Mary's Academy	Belmont Abbey College
Saint Mary's Academy	Marylhurst University
Saint Mary's Academy	Saint Mary College
Saint Mary's Academy	Saint Mary's College
Saint Mary's Academy	Saint Mary's University of Minnesota
Saint Mary's Academy & College	Marylhurst University
Saint Mary's College	Dayton, University of
Saint Mary's College	Mount Mary College
Saint Mary's College of Minnesota	Saint Mary's University of Minnesota
Saint Mary's Convent & Academy	Ohio Dominican College
Saint Mary's Female Institute	Saint Mary-of-the-Woods College
Saint Mary's Female Seminary	Saint Mary's College of Maryland
Saint Mary's Institute	Dayton, University of
Saint Mary's Institute	Mount Mary College
Saint Mary's Institute	Saint Mary's University of San Antonio
Saint Mary's School for Boys	Dayton, University of
Saint Mary's Seminary Junior College	Saint Mary's College of Maryland
Saint Mary's University	Saint Mary's University of San Antonio
Saint Mary-of-the-Woods College	Saint Mary-of-the-Woods College
Saint Michael's College	Santa Fe, The College of
Saint Michael's Institute	Saint Michael's College
Saint Olaf's School	Saint Olaf College
Saint Paul Bible College	Crown College
Saint Paul Bible Institute	Crown College
Saint Paul's Normal & Industrial School	Saint Paul's College
Saint Paul's Polytechnic Institute	Saint Paul's College
Saint Procopius College	Benedictine University
Saint Raphael Seminary	Loras College
Saint Regina Academy	Edgewood College
Saint Rose Junior College	Viterbo University
Saint Rose Normal School	Viterbo University
Saint Stephens College	Bard College

Former Name	Current Name
Saint Teresa College	Avila College
Saint Teresa's Academy	Avila College
Saint Teresa, College of	Avila College
Saint Thomas Aquinas Seminary	Saint Thomas, University of
Saint Thomas College	Scranton, University of
Saint Thomas, College of	Saint Thomas, University of
Saint Vincent's College	DePaul University
Saint Vincent's College	Loyola Marymount University
Saint Xavier College	Saint Xavier University
Saint Xavier College	Xavier University
Saint Xavier College for Women	Saint Xavier University
Salem Academy & College	Salem Academy & College
Salem College	Salem International University
Salem Female Academy	Salem Academy & College
Salem Normal School	Salem State College
Salem School for Girls	Salem Academy & College
Salem Teachers College	Salem State College
Salem-Teikyo University	Salem International University
Salisbury State College	Salisbury University
Salisbury State University	Salisbury University
Salt Lake Collegiate Institute	Westminster College
Salve Regina College	Salve Regina University
Salve Regina-The Newport School	Salve Regina University
Sam Houston Normal Institute	Sam Houston State University
Sam Houston State College	Sam Houston State University
Sam Houston State Teachers College	Sam Houston State University
San Angelo College	Angelo State University
San Diego College for Men	San Diego, University of
San Diego State College	San Diego State University
San Diego State Normal School	San Diego State University
San Diego State Teachers College	San Diego State University
San Fernando Valley Campus of Los Angeles State College of Applied Arts & Sciences	California State University, Northridge
San Fernando Valley State College	California State University, Northridge
San Francisco State College	San Francisco State University
San Francisco State Normal School	San Francisco State University
San Francisco State Teachers College	San Francisco State University
San Isabel Junior College	Southern Colorado, University of
San Jose State College	San Jose State University

Former Name	Current Name
San Jose State Normal School	San Jose State University
San Jose State Teachers College	San Jose State University
Santa Barbara College of the University of California	California, Santa Barbara, University of
Santa Barbara State College	California, Santa Barbara, University of
Santa Barbara State Normal School	California, Santa Barbara, University of
Santa Barbara State Normal School of Manual Arts & Home Economics	California, Santa Barbara, University of
Santa Barbara State Teachers College	California, Santa Barbara, University of
Santa Clara College	Santa Clara University
Santa Clara, University of	Santa Clara University
Sarah Lawrence College for Women	Sarah Lawrence College
Savannah State College	Savannah State University
Scandanavian Department of the Baptist Union Theological Seminary of the University of Chicago	Bethel College
School for Christian Workers	Springfield College
School of Business & Civic Administration of the City College	Bernard M Baruch College of the City University of New York
School of Expression	Curry College
School of Law of the Youngstown Association School	Youngstown State University
School #1	Bowie State University
Schreiner College	Schreiner University
Schreiner Institute	Schreiner University
Scotia Seminary	Barber-Scotia College
Scotia Women's College	Barber-Scotia College
Scripps College for Women	Scripps College
Scripps Institution of Biological Research	California, San Diego, University of
Seattle College	Seattle University
Seattle Pacific College	Seattle Pacific University
Seattle Seminary	Seattle Pacific University
Seattle Seminary & College	Seattle Pacific University
Second District Agricultural School	Arkansas Tech University
Select School	Alfred University
Select School	Mount Union College
Select School at Pine Grove	Grove City College
Seminary for Girls	Queens College
Seton Hall College	Seton Hall University
Seton Hill College	Seton Hill University
Seton Junior College	Seton Hill University

Former Name	Current Name
Shaw Collegiate Institute	Shaw University
Shaw School	Rust College
Shaw School of Business	Husson College
Shaw University	Rust College
Shawnee State Community College	Shawnee State University
Shawnee State General & Technical College	Shawnee State University
Sheldon Jackson College	Westminster College
Shenandoah College	Shenandoah University
Shenandoah College & Conservatory of Music	Shenandoah University
Shenandoah College & School of Music	Shenandoah University
Shenandoah Collegiate Institute & School of Music	Shenandoah University
Shenandoah High School	Shenandoah University
Shenandoah Institute	Shenandoah University
Shenandoah Seminary	Shenandoah University
Shepherd College State Normal School	Shepherd College
Shepherd State Teachers College	Shepherd College
Shippensburg State College	Shippensburg University of Pennsylvania of the State System of Higher Education
Shorter Female College	Shorter College
Siena Heights College	Siena Heights University
Silver Lake College of the Holy Family	Silver Lake College
Simmons College	Hardin-Simmons University
Simmons Female College	Simmons College
Simmons University	Hardin-Simmons University
Simpson Bible College	Simpson College
Simpson Bible Institute	Simpson College
Simpson Centenary College	Simpson College
Sinsinawa Academy	Dominican University
Sioux Falls College	Sioux Falls, University of
Sioux Falls University	Sioux Falls, University of
Skidmore College of Arts of Saratoga Springs	Skidmore College
Slater Industrial Academy	Winston-Salem State University
Slater Industrial & State Normal School	Winston-Salem State University
Slippery Rock State College	Slippery Rock University of Pennsylvania of the State System of Higher Education

Former Name	Current Name
Slippery Rock State Normal School	Slippery Rock University of Pennsylvania of the State System of Higher Education
Slippery Rock State Teachers College	Slippery Rock University of Pennsylvania of the State System of Higher Education
Sonoma State College	Sonoma State University
South Carolina Agricultural College & Mechanics Institute	South Carolina State University
South Carolina at Aiken Center, University of	South Carolina Aiken, University of
South Carolina at Aiken, University of	South Carolina Aiken, University of
South Carolina at Coastal Carolina, University of	Coastal Carolina University
South Carolina College	South Carolina, University of
South Carolina College of Agriculture & Mechanical Arts	South Carolina, University of
South Carolina Industrial & Winthrop Normal College	Winthrop University
South Carolina Military Academy	Citadel, The Military College of South Carolina, The
South Carolina State College	South Carolina State University
South Dakota State College of Agriculture & Mechanic Arts	South Dakota State University
South Dakota, State University of	South Dakota, The University of
South Dakota, University of	South Dakota, The University of
South Florida Institute	Florida Southern College
South Georgia State Normal College	Valdosta State University
South Georgia Teachers College	Georgia Southern University
South Lancaster Academy	Atlantic Union College
South Mississippi College	William Carey College
South Park Junior College	Lamar University
South Texas State Teachers College	Texas A&M University-Kingsville
South Western Normal School	California University of Pennsylvania of the State System of Higher Education
Southeast Missouri State College	Southeast Missouri State University
Southeast Missouri State Teachers College	Southeast Missouri State University
Southeastern Louisiana College	Southeastern Louisiana University
Southeastern Massachusetts University	Massachusetts Dartmouth, University of
Southeastern Normal School	Southeastern Oklahoma State University
Southeastern State College	Southeastern Oklahoma State University

Former Name	Current Name
Southeastern Teachers College	Southeastern Oklahoma State University
Southeastern University of the YMCA of The District of Columbia	Southeastern University
Southern Baptist College	Williams Baptist College
Southern California Bible College	Vanguard University of Southern California
Southern California Bible School	Vanguard University of Southern California
Southern California College	Vanguard University of Southern California
Southern California Junior College	La Sierra University
Southern College	Florida Southern College
Southern College of Seventh-day Adventists	Southern Adventist University
Southern Colorado Junior College, The	Southern Colorado, University of
Southern Colorado State College	Southern Colorado, University of
Southern Connecticut State College	Southern Connecticut State University
Southern Illinois Normal University	Southern Illinois University Carbondale
Southern Illinois University	Southern Illinois University Carbondale
Southern Illinois University at Edwardsville	Southern Illinois University Edwardsville
Southern Industrial School	Southern Adventist University
Southern Junior College	Southern Adventist University
Southern Missionary College	Southern Adventist University
Southern Oregon College	Southern Oregon University
Southern Oregon College of Education	Southern Oregon University
Southern Oregon State College	Southern Oregon University
Southern Oregon State Normal School	Southern Oregon University
Southern State College	Southern Arkansas University
Southern Training School	Southern Adventist University
Southern University	Birmingham-Southern College
Southern University	Southern University & Agricultural & Mechanical College
Southern Utah State College	Southern Utah State University
Southern Utah, College of	Southern Utah State University
Southern & Western Theological Seminary	Maryville College
Southestern Junior College	Alaska Southeast, University of

Former Name	Current Name
Southwest Baptist College	Southwest Baptist University
Southwest Kansas Conference College	Southwestern College
Southwest Minnesota State College	Southwest State University
Southwest Missouri State College	Southwest Missouri State University
Southwest Missouri State Teachers College	Southwest Missouri State University
Southwest Texas State College	Southwest Texas State University
Southwest Texas State Normal College	Southwest Texas State University
Southwest Texas State Normal School	Southwest Texas State University
Southwest Texas State Teachers College	Southwest Texas State University
Southwest Virginia Institute	Virginia Intermont College
Southwestern Adventist College	Southwestern Adventist University
Southwestern at Memphis	Rhodes College
Southwestern Baptist University	Union University
Southwestern College	Rhodes College
Southwestern Collegiate Institute	John Brown University
Southwestern Institute of Technology	Southwestern Oklahoma State University
Southwestern Junior College	Southwestern Adventist University
Southwestern Louisiana Industrial Institute	Louisiana at Lafayette, University of
Southwestern Louisiana Institute of Liberal & Technical Learning	Louisiana at Lafayette, University of
Southwestern Louisiana, The University of	Louisiana at Lafayette, University of
Southwestern Massachusetts Technical Institute	Massachusetts Dartmouth, University of
Southwestern Normal School	Southwestern Oklahoma State University
Southwestern Presbyterian University	Rhodes College
Southwestern State College	Southwestern Oklahoma State University
Southwestern State College of Diversified Occupations	Southwestern Oklahoma State University
Southwestern State Teachers College	Southwestern Oklahoma State University
Southwestern Union College	Southwestern Adventist University
Southwest, College of the	Southwest, College of the
Spalding College	Spalding University
Spartanburg Regional Campus	South Carolina Spartanburg, University of

Former Name	Current Name
Spearfish Normal School	Black Hills State University
Spelman Seminary	Spelman College
Spring Arbor College	Spring Arbor University
Spring Arbor Seminary	Spring Arbor University
Spring Arbor Seminary & Junior College	Spring Arbor University
Spring Creek Normal & Collegiate Institute	Bridgewater College
Springfield College	Drury University
Stanislaus State College	California State University, Stanislaus
State Agricultural College	Oregon State University
State Agricultural College of Oregon	Oregon State University
State Agricultural College of the State of Oregon	Oregon State University
State Agricultural College, The	Michigan State University
State Agricultural School	Rhode Island, University of
State Agricultural & Mechanical College for Negroes	Alabama Agricultural & Mechanical University
State Agricultural & Mechanical College: Third District	Southern Arkansas University
State Agricultural & Mechanical Institute for Negroes	Alabama Agricultural & Mechanical University
State College at Bridgewater	Bridgewater State College
State College at Fitchburg	Fitchburg State College
State College at Framingham	Framingham State College
State College at Salem	Salem State College
State College at Westfield	Westfield State College
State College at Worcester	Worcester State College
State College for Alameda County	California State University, Hayward
State College for Colored Students	Delaware State University
State College of Agriculture & the Mechanical Arts	Maine, University of
State College of Arkansas	Central Arkansas, University of
State College of Iowa	Northern Iowa, University of
State College of Washington, The	Washington State University
State Colored Normal School	Fayetteville State University
State Colored Normal & Industrial School	Fayetteville State University
State Female Normal School	Longwood College
State Normal College for Colored Students	Florida Agricultural & Mechanical University
State Normal School	Fayetteville State University

Former Name	Current Name
State Normal School	Fitchburg State College
State Normal School	Framingham State College
State Normal School	New York College at Fredonia, State University of
State Normal School	Northern Colorado, University of
State Normal School	Western State College of Colorado, The
State Normal School at Alamosa	Adams State College
State Normal School at Castleton	Castleton State College
State Normal School at Chadron, Nebraska	Chadron State College
State Normal School at Cheney	Eastern Washington University
State Normal School at New Watcom	Western Washington University
State Normal School at Saint Cloud	Saint Cloud State University
State Normal School at Watcom	Western Washington University
State Normal School at Worcester	Worcester State College
State Normal School for Colored Persons	Kentucky State University
State Normal School for Colored Students	Alabama State University
State Normal School for Second Normal District of Missouri	Central Missouri State University
State Normal School for the Negro Race	Fayetteville State University
State Normal School for Women	Longwood College
State Normal School for Women at Harrisonburg	James Madison University
State Normal School of West Virginia: Glenville Branch	Glenville State College
State Normal School #2 at Frostburg	Frostburg State University
State Normal School & State Teachers College at Wayne	Wayne State College
State Normal School & University for Colored Students & Teachers	Alabama State University
State Normal School, Mansfield	Mansfield University of Pennsylvania of the State System of Higher Education
State Normal School, Valley City	Valley City State University
State Normal & Industrial College	North Carolina at Greensboro, The University of
State Normal & Industrial College for Colored Students	Florida Agricultural & Mechanical University
State Normal & Industrial School	North Carolina at Greensboro, The University of
State Normal & Industrial School for Women at Radford	Radford University

Former Name	Current Name
State Normal & Industrial School for Women, Fredericksburg	Mary Washington College
State Normal & Training School	New York College at Buffalo, State University of
State Teachers College	Alabama State University
State Teachers College	Fitchburg State College
State Teachers College	Radford University
State Teachers College at Brockport	New York College at Brockport, State University of
State Teachers College at Buffalo	New York College at Buffalo, State University of
State Teachers College at Cortland	New York College at Cortland, State University of
State Teachers College at Farmville	Longwood College
State Teachers College at Fredonia	New York College at Fredonia, State University of
State Teachers College at Frostburg	Frostburg State University
State Teachers College at Geneseo	New York College at Geneseo, State University of
State Teachers College at Harrisonburg	James Madison University
State Teachers College at Lowell	Massachusetts Lowell, University of
State Teachers College at New Paltz	New York College at New Paltz, State University of
State Teachers College at North Adams	Massachusetts College of Liberal Arts
State Teachers College at Oneonta	New York College at Oneonta, State University of
State Teachers College at Oswego	New York College at Oswego, State University of
State Teachers College at Plattsburgh	New York College at Plattsburgh, State University of
State Teachers College at Potsdam	New York College at Potsdam, State University of
State Teachers College at Shippensburg	Shippensburg University of Pennsylvania of the State System of Higher Education
State Teachers College at Westfield	Westfield State College
State Teachers College, Chico	California State University, Chico
State Teachers College, Fredericksburg	Mary Washington College
State Teachers College, Fresno	California State University, Fresno
State Teachers College, Johnson City	East Tennessee State University
State Teachers College, Livingston	West Alabama, University of
State Teachers College, Murfreesboro	Middle Tennessee State University
State University College for Teachers at Buffalo	New York College at Buffalo, State University of

Former Name	Current Name
State University College of Education at Albany	New York University Center at Albany, State University of
State University College of Education at Brockport	New York College at Brockport, State University of
State University College of Education at Buffalo	New York College at Buffalo, State University of
State University College of Education at Cortland	New York College at Cortland, State University of
State University College of Education at Fredonia	New York College at Fredonia, State University of
State University College of Education at Geneseo	New York College at Geneseo, State University of
State University College of Education at New Paltz	New York College at New Paltz, State University of
State University College of Education at Oswego	New York College at Oswego, State University of
State University College of Education at Plattsburgh	New York College at Plattsburgh, State University of
State University College of Education at Potsdam	New York College at Potsdam, State University of
State University College of Forestry at Syracuse University	New York College of Environmental Science & Forestry at Syracuse, State University of
State University of Science & Engineering on Long Island	New York University Center at Stony Brook, State University of
State University Teachers College at Brockport	New York College at Brockport, State University of
State University Teachers College at Cortland	New York College at Cortland, State University of
State University Teachers College at Fredonia	New York College at Fredonia, State University of
State University Teachers College at Geneseo	New York College at Geneseo, State University of
State University Teachers College at New Paltz	New York College at New Paltz, State University of
State University Teachers College at Oneonta	New York College at Oneonta, State University of
State University Teachers College at Oswego	New York College at Oswego, State University of
State University Teachers College at Plattsburgh	New York College at Plattsburgh, State University of
State University Teachers College at Potsdam	New York College at Potsdam, State University of
State University: Long Island Center	New York University Center at Stony Brook, State University of
Staten Island Community College	Staten Island of the City University of New York, The College of

Former Name	Current Name
Stephen F Austin State College	Stephen F Austin State University
Stephen F Austin State Teachers College	Stephen F Austin State University
Stephenville College	Tarleton State University
Steubenville, College of	Franciscan University of Steubenville
Steubenville, University of	Franciscan University of Steubenville
Stevens Point State Normal School	Wisconsin-Stevens Point, University of
Stewart College	Rhodes College
Stillman Institute	Stillman College
Stockton Business College, Normal School, & Telegraphic Institute	Humphreys College
Stockton State College	Richard Stockton College of New Jersey, The
Storrs Agricultural College	Connecticut, University of
Storrs Agricultural School	Connecticut, University of
Stout Institute	Wisconsin-Stout, University of
Stout Manual Training & Domestic Science School	Wisconsin-Stout, University of
Stout State College	Wisconsin-Stout, University of
Stout State University	Wisconsin-Stout, University of
Straight College	Dillard University
Straight University	Dillard University
Strayer College	Strayer University
Strayer College of Accountancy	Strayer University
Strayer Junior College of Finance	Strayer University
Strayer's Business College	Strayer University
St. Leo Academy	Saint Leo University
St. Leo College	Saint Leo University
St. Leo College & Preparatory School	Saint Leo University
St. Leo High School	Saint Leo University
St. Leo Military Academy	Saint Leo University
St. Leo's College	Saint Leo University
Suffolk Law School	Suffolk University
Sul Ross Normal College	Sul Ross State University
Sul Ross State College	Sul Ross State University
Sul Ross State Teachers College	Sul Ross State University
Sullivan Business College	Sullivan University
Sullivan College	Sullivan University
Sullivan Junior College of Business	Sullivan University
Sumner Academy	Whitworth College
Superior Normal School	Wisconsin-Superior, University of

Former Name	Current Name
Superior State Teachers College	Wisconsin-Superior, University of
Suwannee River, The Seminary West of the	Florida State University, The
Swayne School	Talladega College
Swedish Evangelical Mission Covenant College & Seminary	North Park University
Sweet Briar Institute	Sweet Briar College

Former Name	Current Name
Tampa Junior College	Tampa, The University of
Tarleton State College	Tarleton State University
Teacher Training School, Blue Island	Chicago State University
Teachers College of Connecticut	Central Connecticut State University
Tempe State Teachers College	Arizona State University
Temple College	Temple University
Tennessee Agricultural & Industrial State College	Tennessee State University
Tennessee Agricultural & Industrial State Normal College	Tennessee State University
Tennessee Agricultural & Industrial State Normal School	Tennessee State University
Tennessee Agricultural & Industrial State University	Tennessee State University
Tennessee Junior College	Tennessee: Martin, The University of
Tennessee Polytechnic Institute	Tennessee Technological University
Tennessee Technological University	Tennessee Technological University
Territorial Normal School	Western New Mexico University
Territorial Normal School of Oklahoma	Central Oklahoma, University of
Territorial University of Washington	Washington, University of
Texas A & I University	Texas A&M University-Kingsville
Texas A&I University at Corpus Christi	Texas A&M University-Corpus Christi
Texas A&M University at Laredo	Texas A&M International University
Texas College of Arts & Industries	Texas A&M University-Kingsville
Texas College of Mines & Metallurgy	Texas at El Paso, The University of
Texas Holiness College	Southern Nazarene University
Texas Lutheran College	Texas Lutheran University
Texas Normal College & Teacher Training Institute	North Texas, University of
Texas State College for Women	Texas Woman's University
Texas State School of Mines & Metallurgy	Texas at El Paso, The University of
Texas State University for Negroes	Texas Southern University

Former Name	Current Name
Texas Technological College	Texas Tech University
Texas University	Southwestern University
Texas Western College	Texas at El Paso, The University of
Texas Woman's University	Texas Woman's University
Texas, Department of Mines & Metallurgy, University of	Texas at El Paso, The University of
Texas, The University of	Texas at Austin, The University of
Textile Division of the Philadelphia Museum & School of Industrial Art	Philadelphia University
Thames College	Connecticut College
Theological School of the Christian Reformed Church, The	Calvin College
Theological Seminary of the Evangelical Lutheran Synod of Ohio	Capital University
Theological Seminary of the Protestant Episcopal Church, The	Kenyon College
Thiel Hall	Thiel College
Third District Agricultural School	Southern Arkansas University
Third District Agricultural & Mechanical College	Georgia Southwestern State University
Third District Agricultural & Mechanical School	Georgia Southwestern State University
Third District Normal School of Southeast Missouri	Southeast Missouri State University
Third State Normal School	Saint Cloud State University
Thomas College	Thomas University
Thomas County Community College	Thomas University
Thomas Jefferson College of Chicago	Roosevelt University
Thomas S Clarkson Memorial College of Technology	Clarkson University
Thomas S Clarkson Memorial School of Technology	Clarkson University
Throop College of Technology	California Institute of Technology
Throop Polytechnic Institute	California Institute of Technology
Throop University	California Institute of Technology
Toledo University	Toledo, The University of
Toledo University of Arts & Trades	Toledo, The University of
Toledo, University of the City of	Toledo, The University of
Towson State College	Towson University
Towson State University	Towson University
Training School for Christian Workers	Azusa Pacific University
Transylvania College	Transylvania University
Transylvania Seminary	Transylvania University

374

Former Name	Current Name
Trenton Business College	Rider University
Trenton State College	New Jersey, The College of
Trevecca College	Trevecca Nazarene University
Trevecca Nazarene College	Trevecca Nazarene University
Trinity College	Duke University
Trinity Seminary	Dana College
Trinity Seminary & Blair College	Dana College
Triple Cities College of Syracuse University	New York University Center at Binghamtom, State University of
Tri-State College	Tri-State University
Tri-State Normal College	Tri-State University
Troy Conference Academy	Green Mountain College
Troy State College	Troy State University
Troy State Normal School	Troy State University
Troy State Teachers College	Troy State University
Tualatin Academy	Pacific University
Tualatin Academy & Pacific University	Pacific University
Tufts College	Tufts University
Tuscaloosa Institute	Stillman College
Tuskegee Female College	Huntingdon College
Tuskegee Institute	Tuskegee University
Tuskegee Normal School	Tuskegee University
Tuskegee Normal & Industrial Institute	Tuskegee University
Tuskegee State Normal School	Tuskegee University

U

U S Grant Memorial University	Tennessee at Chattanooga, The University of
U S Grant Memorial University	Tennessee Wesleyan College
Union Baptist Institute	Brewton-Parker College
Union Female College	Averett University
Union for Experimenting Colleges & Universities, The	Union Institute & University
Union Institute	Duke University
Union Institute, The	Union Institute & University
Union Seminary	Albright College
United States International University	Alliant International University
Unity Institute of Liberal Arts & Sciences	Unity College
University Farm School	California, Davis, University of

Former Name	Current Name
Unknown name; sponsored by the YMCA of The District of Columbia	Southeastern University
Unnamed academy	Union University
Unnamed Bible training school	Lee University
Unnamed Christian school	Eastern Nazarene College
Unnamed girls boarding school	Moravian College & Moravian Theological Seminary
Unnamed Indian boarding school	Fort Lewis College
Unnamed junior college	Mount Ida College
Unnamed normal school	Framingham State College
Unnamed preparatory school	Dominican University of California
Unnamed teachers seminarium for the education of sisters	Alvernia College
Unnamed teachers seminary	Wartburg College
Unnamed theological school	Bryn Athyn College of the New Church
Urbana College	Urbana University
Urbana Junior College	Urbana University
Ursuline College for Women	Ursuline College
Utah State Agricultural College	Utah State University of Agriculture & Applied Science
Utica College of Syracuse University	Utica College

V

Former Name	Current Name
Valdosta State College	Valdosta State University
Valley City State College	Valley City State University
Valley City State Teachers College	Valley City State University
Valley Union Seminary	Hollins University
Valparaiso College	Valparaiso University
Valparaiso Male & Female College	Valparaiso University
Vanguard University of Southern California	Vanguard University of Southern California
Vanport Extension Center of the Oregon State System of Higher Education	Portland State University
Vassar Female College	Vassar College
Vermont Classical High School	Castleton State College
Vermont Institute of Community Involvement	Burlington College
Vermont, University of	Vermont, University of & State Agricultural College
Villa Maria Academy for Girls	Immaculata University
Villa Maria College	Immaculata University

Former Name	Current Name
Virginia A & M College & Polytechnic Institute: Women's Division	Radford University
Virginia Agricultural & Mechanical College	Virginia Polytechnic Institute & State University
Virginia Agricultural & Mechanical College & Polytechnic Institute	Virginia Polytechnic Institute & State University
Virginia Baptist Seminary	Richmond, University of
Virginia Christian College	Lynchburg College
Virginia Collegiate Institute, The	Roanoke College
Virginia Institute	Virginia Intermont College
Virginia Institute, The	Roanoke College
Virginia Normal College	Bridgewater College
Virginia Normal & Collegiate Institute	Virginia State University
Virginia Normal & Industrial Institute	Virginia State University
Virginia State College	Virginia State University
Virginia State College for Negroes	Virginia State University
Virginia State College: Norfolk Division	Norfolk State University
Virginia Union University: Norfolk Unit	Norfolk State University
Viterbo College	Viterbo University
Voorhis Unit of the California Polytechnic School	California State Polytechnic University, Pomona

W

Former Name	Current Name
Wabash Manual Labor College & Teachers Seminary	Wabash College
Wadsworth Normal & Training School	New York College at Geneseo, State University of
Wagner Lutheran College	Wagner College
Wagner Memorial Lutheran College	Wagner College
Wake Forest College	Wake Forest University
Wake Forest Institute	Wake Forest University
Walden Seminary	Philander Smith College
Walnut Grove Academy	Eureka College
Walnut Grove Seminary	Eureka College
Walsh College	Walsh University
Ward-Belmont School	Belmont University
Warren Wilson Vocational Junior College	Warren Wilson College
Washburn College	Washburn University of Topeka
Washington Academy	Washington & Jefferson College
Washington Academy	Washington & Lee University

Former Name	Current Name
Washington Agricultural College & School of Science	Washington State University
Washington College	Trinity College
Washington College	Washington & Jefferson College
Washington College	Washington & Lee University
Washington Foreign Mission Seminary	Columbia Union College
Washington Institute in Saint Louis	Washington University in Saint Louis
Washington Missionary College	Columbia Union College
Washington State College	Maine at Machias, University of
Washington State Normal School	Central Washington University
Washington State Normal School	Maine at Machias, University of
Washington State Normal School at Bellingham	Western Washington University
Washington State Teachers College	Maine at Machias, University of
Washington State Teachers College of the University of Maine	Maine at Machias, University of
Washington Training College	Columbia Union College
Waterbury Business College	Teikyo Post University
Waterville College	Colby College
Wautaga Academy	Appalachian State University
Wayland Baptist College	Wayland Baptist University
Wayland Literary & Technical Institution	Wayland Baptist University
Wayne Normal School	Wayne State College
Wayne University	Wayne State University
Waynesburg College	Waynesburg College
Weber Academy	Weber State University
Weber College	Weber State University
Weber Normal School	Weber State University
Weber Stake Academy	Weber State University
Weber State College	Weber State University
Webster College	Webster University
Wellesley Female Seminary	Wellesley College
Wells Seminary for the Higher Education of Young Women	Wells College
Welsh Neck Academy	Coker College
Wesley Collegiate Institute	Wesley College
Wesley Junior College	Wesley College
Wesleyan Female College	Wesleyan College
Wesleyan Institute	Florida Southern College
Wesleyan Methodist Bible Institute	Southern Wesleyan University

Former Name	Current Name
Wesleyan Methodist College	Southern Wesleyan University
Wesleyan Seminary	Florida Southern College
Wesleyan Seminary at Albion, The	Albion College
Wesleyan Seminary & Female College at Albion	Albion College
Wesleyan University	North Alabama, University of
Wesleyan University of West Virginia	West Virginia Wesleyan College
West Central School of Agriculture	Minnesota, Morris, University of
West Chester Academy	West Chester University of Pennsylvania of the State System of Higher Education
West Chester Military Academy	Widener University
West Chester State College	West Chester University of Pennsylvania of the State System of Higher Education
West Chester State Normal School	West Chester University of Pennsylvania of the State System of Higher Education
West Chester State Teachers College	West Chester University of Pennsylvania of the State System of Higher Education
West Georgia College	West Georgia, State University of
West Kentucky Baptist Bible Institute	Mid-Continent College
West Liberty Academy	West Liberty State College
West Liberty State Normal School	West Liberty State College
West Liberty State Teachers College	West Liberty State College
West Tennessee Christian College	Freed-Hardeman University
West Tennessee College	Union University
West Tennessee Normal School	Memphis, The University of
West Tennessee State Teachers College	Memphis, The University of
West Texas State College	West Texas A&M University
West Texas State Normal College	West Texas A&M University
West Texas State Teachers College	West Texas A&M University
West Texas State University	West Texas A&M University
West Virginia Collegiate Institute	West Virginia State College
West Virginia Colored Institute	West Virginia State College
West Virginia Conference Seminary	West Virginia Wesleyan College
West Virginia Institute of Technology	West Virginia University Institute of Technology
West Virginia Trades School	West Virginia University Institute of Technology
West Virginia University: Montgomery Preparatory Branch	West Virginia University Institute of Technology

Former Name	Current Name
West Virginia, The College of	Mountain State University
Western Baptist Bible College & Theological Seminary	Western Baptist College
Western Bible College	Westmont College
Western Carolina College	Western Carolina University
Western Carolina Teachers College	Western Carolina University
Western Connecticut State College	Western Connecticut State University
Western Holiness College & Bible Training School	Oklahoma Wesleyan University
Western Illinois State College	Western Illinois University
Western Illinois State Normal School	Western Illinois University
Western Illinois State Teachers College	Western Illinois University
Western Kentucky State College	Western Kentucky University
Western Kentucky State Normal School	Western Kentucky University
Western Kentucky State Normal School & Teachers College	Western Kentucky University
Western Kentucky State Teachers College	Western Kentucky University
Western Maine Normal School	Southern Maine, University of
Western Maryland College	McDaniel College
Western Michigan College	Western Michigan University
Western Michigan College of Education	Western Michigan University
Western Montana College	Montana-Western, The University of
Western Montana College of Education	Montana-Western, The University of
Western Montana College of the University of Montana	Montana-Western, The University of
Western Oregon State College	Western Oregon University
Western Reserve College	Case Western Reserve University
Western Reserve Eclectic Institute	Hiram College
Western Reserve University	Case Western Reserve University
Western State Normal School	Maine at Farmington, University of
Western State Normal School	Western Michigan University
Western State Teachers College	Western Michigan University
Western University of Pennsylvania	Pittsburgh, University of
Western Washington College of Education	Western Washington University
Western Washington State College	Western Washington University
Westminster College of Salt Lake City	Westminster College
Westminster Collegiate Institute	Westminster College

Former Name	Current Name
Wheaton Female Academy	Wheaton College
Wheeling College	Wheeling Jesuit University
Wheeling Jesuit College	Wheeling Jesuit University
Wheelock School	Wheelock College
Whitewater Normal School	Wisconsin-Whitewater, University of
Whitewater State Teachers College	Wisconsin-Whitewater, University of
Whitman Seminary	Whitman College
Wichita Falls Junior College	Midwestern State University
Wichita, Municipal University of	Wichita State University
Wichita, University of	Wichita State University
Widener College	Widener University
Wilberforce State College	Central State University
Wiley University	Wiley College
Wilkes College	Wilkes University
William J Porter University	Jacksonville University
William Jennings Bryan College	Bryan College
William Jennings Bryan University	Bryan College
William Marsh Rice Institute for the Advancement of Letters, Science, & Art	Rice University, William Marsh
William Paterson College of New Jersey, The	William Paterson University of New Jersey, The
William Penn College	William Penn University
William Warren School	Menlo College
William Woods College	William Woods University
William Woods College for Girls of the Christian Church of Mississippi	William Woods University
William & Mary College: Newport News Branch	Christopher Newport University
Williamsburg Institute	Cumberland College
Williamsport Academy	Lycoming College
Williamsport Area Community College	Pennsylvania College of Technology
Williamsport Technical Institute	Pennsylvania College of Technology
Williamston Female College	Lander University
Willimantic State College	Eastern Connecticut State University
Willimantic State Normal School	Eastern Connecticut State University
Willimantic State Teachers College	Eastern Connecticut State University
Wilmington College	North Carolina at Wilmington, The University of
Wilmington Conference Collegiate Institute	Wesley College
Wilson Female College	Wilson College

Former Name	Current Name
Wingate Academy	Wingate University
Wingate College	Wingate University
Winona State College	Winona State University
Winona State Normal School	Winona State University
Winona State Teachers College	Winona State University
Winston-Salem State College	Winston-Salem State University
Winston-Salem Teachers College	Winston-Salem State University
Winthrop College	Winthrop University
Winthrop Normal & Industrial College of South Carolina	Winthrop University
Winthrop Training School for Teachers	Winthrop University
Wisconsin State College at Eau Claire	Wisconsin-Eau Claire, University of
Wisconsin State College at La Crosse	Wisconsin-La Crosse, University of
Wisconsin State College at Milwaukee	Wisconsin-Milwaukee, University of
Wisconsin State College at Oshkosh	Wisconsin-Oshkosh, University of
Wisconsin State College at Platteville	Wisconsin-Platteville, University of
Wisconsin State College at River Falls	Wisconsin-River Falls, University of
Wisconsin State College at Stevens Point	Wisconsin-Stevens Point, University of
Wisconsin State College at Superior	Wisconsin-Superior, University of
Wisconsin State College at Whitewater	Wisconsin-Whitewater, University of
Wisconsin State College & Institute of Technology at Platteville	Wisconsin-Platteville, University of
Wisconsin State Normal School, Platteville	Wisconsin-Platteville, University of
Wisconsin State University at Eau Claire	Wisconsin-Eau Claire, University of
Wisconsin State University at La Crosse	Wisconsin-La Crosse, University of
Wisconsin State University at Oshkosh	Wisconsin-Oshkosh, University of
Wisconsin State University at Platteville	Wisconsin-Platteville, University of
Wisconsin State University at River Falls	Wisconsin-River Falls, University of
Wisconsin State University at Stevens Point	Wisconsin-Stevens Point, University of
Wisconsin State University at Superior	Wisconsin-Superior, University of
Wisconsin State University at Whitewater	Wisconsin-Whitewater, University of
Wisconsin, University of	Wisconsin-Madison, University of
Wittenberg College	Wittenberg University

Former Name	Current Name
Woman's College of Baltimore	Goucher College
Woman's College of Baltimore City	Goucher College
Woman's College of Fredericksburg	Hood College
Woman's College of Georgia, The	Georgia College & State University
Women's College of Alabama	Huntingdon College
Women's College of the University of North Carolina, The	North Carolina at Greensboro, The University of
Woodbury College	Woodbury University
Wooster, University of	Wooster, The College of
Worcester County Free Institute of Industrial Science	Worcester Polytechnic Institute
Worcester State Teachers College	Worcester State College

X

Xavier University	Xavier University of Louisana

Y

Yale College	Yale University
Yeshiva Eitz Chaim	Yeshiva University
YMCA Institute	Roger Williams University
YMCA Institute of Engineering & Finance	Roger Williams University
York Academy	York College of Pennsylvania
York Collegiate Institute	York College of Pennsylvania
York Collegiate Institute, The Junior College of the	York College of Pennsylvania
York County Academy	York College of Pennsylvania
York Junior College	York College of Pennsylvania
Young Ladies Seminary of Benecia	Mills College
Young Women's Industrial Club of Saratoga	Skidmore College
Youngstown College	Youngstown State University
Youngstown Institute of Technology	Youngstown State University
Youngstown University	Youngstown State University

Z

Zion Wesley College	Livingstone College
Zion Wesley Institute	Livingstone College

ABOUT THE AUTHOR

Morgan G. Brenner, a retired life insurance company executive and consultant to the industry, is a sports historian who became a college name historian in the process of compiling his first book, *College Basketball's National Championships*. A native of York, Pennsylvania, he resides in Havertown, Pennsylvania.